# KIBBUTZ GOSHEN
## An Israeli Commune

### Alison M. Bowes
University of Stirling, Scotland

WAVELAND
PRESS, INC.
Prospect Heights, Illinois

For information about this book, write or call:

Waveland Press, Inc.
P.O. Box 400
Prospect Heights, Illinois 60070
(312) 634-0081

Printed in the United States of America

7   6   5   4   3   2   1

# Contents

# Introduction

There is only one all-out effort to create a Full Cooperative, which justifies our speaking of success in the socialistic sense, and that is the Jewish Village commune in its various forms, as found in Palestine. (Buber 1949:141)

Since the foundation of the first kibbutz, Degania, in 1910, the kibbutzim of Palestine/Israel have attracted the attention of the outside world. For Buber, who wrote during the heyday of the kibbutz movement, the kibbutz was a utopian "experiment that did not fail," an example of socialism in living practice. For the Zionist movement, the kibbutzim offered a particularly effective method of Jewish settlement in Palestine before the foundation of the State of Israel in 1948. Once some initial suspicion of the "communist" way of life of the kibbutzim had been overcome, and the special economic and military advantages of kibbutz settlement had been recognized, the kibbutzim started to become part of the Zionist establishment. Until 1977 when a right wing government under Menachem Begin was elected, the kibbutzim were involved at the highest political level in government and influenced life in Israel much more fundamentally than their numbers would suggest. Even at its peak in the late 1940s and early 1950s, the kibbutz movement has never contained more than eight percent of the Israeli Jewish population; today, it numbers less than three percent.

That such a tiny group of people could be so influential is perhaps not very surprising. Similar things, after all, happen in other societies. What is far more surprising about the kibbutzim is that they have attracted so much attention, which has been focused not on their undisputed place in the Israeli elite but on the unique structure of community life in the kibbutz. Two main groups have been involved. First, thousands of young people—Jews and Gentiles alike—have spent time on kibbutzim as volunteer workers, providing much hard work in return for the

1

experience of a totally different way of life. Secondly, a seemingly endless stream of academic research has been done in the kibbutzim, minutely scrutinizing every conceivable aspect of kibbutz life. One bibliography (Shur 1972) lists more than a thousand scholarly books and articles. As if that were not enough, there are at least three research institutes, two in Israel and one at Harvard, entirely devoted to the study of the kibbutz which now pour out even more books and articles.

What can be the point then of another book on the kibbutz? After all, even if people are not academically minded, they could go and see for themselves. The problem with that approach is that the kibbutzim, faced with a flood of strangers wanting to know about kibbutz life, have found ways of containing potentially disturbing invasions and protect themselves and their way of life from intrusions. So one may learn a little from spending time as a volunteer worker, but not very much. Like other communities, kibbutzim are intolerant of pests. While they welcome volunteers and the work they do, they are not prepared to open all aspects of their daily life to several hundred outsiders a year.

Reading can also be unsatisfying. It is not hard to find a general account of the organization of a kibbutz; most readers will soon come across Spiro's (1956) standard study which gives a general idea of a kibbutz thirty years ago. But Spiro today, even after two new editions (1970, 1975) raises more questions than he answers. How, for example, have the kibbutzim changed since the 1950s? How does the organization actually work in everyday life? What are the similarities and differences between one kibbutz and another? For answers to these questions, the reader may well turn to more recent academic research. S/he will find that there is no contemporary study comparable to Spiro's, and that the literature tends to focus on very minute and esoteric aspects of kibbutz life. Much of it is of great interest to the specialist, but for the beginner in kibbutz studies, it has little to offer. It does not connect with the ordinary reader's experience of the world, nor with the old general account. Thus, there is a gap in the literature, which this book hopes to help fill.

This book proposes to offer the ordinary reader some answers to common questions about the kibbutz such as: What is life like on a kibbutz? How do all these communalistic ideas work in practice? Starting with those questions, and starting always with everyday life in one kibbutz, the idea is to connect what happens in everyday life to more general aspects of the social and historical context of the kibbutz, and suggest ways of understanding kibbutz life. In other words, I want to take the study of the kibbutz back to the very basics of anthropology and examine how a kibbutz works and what makes it work.

I call the kibbutz in question Goshen: this is not its real name, but I have changed it to prevent identification, as I have also changed the names of the people I talk about. I did the fieldwork for the study in 1974 for two months, then returned for a year between March 1975 and March 1976. Some of the data I use are quite particular, even intimate, but since the time of study, Goshen has lost some members and acquired new ones: one member said to me "It is not the same place any more." It would be difficult even for a very determined detective to trace the people and events I describe back to their origins, and I hope that no one will try. The details of people and events are very important: they are Malinowski's "minutiae of everyday life," the starting point for anthropological study. Therefore, I always begin with them and then move gradually outwards into different and widening levels of social structure which, in the end, afford explanations of the original details.

When an anthropologist starts a field study, s/he meets the minutiae of everyday life first and wonders how s/he will ever make sense of all the different personalities and strange happenings that crowd in from every direction. Sometimes, s/he manages the task in the end, but the steps used in doing so are often lost in the final account. In the book, I try to show how my understanding of the kibbutz has developed, how I looked for patterns in the apparent everyday muddle, how these patterns led to a grasp of the structure of this community, its principles, and how eventually the community structure accommodated the wider context. At each stage, new pieces were added to the jigsaw puzzle of explanation, and the reader will find that in each chapter explanation is built up gradually. The jigsaw still has pieces missing, but that is inevitable, given the nature (even arrogance) of the enterprise.

The book cannot, therefore, offer a complete explanation for all aspects of life in the kibbutz. By making reference to other literature, it does suggest to the reader where alternative explanations are to be found and ways of researching the questions which the material may raise in the reader's mind. For those anxious to learn more as well as for those reading in preparation for a visit to a kibbutz, it can be a starting point for further work.

Social anthropology is that branch of social science which deals with the multi-faceted nature of human social life of all kinds. It involves looking at the kibbutz movement from all sides and gradually unifying those pieces into a whole. Ultimately, the perspective includes the notion that every element of a society is interconnected with every other element. To have any coherence however, the material has to be divided into sections. Each chapter in the book therefore focuses on a different aspect of kibbutz life. I begin with a discussion of my first, lasting and discarded impressions. Next, I provide a general history of the kibbutz movement and show how Goshen both fits into the general history and how far it differs in its own distinctive history. In "Working on a Kibbutz," I focus on the economic side of kibbutz life. The material here can be related to the outsider's experience of kibbutz life as a volunteer worker. "Controlling the Community" is about how people are kept in line and how decisions are made. Here too, the starting point is one of the immediately striking characteristics of kibbutz life—the fact that people spend so much of their time gossiping. "Women and Men" is about each gender's experience of kibbutz life, how these differ according to generations and how relationships between men and women in the kibbutz work. It expands explanations of contemporary gender roles introduced in the chapters on the economy and politics and social control. In "New Generations," I look at a development which faces all kibbutzim at some time in their history and which Goshen faced in 1975-6: What would the children of the kibbutz make of their lives, and how would their reaching adulthood and making their decisions about their futures affect the kibbutz as a whole? "Ceremonies and Festivals" works at celebration of kibbutz life and discusses how these reflect ideology and interaction in kibbutz life, and explains the place of the kibbutz movement in Israeli society. Finally, in "Studying the Kibbutz," I examine where kibbutz research might go from here, both in terms of academic questions and in terms of the interested individual who might want to learn more about the kibbutz through reading or experience.

# - 1 -

# First and Lasting Impressions

I arrived in Israel in midsummer 1974 with a scholarship, a new notebook and a list of addresses. The first day, I was sunburned on the beach in Tel Aviv; the second, I went to find a kibbutz. One of my addresses listed an official of the British Zionist Federation. I met him in his office and explained confidently that I was working on a doctorate. After some months of work, I had decided that my field research should be in a kibbutz. I had come to Israel for the summer to find a community, intending to work there briefly as a volunteer worker and to consider the feasibility of doing a year's fieldwork later on. He explained, denting my confidence somewhat, that it was the middle of the summer, that Israel was full of vacationing students who wanted to go to a kibbutz, and that a kibbutz would not like a volunteer worker ("a slave") studying it because she might get a bad picture of the place. At that point, a middle-aged man, very tanned and fit-looking wearing shorts, walked into the office and sat down obviously interested in our conversation. The official started to talk to him in Hebrew, and I understood that he was explaining what I wanted. They talked for some minutes, the official remarking to me in English as the discussion went on: "He's a kibbutznik you know—you can tell by the clothes," "Now I'm persuading him you can go there." When they had finished, the kibbutznik said, in halting English, that he would ask if I could go to his kibbutz. The official explained that this was a favor to a friend: I was to telephone in a day or two to see if everything was all right.

That was my introduction to Israel, and very important it was too. I had acquired "protektsia"—connections in the right places—who could help me get what I wanted. At the start of the interview, going to a kibbutz had looked impossible. By the end after the string pulling, it looked easy, and I had the best kind of introduction, from a member of the kibbutz. So, I thought, I would not arrive as an anonymous outsider.

5

In the next three days, I began to explore Israel, my senses assaulted by an incredible variety of impressions. On the day of the interview, the banks were closed in memory of the destruction of the temple. Exchanging money in a first class hotel, I discovered it to be the coolest place in the city. When I came out, the heat seemed far worse. I met a girl who said she never handled money on the Sabbath and two Americans who were disappointed in Israel, saying that it only survived through US support. I went to Jerusalem on a very noisy, very slow and very full train. In Jerusalem, I went to see the sights. The Dome of the Rock was so dazzling in the sunlight, I could not bear to look; the Wailing Wall was divided into a men's (large) and a women's (small) section; the Orthodox Jewish men had sidelocks a foot long, curled into perfect ringlets; I got lost in the back streets of the Old City, and somebody threw an old brush at me from an upstairs window. I went to visit more of the addresses on my list collecting books and pamphlets to help with my work. When asked what I thought of Israel, I was completely unable to reply. How could I when there was something and someone new wherever I turned?

I managed to telephone my contact in the BZO who confirmed that I could go to Kibbutz Goshen. I had to find and catch two buses; the second one seemed to be going to the middle of nowhere. I looked hopefully over the other passengers to see if they might be going where I was. There were three girls with rucksacks who looked like kibbutz volunteers, but they were signing to one another, and I realized they were deaf. When the bus drew into Goshen, I stepped off and stood in the middle of the parking lot wondering what to do next. It was mid-afternoon, and there was nobody about. One of the deaf girls, who could speak, asked me in German if I was a new volunteer. She took me along a series of winding paths passing many apparently deserted one story buildings, and awakened a man from his afternoon sleep. "Put her in one of the barracks," he said, "And go away: I'll see to her later." So there I was, in a wooden hut with a stone-tiled floor and three cactus plants outside, still wondering what to do. The other volunteers soon initiated me into their work which clearly had little to do with the work of the members. They showed me the dining room where everyone took their meals, the showers which all the volunteers shared, and the swimming pool on the other side of the kibbutz.

I quickly realized the importance of my "protektsia" which extended to Goshen. The kibbutznik who had been in the BZO soon met and talked with me. The volunteers were surprised, saying that "he *never* talks to volunteers." And I found the kibbutz secretary, whose name I had also been given. He was very interested in my study and very helpful, agreeing (thankfully, I later discovered) with my proposal to proceed very gently to begin with.

Straight away, I started to see some of the strains and tensions of kibbutz life. There was some separation between the volunteers and the members; there were some members who avoided volunteers completely and others (mainly young men) who were often in the volunteers' area. The young women of the kibbutz were said to be hostile to volunteers because they feared they would take away the men.

The next thing was to start work. I got up at 4:30 a.m. to work in the chicken houses and spent the day moving small and very dirty chickens from one set of pens to another. The smell was appalling, and a graphic description of the factory in Jerusalem where the chickens would soon go for meat did not help my already queasy insides. My second job was in the hothouses planting new rose bushes and pinching out shoots from mature ones; my third, ironing clothes; my fourth, washing cooking pots; my fifth, serving in the dining room. On the day Nixon resigned, I was cleaning tables in that dining room.

I stayed on Goshen for two months. At the end of that time, I had concluded that I would go back for the planned year, starting the next spring. During the two months, many of my preconceptions about the kibbutz, which I had gained from reading the available literature, had been shattered, and I had started to formulate both what questions I should be asking and how I should do the main piece of fieldwork. I was also beginning to learn about Goshen — what was its physical layout, who were its people, what were its special rules, what would life be like for me as an anthropologist and worker.

One of the particular advantages of the kibbutz as a fieldwork location seemed to be that it offered a readymade opportunity for participant observation. As a volunteer worker, I thought I would be able to participate in kibbutz life readily, in a recognized role which would allow me to contribute to the community while getting to know the people in it and learning about their way of life. There would, I thought, be an exchange relationship involved; I would be giving work in exchange for information. This appealed to my ethical sense, as I had become critical of the kind of fieldwork which had no return for the community, only allowing the advance of an anthropological career. My visit to the BZO was an attempt to enter a kibbutz as a volunteer in the normal way, that is, through a direct introduction by an outside formal agency. The invitation to Goshen from a member was, as it turned out, an important stroke of luck. When I arrived in Goshen, the gap between the volunteers and the permanent residents (the members) was very quickly apparent. There were a number of volunteers who, though they had hoped to learn about kibbutz life, had been completely unable to make any more than passing acquaintance with the members. This was especially the case with those volunteers who had come in groups from the same country; they were often put to work together and spent most of their nonwork time together as well. Some of those who had come as individuals, as I had, did manage to make more contact with the community but had achieved this over a series of visits and often with only a restricted circle of members. One reason for this general lack of contact lay in the nature of the situation; the volunteers had been a constant feature of life on Goshen since at least the 1967 war. However, they were a constantly changing population with individuals staying, on average, about two and a half months each. It would have been a considerable effort for members to befriend all these people and teach them about kibbutz life. Also, the members had had some unhappy experiences with volunteers, and many had become suspicious of them as a group, thus wishing to stay aloof and to keep them under control. Despite this, volunteers with experience at other kibbutzim insisted that they found Goshen a particularly friendly place, especially in comparison with larger, richer and older established kibbutzim. My 'protektsia' therefore proved a considerable asset in helping me to meet the people from Goshen who would otherwise have been unwilling to have anything to do with volunteers.

Although there was a clear separation between volunteers and members on Goshen, it was clear that the volunteer category, if not the particular individuals in it, was a permanent part of the community. This too was a departure from what I had been led to expect from kibbutz literature. All the standard works on kibbutzim concentrated on the members, that is, on those people who had been formally elected to have a share in the commune and a stake in running it. When the studies were not focusing on the members, they were talking about the members' children. This, I realized, was misleading. In addition to the volunteers who on Goshen comprised at least 12% of the workforce, there were many other people besides members and their children. There were hired laborers, permanent or temporary; others living and working there as part of their army service for several months; the aged parents of members who had come to spend their last days near their families. Also, there were many contacts between people on Goshen and people elsewhere, both in Israel and abroad, which affected life on the kibbutz very directly. It was, I realized, too easy to define a kibbutz as a commune whose members share production and consumption. Although that is true in some respects, all the other people and relationships must be taken into account.

One of my main interests in preparing the study had been kibbutz ideology. The theoretical dimension of my research related to the relationship between ideas and social action, and I was especially interested in communes because I thought they must have firm and clear ideological bases. Reading about the kibbutz, I quickly discovered that this was not exactly the case. First, kibbutz ideology had developed with the kibbutz movement through the interaction of ideas and action, and was continuing to do so. Second, the ideology had never been very clear or unambiguous. There had been constant debates about every aspect, including such "basic" matters as equality, labor, democracy and so on. That much, I had understood, but I had expected lively ideological debate to be going on in Goshen. In fact, I found that most people's conversation was concerned either with the day-to-day affairs of the community or with one anothers' lives. Occasionally, there would be a formal, ideological debate in a kibbutz meeting, but lengthy discussion was thought of primarily as the concern of officials in the federation to which Goshen was affiliated. As it turned out, I had been right to think of ideology as an important dimension of kibbutz life but misled by my reading to think of it as a constant topic of conversation. The kibbutz was, after all, established as a way of life, and people were "living their ideology." There were values, unfamiliar to an outsider like me, which a kibbutznik did not need to reflect upon all the time because s/he was intimately involved with them. Of course, ideology constantly impinged on peoples' lives, but it did so in subtle and indirect ways. Although people appeared on the surface to be concerned mainly with everyday events and activities, they were, implicitly, constantly relating and referring to their ideology. The ideological debates in the kibbutz provided occasional opportunities (which few people actually took) to bring these undercurrents to the surface, and the articulation of ideology was left primarily to the federation officials.

My impression from reading about the early years of the kibbutz movement was that ideological debate had been much more intense and explicit. A possible interpretation of the change was that the kibbutz was in decline. The declining proportion of the Israeli population found in the kibbutzim was probably due to a number of factors including increasing material prosperity, the development of industrial enterprises, the concentration of women in the "service" branches of the economy and the seeming resurgence of nuclear family life at the expense of communal child rearing. To conceive of these events as "decline" however involved making assumptions about a fixed ideological starting point which I already knew had not existed. To see the new developments as "bad" or "wrong" entailed elevating the early kibbutz to a "pure" status which was unreal. For example, one would have to assume that all Israelis could and should be kibbutz members, that poverty was a virtue, that agriculture was "better" than industry and so on. These assumptions have certainly been made, but they reflect values which are not necessarily kibbutz values. People in Goshen were highly critical of their community and its workings, but their criticisms were related to quite different values. Of course, their views were not the only ones relevant to the question of whether or not the kibbutz might be in decline, but it was clear that change and decline are not the same thing and that if any assumptions of decline were to be found, they would not lie *outsiders'* assumptions about the relative merits of past and present kibbutz life.

Inevitably the issue of Zionism arises in relation to the kibbutz or, indeed, any aspect of Israeli society. It was such an "issue" in Britain that my decision to go to Israel at all was not lightly made. Accustomed to constant discussion of Zionism at home, I was at first taken aback by the almost complete absence of any comments in Goshen. I had failed to understand, I think, the difference between being an Israeli and being a Zionist. The debates at home had centered on whether or not one could accept Zionism; an Israeli did not have a choice in the matter. Zionism was a fact of life, and political discussion centered not on whether Israel would exist or not, but on questions of Israeli politics. At that time, the Labor government was still in power. The election of Begin's right wing Likud in 1977 was to alter the issues, especially as it granted increasing license to Jewish settlements in the occupied territories. These settlements were being attempted when I returned to Israel in 1975 but were officially opposed by the government.

Reading about the Israeli-Arab question had made me somewhat fearful of being in Israel, which seemed in a state of constant and dangerous war. There were signs of "the war" (the term used for the general Israeli-Arab situation), such as many uniformed soldiers carrying guns, and some, though very little, evidence of bomb damage. These were, for me, a disturbing reminder of the tensions in the Middle East. My Israeli friends told me that they were used to such sights and as army reservists themselves often joined the parties of uniformed hitchhikers. Their feelings about the war were based on direct experience of it. When I arrived in Israel in the summer of 1974, the Yom Kippur War was a very recent memory, and many of those who had fought in it had only recently arrived home. Some talked about it, some would not, but all had been very deeply affected by it. It had been a blow, not only to national but also to individual morale: for those young men and women who had been regular soldiers at the time, for the older men whose second, third or fourth war it had been, for the older women who had been left to run the kibbutz while the men were away fighting and for some volunteers who had been on Goshen at the time. During that first visit then, if people discussed "the war," they discussed the Yom Kippur War. When I returned, the talk was more general: of the rapidly worsening situation in Lebanon, of the occasional terrorist attack in the North, and of the Syrians, who had become the most feared enemy. From time to time, the question became immediate and personal again. Once or twice during the year, the army came to Goshen during the night to take reservists. The next day, there would be real tension and fear in the kibbutz until the immediate danger had passed, the reservists returned, and life went back to normal. So people did not live in constant fear, but fear was just under the surface of life all the time. The sight of soldiers and guns and even the occasional tank was commonplace for kibbutzniks; I never got used to it.

Many of the books about kibbutzim have subtitles giving them a distinctly romantic aspect. Spiro's (1972) "venture in utopia," Darin-Drabkin's (1962) "other society," Buber's (1949) "experiment that did not fail" all suggested the kibbutz to be unique and exciting, full of committed and idealistic Socialists. This image was reinforced for me by the notion of a constant stream of volunteer workers trying their own Socialist experiments by living for a time on a kibbutz. I found that the kibbutz was indeed very special in some respects, such as the degree of communalism practiced, the remarkable equality of all members, the material and nonmaterial security provided by the community, the peaceful environment, the wonderful times the children seemed to have and so on. In other respects, life there was very ordinary and mundane; people spent their days at work and their afternoons and evenings with their families and friends. There was housework and gardening to do, children to play with, parties to go to, etc. And it was hard to think of the kibbutz as an experiment. It was a community where people lived and worked all their lives and planned to continue doing so. For volunteers perhaps it was an experiment, less successful from their point of view if they found only limited contact with the members.

To ask successful questions about the kibbutz then, I had first of all to abandon all these preconceptions. I had to recognize the nature of my own position as a rather unorthodox volunteer, which led me to question previous notions not only about relationships within the kibbutz but also about what exactly the kibbutz was, and to recognize the interrelationships between kibbutzniks and people outside the kibbutz. The question of the relationship between ideology and everyday life needed to be more subtly approached. The two were so closely interwoven and covered the whole of kibbutz life so that any information about the kibbutz was relevant to the topic. Therefore a general ethnographic study of Goshen was in order: fortunately, the community was small enough for me to be able to do this in the time at my disposal. Whether or not the kibbutz was in decline had turned out to be an assumption-ridden question. However, it still appeared worthwhile to look at kibbutzniks' own view of their community and also to look at its place in Israeli society. This was to become more and more important as a topic as the study proceeded. Zionism was a part of everyday kibbutz life, although not in the way I had expected. My particular interest in the relationship between ideology and everyday life needed to be explored in the context of the general ethnography. "The war" too, was related to this general overview. I had erroneously singled it out as a distinctive issue when, of course, it was bound up with kibbutz thinking and kibbutz social activity.

The issues raised by my reading did not develop precisely into those I would investigate. This is not to say that the reading was irrelevant or pointless. I could not have exposed these misconceptions had I not acquired them in the first place. Once I had begun the fieldwork, I had perforce to follow Emmanuel Marx's (1967:xiii) injunction which he attributes to Max Gluckman to "follow your material, wherever it may lead you." Having done the fieldwork I could, on the basis of the material I had collected, evaluate the previously published studies more productively. My discussion of the kibbutz in this book is based on an interaction of my field material, anthropological theory, and previously published kibbutz studies, with my field material as the baseline.

As to how I was going to conduct the fieldwork, this too was much clearer after my visit. I planned to continue in my role as a volunteer. This was a role I could easily take on as a young, single foreigner. I was not however an ordinary volunteer. As I have described, my entry to Goshen had been through 'protektsia,' which I needed and was lucky to have.

From the beginning, I clearly established that I was an anthropologist and that I was planning to collect field material during my stay. The Secretariat of Goshen (the elected officials of the community) told me that they had informed the members of this and that it had been approved. As time went on, I became aware that not all the members did, in fact, know exactly what I was doing. Others did not fully understand, and it became apparent that the message about my studying Goshen had been passed to the members rather less straightforwardly that I had thought. This was not, I think, a plot by the Secretariat, merely an example of their ability to present possibly unwelcome information in an acceptable and noncontentious manner. I am sure that many of the members simply forgot what I was doing. Some could not take it seriously, since in the Israeli context, I was "far too young" to be doing a doctorate.

My nationality and language made me conspicuous. For months at a time, I was the only British volunteer and the only native English-speaking one. This was an advantage in the sense that I could not be categorized as one of the French or the Swiss, as most other volunteers were, and treated as an anonymous member of the group. It was a disadvantage in the sense that there were rather too many people around anxious to practice their English. This helped me make contacts but did not help my language study, which was very complicated as I will explain shortly.

Understanding the relationship between the volunteers and the members of the kibbutz taught me how I should behave. Most importantly, it was clear that I would have to work hard for the kibbutz. Volunteers who arrived on Goshen as individuals rather than as members of groups very quickly acquired reputations as good or bad workers. I managed to gain a reputation as a good worker, which was enhanced during my second stay by doing more skilled work. Fortunately, I knew how to sew and could alter clothes quite well. This was especially useful as it engendered good relationships with the influential women who worked in the *communa,* the clothing store where laundry was ironed and sorted and various sewing jobs were done. The second skill I learned on Goshen. Roses were grown in hothouses to be exported to Europe as cut flowers in the winter. The flowers had to be cut carefully, then sorted into bundles of twenty identical blooms. Happily, I developed a knack for this and it also helped in establishing many good relationships. Originally, I worked in several branches of the kibbutz economy. Later during my year's fieldwork, I spent longer periods in the *communa* and the roses branch. This was ideal, since I first was exposed to a general view of most of the branches and then enjoyed a more specialized and longer-term view of the latter two. The price of working hard and writing up my field notes every day was both physical and mental exhaustion. Fieldwork on a kibbutz is definitely not for the weak or fainthearted. I was fortunate in being allowed two days off per week (customary for a volunteer) throughout my stay. Normally after six months, I should have moved to a six-day working week as kibbutz members did. I am eternally grateful to Goshen for allowing this; without it, fieldwork would have been impossible.

As well as working hard, I had to avoid becoming involved with any of the young men of Goshen. One of the main reasons for the strain in the volunteer member relationships which developed while I was there was that several foreign women, who had originally gone there as volunteers, had married kibbutz men. They were characterized as having "taken away" these men from the community, either by going abroad with them or by decreasing their involvement with the other members. Any sign of a liaison between a female volunteer and a male member of Goshen became a matter of serious concern. Somewhat less serious, although still criticized were relationships between male volunteers and female members (because it was thought so important for women to get married).

As well as participating in work in the kibbutz, I was involved with other aspects of social life. These events were both formal and informal and included a full year's cycle of ceremonial activity (except for one festival, Purim), many collective social events, and a constant round of visiting with members and volunteers. Formal political life was the one aspect of life in Goshen in which I was unable to participate directly. In order to overcome this disadvantage, I made special efforts to collect reports of formal meetings from as many people as possible. I was not alone in not going to the meetings; many kibbutz members also failed to attend. They kept up with formal political happenings in much the same way as I did.

When I originally planned the fieldwork, I had thought of doing a demographic survey of the kibbutz and a full set of life history interviews, as the literature on anthropological methodology suggested. This turned out not to be feasible. In such an intimate community as Goshen, I could easily have alienated people by insisting on formal interviews. Also, there were many people there who preferred not to recall their pasts which had been steeped in persecution and oppression of the most extreme and violent kind. For the demographic survey, I compiled a set of index cards, one for each permanent or temporary resident of Goshen over the period of fieldwork, and filled in details such as ages, countries of origin, relatives, etc. which cropped up in conversation. My collection of life histories was incremented in a similar way as well as from items of "common knowledge" on Goshen. Some people talked at great length about their lives, although I did not press them to do so.

I carried out a limited number of more formal interviews during my fieldwork, usually to give me a framework to help order other material. For example, I interviewed one of the veterans about the history of Goshen and the Economic Manager about the kibbutz economy. The first gave me at least an outline (not entirely accurate, as other information showed) of who had come and gone to and from Goshen. The inaccuracies in his account were as interesting as the accurate sections. The second gave me basic economic data on Goshen, which I could not otherwise have obtained. Other formal interviews were with various officials and researchers of the kibbutz movement, who provided valuable background data, as well as insight into the attitudes of officials towards Goshen and towards foreign, female Ph.D. candidates.

Before going to Israel, I attended an evening class in Hebrew. By the time of my first visit, I had an elementary grasp of the language. I hoped to improve my vocabulary once there, aiming in the tradition of anthropological fieldwork to work in the vernacular. When I arrived, I found that the vernacular was not quite as I had expected: the people of Goshen used several different languages, only one of which was Hebrew. The major alternative was French, used by many North Africans as well as people from France. Fortunately, my French was good enough to interact with these people who used the language for their everyday purposes, reserving Hebrew for more formal occasions or for conversation with people who did not know French. There were a few families who used English amongst themselves, and Hebrew elsewhere. I could, of course, operate in English and did talk to people who had studied English and wanted to practice it. Some members and many volunteers also used German. This too, I already knew. Generally, a majority of the adult population knew and regularly used more than one language. The record, seven languages, was claimed by one of the original settlers of Goshen who had come from Alexandria in Egypt (I heard him use Hebrew, Arabic, English and French with considerable facility, and he said he knew Greek, Spanish and Italian as well). The choice of language depended both on the situation and the person with whom one was speaking. Hebrew was the "official" language, used for all formal meetings and ceremonies, and it was also used with the children of the kibbutz. Other languages were used at work and in more general social interaction. People would select one which was comfortable for all participants, sometimes with the intention of excluding particular listeners. Less than half of all the members of Goshen had Hebrew as a native language; many of those who had learned it after coming to Israel did not speak it well. For myself, this lack of facility in the language was an advantage, as it meant that the Hebrew spoken on Goshen tended to be rather simple and hence comprehensible for a learner.

The members of Goshen came from many different countries. The first had come from Egypt in the late 1940s, and later settlers had come from Europe, Belgium, Morocco, France and many other countries. During my stay, the arrival of some young settlers from Argentina was eagerly awaited. The variety of people in Goshen was as great as the variety of people in Israel itself. The rather uniform kibbutz work clothes, the common standard of living and the general similarity of people's life-style tended to minimize the visual variety.

Walking around the residential areas of the kibbutz, several different kinds of houses could clearly be seen. The least comfortable were wooden huts with stone floors (the earliest permanent houses of the settlement) which were by now used mainly by volunteers and some visiting soldiers. The next were more substantially built rooms, each with its own small bathroom. These were occupied by young, mainly single kibbutz members. Young married couples, single parents, and some older members had small two room flats; more senior members lived in three room flats with a living room, bedroom and kitchen (all these had their own bathrooms). Thus, better accommodations came with seniority of membership and bore no relationship to one's economic assets or activity. In addition to the members' and volunteers' houses, there were several children's houses, one for each (approximately) eighteen-month age group, where children spent most of their time and which included shared bathrooms. After about twelve years of age, Goshen's children lived and went to school on another kibbutz, returning home two or three times a week and during school holidays when they would stay at their parents' homes or in one of the huts. Once they began their army service, at about eighteen years old, they would be allocated rooms to themselves for use when they returned to Goshen most weekends.

Other buildings were for communal use. The main gathering place, used for social events and formal settings as well as meals, was the dining hall, a rather dilapidated wooden building with a stone floor. Behind this was the kitchen, where all the food was prepared. During my stay, a new kitchen was built, to the delight of the women workers who had suffered hot, cramped and wholly inadequate conditions for years. From the point of view of the volunteers, many of whom had done dishes three times a day for the whole community, the main advantage of the new kitchen was the dishwasher which came with it.

The laundry and the *communa* (clothing store) were a short walk from the dining room and also occupied wooden buildings. Next to these was a relic of Goshen's early days, a dilapidated shack containing communal showers. It was now occupied by pigeons whose cooing provided a pleasant accompaniment throughout the working day.

Opposite the dining room was the *moadon,* or clubhouse, which consisted of a television room, a small library and a sitting room with a coffeemaking machine. This *moadon,* built early in Goshen's history, had been its pride and joy, a considerable asset for a small, new kibbutz, but was getting rather cramped by the time of my fieldwork.

Throughout the site, as throughout the country, there were bomb shelters. On Goshen, these were used for other purposes too. One contained another communal television set, another a table tennis table and a third was designated as a youth club, to supplement the facilities of the *moadon.*

The administrative offices of Goshen occupied more wooden huts. One housed the main office and the Post Office, where the mobile post van visited daily. Another (which also doubled as a storeroom for shoes), housed the labor organizer, elected for six months at a time whose job it was to match available workers to necessary jobs. This unenviable task involved delicate negotiations with representatives of the various branches of the kibbutz economy who would insist they were permanently short of workers and with people who were available to move from one branch to another but who had firm likes and dislikes in the work field. Often, loud arguments from the Work Office would echo around the nearby parking lot.

The parking lot contained the vehicles belonging to Goshen. There were two cars reserved for physically disabled members, and two more for communal use. There was a minibus which took the workers to the secondary school each day; two more minibuses were used to ferry members to and from the city and for deliveries as well as a large lorry, the pride and joy of its driver. Tractors and jeeps were parked there which had brought people in from the fields at mealtimes or at the end of the working day. Four times a day, except on the Sabbath, the public bus drove into Goshen. Since the vehicles were used primarily for "kibbutz business," the bus was most people's principal mode of transport if they wanted a day in town. Despite being only a twenty-minute bus ride out of town, Goshen was fairly isolated. The town was too far away to walk, and hitchhiking was difficult as there was very little traffic on the road. Most of the time, people had to arrange to catch the bus. Those travelling were normally either kibbutz members with business in town such as a job or an official visit to the offices of the federation of kibbutzim, or members on pleasure trips to town, or volunteers. Many of the members left Goshen only very rarely. They had little reason to do so and every reason to economize with the very small amount of money available to them.

Actual cash was very rarely seen on Goshen. In the center of the site was a small store stocked with tea, coffee, biscuits, cigarettes, toiletries, cleaning materials, candy, and a few very simple consumer goods where, twice a week, people would go and collect whatever they needed in their houses. Much of the stock was simply there for the taking. Expensive brands of goods and "extras" like small presents would be "paid for" with the personal budget, an amount allocated to each family annually for small items like this. Only volunteers used cash in the store, some of which was their monthly pocket money. If a kibbutz member needed cash, s/he would have to apply for it in the kibbutz office.

Not all a member's needs were satisfied by the store. For clothes, both work and dress, s/he would go to the *communa* where selections of clothes were available from time to time. If these were not suitable, the member would be given a token to take to a kibbutz store in town where the stock was more varied. Shoes were obtained from the shoe store in a similar fashion. For furniture, the member would have a fixed amount to spend at a specified shop. For most of these things, there were fixed annual allowances — furniture came with seniority or a move to a new flat. For any special needs, individuals had to apply to the officials of Goshen. "Special needs" might be artists' materials, the repair of a musical instrument, extra bookshelves, toys for a handicapped child, etc. — anything out of the ordinary. Volunteers did not normally receive the allowances or the extras unless they stayed on Goshen for more than six months. Visiting soldiers were paid allowances on a pro rata basis and hired workers received only their pay.

Goshen's buildings included a handsome clinic staffed daily by a nurse and visited twice a week by a doctor. The visiting dentist worked in another hut; he came once a week. Other huts were reserved for various purposes. One was occupied by a rather disabled elderly woman who made cosmetics and gave beauty treatments to the women of Goshen. Another contained a piano and was used by a succession of musicians. During my stay, Goshen's own pop group would attempt to play there. However, they were so unpopular with those living nearby that the electrical fuses would regularly and mysteriously disappear. Additional huts served as a common room for the volunteers or a discotheque assuming someone could locate sufficiently powerful stereo equipment. That hut was painted with very wild and very bright murals and was the farthest away from any living quarters.

Interspersed among the buildings were various sports facilities: a football field, basketball court (both games were very popular), and a swimming pool, where most people of Goshen would congregate on summer afternoons.

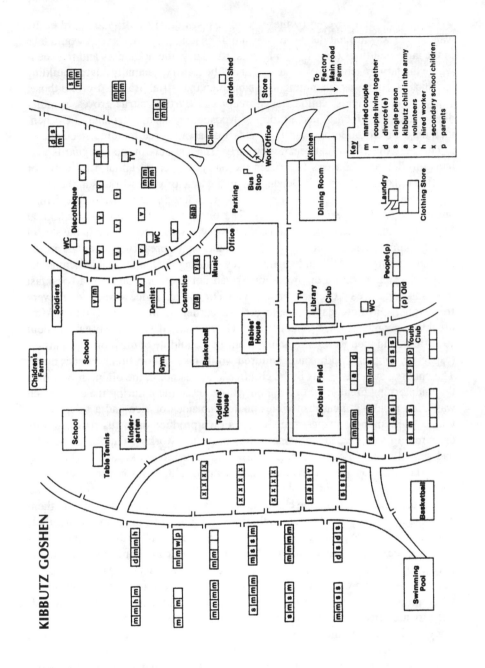

KIBBUTZ GOSHEN

**Key**

m married couple
l couple living together
d divorcé(e)
s single person
a kibbutz child in the army
v volunteers
h hired worker
x secondary school children
p parents

To
Factory
Main road
Farm

The area of land covered by these buildings was quite small; you could easily walk all the way around the perimeter in half an hour. A wider sweep would take in the farm buildings (the chicken houses, the dairy, the hothouses and the sheds where the farm machinery was stored) and "the factory," actually a large building in which Goshen was attempting to establish an industrial branch. Beyond those, you were in the fields: cotton fields predominantly then citrus groves, a rather dilapidated pear orchard, and a group of avocado trees. The total area of Goshen, including all the buildings and the fields was about three hundred hectares.

The daily life of Goshen began very early. The last duty of the two guards who had patrolled all night was to awaken the dairy workers at about 4:00 a.m. for the first milking of the cows. Depending on the time of year, workers in the fields would rise next. At dawn, they would go to the dining room for tea before setting out for the fields in jeeps and trailers. The bus left for the secondary school at 5:30 a.m. with teachers and a volunteer or two who would be helping in the school dining room. Then the service workers would begin preparing breakfast in the kitchen, waking the children in their houses, starting the laundry and opening the office. Starting at 7:30 a.m., workers arrived in the dining room for a breakfast of salads, eggs, cream cheeses, bread and tea or coffee. Twice a week, there were fresh rolls. On these days, people arrived earlier to insure their treat. After breakfast, people returned to their work. They would take a coffee break at about 10:00 a.m. and then work until about noon. In the middle of the morning, parents (especially mothers) with young children would take a short break to visit them. The children ate their meals in the children's houses not in the dining room, thus the midmorning break might be the only time to see them during the day. Lunch was a hot meal—a meat dish with noodles, potatoes or rice and a salad, often with a fruit compote made from Goshen's own produce or citrus fruit from its orchards. In summer, lunch marked the end of the working day for those who had started early. In the winter, people would return to work until 2:00 or 3:00 p.m. The afternoon was for showering and sleeping, although some more energetic souls would head straight for the swimming pool. At 4:00 p.m., parents would collect their children from the children's houses and would spend time with them until about 7:00 p.m., when the children would return to their houses for their evening meal before going to bed. From the age of six months, this was the child's daily routine. Some kitchen workers returned to work at about 5:30 p.m. to set out the supper: people started to come to eat at 6:00 p.m. Supper was like breakfast, with salads and so on, although once a week there was an "Oriental evening" when children came to eat in the main dining room and there were *pittot* (round, flat Oriental bread) and *felafel* (balls of chickpea paste, deep-fried).

By 8:00 p.m., the meal was over. Parents would go to the childrens' houses to say goodnight to their offspring (or to return them there) and return home; there was some evening visiting, but most people would retire early. The guards would be on duty by suppertime. Later, a woman would station herself beside an intercom in the area of the children's houses to attend to any children who woke during the night. Everything would then be quiet until morning.

On the Sabbath, the daily routine varied. The Sabbath began on Friday night with a hot meal and tablecloths (only seen otherwise at festivals). Friday nights often entailed some social events such as parties or films. On Saturday morning only absolutely essential work would be done: the cows had to be milked and food had to be cooked and served. Most people, however, had the day off to spend with their family or friends. The General Assembly of the kibbutz was held every Saturday evening. Members and candidates who had formal rights to participate in running Goshen could attend; volunteers could not. Attendance at the meeting varied. Usually about one-third to one-half of the members would be there, unless there was an issue of special interest when more people might attend. If members did not go to the meetings, they were not necessarily out of touch with events. To a large extent, the General Assembly acted as a "rubber stamp" to decisions which had already been made informally. After the meeting it was easy to find out what had happened from the postmortems that would inevitably be conducted throughout the next day and possibly longer.

For the members of Goshen, the Sabbath was a day of rest without religious significance. Goshen was affiliated with a federation of kibbutzim which added atheism to the two main principles of socialism and Zionism. Further breaks in the daily routine occurred at festival celebrations. Some of these were traditional festivals of Judaism which were divested of their religious dimensions and treated by kibbutzniks as agricultural and historical. Other festivals were Zionist (such as Israeli Independence Day) or Socialist (such as May Day) and had no religious referents. Volunteers saw things differently. Jewish volunteers (a minority on Goshen) tended towards atheism; if their inclinations had been different, they would have gone to agnostic or religious kibbutzim. They could understand the members' celebrations. For the non-Jewish volunteers, the celebrations were often rather mysterious. Those who were practicing Christians would celebrate their own festivals, separate from the members. The most devout (there were very few) held a prayer meeting and their own Sabbath activities in the volunteers' area of Goshen. For some of these people, being in the "Holy Land" was in itself an intense religious experience.

For me, fieldwork was an intense experience, a *rite de passage* which enabled me to acquire my professional credentials as an anthropologist and a fundamentally personal challenge to my own values and a way of life. When I finished the fieldwork in the Spring of 1976, I was ready to go home. I felt that I would never want to return to Israel or Goshen. Having had time to reflect on my work, having written and talked about it for several years, I begin to feel that I might go back one day. Many people of Goshen have read my work, and I have discussed it with some of them who have visited me in Britain. The most common reactions have been "you know more about Goshen than we do" and "how can you have so much to say about us?" In some ways I suppose I do "know" more than they do, having registered in my fieldnotes the detailed events of some fourteen months and having reflected on them in the light of other studies of kibbutzim and the insights of social anthropology. In other ways, I feel my work has only scratched the surface of what kibbutz life is like and how it works. This is, I suppose a customary act for an anthropologist—to apologize for what she has written. Although it is inevitably inadequate, I feel the account is worth giving.

In what follows, I will offer some answers to the questions I have raised and perhaps to those which have arisen in my reader's mind. The first thing is to examine the origins of the kibbutzim generally and Goshen in particular.

# - 2 -

# Background to
# the Study

## History of the Kibbutz Movement

The history of the kibbutz movement began in Europe in the latter part of the nineteenth century. At that time, anti-Semitism had reached fever pitch, especially in Russia and Poland, and many Jews were reflecting yet again on their position in the Diaspora. Their reflections were fueled by the emerging Zionist movement. In 1896, Theodor Herzl wrote:

> The Jews who wish will have their State. We shall live at last as free men on our own soil, and die peacefully in our own homes. The world will be freed by our liberty, enriched by our wealth, magnified by our greatness. And whatever we attempt there to accomplish for our own welfare will react powerfully and beneficently for the good of humanity. (Herzl 1896:79)

In 1897, the first Zionist Congress was held in Basel, Switzerland attracting attention and support from Jews all over Europe, especially from Russia (Grayzel 1968).

As anti-Semitism increased in fury, as Zionism and rival European nationalisms became consolidated, the Jewish communities were increasingly beleaguered. Great waves of emigrants moved West, into Western Europe, the United States and South America. For some Jews, Zionism meant settlement in Palestine. In the 1880s, Jews started to arrive there in significant numbers. There had been Jewish communities in Palestine since ancient times and some immigration, mainly as pilgrimage, at least since the thirteenth century. Modern immigration, which has to be clearly distinguished from the old pilgrimage (Eisenstadt 1967), involved members of the Zionist movement and of certain other organizations with similar, if less explicitly political, philosophies. Although between 1882 and 1903 some twenty-five thousand Jews entered Palestine, they were only a small minority of

21

those leaving their old homes. These settlers are often referred to as the first *aliya* (pl. *aliyot*), a Hebrew word meaning "ascent," which indicates the value attached to settlement in Palestine by Zionists. This "ascent" however was less grand than its name suggests. Some settlements were controlled by officials from the Zionist movement based in Europe and were not allowed to decide for themselves how they wished to live; other settlers found conditions in Palestine physically intolerable and there were many departures and even deaths, most commonly from malaria or suicide (Elon 1972).

There is no evidence of efforts at communal living in the first *aliya* (Eisenstadt 1967, Viteles 1967), although if the settlers had had any ideas of this kind, they would probably have been stifled by the foreign administrators and financiers in Europe who controlled the settlements. However, the experience of the settlers of the first *aliya*, especially the many hardships they undoubtedly faced has to be seen as an important predecessor of and influence on the kibbutz movement (Amitai 1966).

The first clearly documented attempts at communal living appear in the second *aliya* (1904-1914). One example is related by Viteles (1967), who describes the experiences of a group of about ten young people from a town called Romani in the Ukraine. After meeting on the boat to Palestine, they decided to stick together in the new country, sharing a household, pooling their incomes and working together. They called themselves Hakommuna Haromanit (the Romani Commune) and were one of several groups of youngsters living and working together, much as young people today might do in a foreign and somewhat hostile land. The special significance of Hakommuna Haromanit was that after reflecting on their experience and discussing their lives together, its members began to see that they could design a whole way of life based on communality. After many difficulties, they persuaded the Jewish National Fund (which was already purchasing land for Jewish settlement in Palestine) to allocate a plot of land near the Sea of Galilee where they settled in 1910. They called their settlement Degania (meaning "cornflower") and it is now universally considered to have been the first kibbutz. Other groups, whose experiences had been similar to those of the Romani Commune, quickly followed the example of Degania and started to settle on land acquired by the JNF. (Zureik 1979 gives more information on land acquisition). By 1919, there were at least five such communal settlements in Palestine (Criden and Gelb 1974). There may well have been more, but it has proved impossible to obtain figures on kibbutzim which did not survive to the present day. By 1922, the total number of settlers had reached more than a thousand (Ben David 1964). In these early years, they comprised less than one percent of the Jewish population in Palestine. Their heyday was to come later, between the 1920s and the 1950s.

Early days in Degania and the other communal settlements were filled with hard work and long discussion about the new life in Palestine. Also, as Miriam Baratz, a member of Degania, writes:

> After a day of hard and grinding labor, we would sit in a circle, begin with romantic songs, pour out all our heart, and then go over to Hassidic tunes, which bring all of us to our feet dancing, and perspiring without an end. (quoted by Viteles 1967:30)

The emotional intensity of the period is stressed by many commentators, as well as by the settlers themselves. Miriam's husband, Joseph:

> [It] . . . was a kind of communal 'honeymoon.' We used to go out in the morning to plough while it was still dark. There were six pairs of mules and six fresh, energetic riders upon them. Here we are on the banks of the Jordan, and a mighty song burst from our throats. . . . We felt we had become farmers, workers of the soil — our homeland's soil. When dusk fell, we used to return. . . . We used to sit . . . crowded together, and talk about the farm. (quoted by Amitai 1966:26 — and see Baratz 1954, his personal recollections of Degania)

The life of the pioneers has often been compared with the Hassidic movement, a Jewish ecstatic cult of eighteenth century Europe (Spiro 1972, Viteles 1968). Viteles (1968:233) says that, like the Hassidic congregation, the settlements were:

> . . . based on inspirations and emotion, on momentary instead of steady permanence of the everyday, in brief on an intoxicating narcosis.

The settlers too recognized their links with Hassidism (see Miriam Baratz' comments above), borrowing its songs and dances, especially the *hora*, a circular dance in which the participant is inevitably caught in a frenzied group movement which becomes a sign of group unity, each dancer relying on the next for physical support (cf. Spiro 1972:58).

The settlers' ideas evolved as they discussed their new experiences, the problems they faced (both personal and practical), and the kind of society they wanted to build. Their conclusions, while generally socialist and generally Zionist and opposed to the conditions of Jewish existence in the Diaspora (Diamond 1957), could not have been predicted in detail. When they arrived in Palestine, they had had little idea of what the country was like or what they would do there. The foundation of Degania and the other settlements resulted from what Ben David (1964:47) calls "an almost pure process of trial and error": development continued in this fashion, with ideas and organizational forms being crystallized only gradually.

News of the young pioneers' efforts in Palestine filtered back to Zionist youth groups in Europe, and these groups began to see a clear aim for their efforts: they would train people to go to Palestine and to settle on the land, working it communally as the pioneers were doing. Thus the Jewish people would tie themselves firmly to the land and would regain the self-respect they had lost after centuries of oppression. A new Jewish people would be born.

In the 1920s the settlements themselves started to try and consolidate their activities by meeting together and attempting to set up federations which would coordinate settlements and organize joint activities. In 1923, settler representatives met at Degania Aleph (there were now two Deganias — Aleph and Beth) to prepare for a congress of all the settlements. Their efforts resulted in the formation in 1926 of Chever Hakvutzot, a body consisting of representatives from all member settlements. The aim was to further the cause of communal living both among settlers and among the authorities of the Yishuv (the name given to the pre-1948 settlement of Jews in Palestine) and to encourage and facilitate cooperation between the member settlements.

Chever Hakvutzot intended to include all the settlements but was unable to do so. There was so much ideological variation between them by this time that they could not agree to join the same federation. Two other federations were set up, Hakibbutz Hameuchad in 1923 and Hakibbutz Haartzi in 1929. We need not dwell on the differences between the federations here. Where relevant, I will elaborate as the discussion proceeds. For the moment, we need only note that Chever Hakvutzot and Hakibbutz Hameuchad are usually considered the right wing of the movement, and Hakibbutz Haartzi the left wing.

Within the federations and within individual settlements, there was not complete agreement on matters of principle or organization. Some settlements were so internally divided that they found themselves unable to participate in any federation, and lengthy arguments took place within all the federations about organizational form, the principles on which they rested, etc. (Viteles 1968 gives details). In consequence, the federations only gradually became established and achieved something like their present form in the 1950s. During the 1950s, several communities split over the issue of which federation they would join (Stern 1965, Viteles 1968) and were involved in bitter internal disputes. In 1951, Chever Hakvutzot became Ichud Hakvutzot Vehakibbutzim. Until 1979, there were three large federations of settlements. In 1979, Ichud and Hameuchad joined together to form a federation called Hatnuah Hakibbitzit Hameuchedet (Takam for short). Hakibbutz Hadati, a federation of religious kibbutzim was founded in 1934. The religious kibbutzim differ considerably from the main body of the kibbutz movement. They have been little studied and are excluded from consideration in this book. Interested readers should consult Viteles 1968, Section 4, and Fishman 1983.

The reader will have noted that I have not been referring to the early settlements as "kibbutzim." In the pioneering days, we are concerned with groups of young people trying out a new way of life. In the literature, their settlements are referred to as *kvutzot* (s. *kvutza*), a Hebrew word for a group which, when applied to the groups of young pioneers, carries strong connotations of communalism and closeness, even emotion. It is hard to establish when the word "kibbutz" (pl. kibbutzim), which is in Hebrew very close to *kvutza* ("b" and "v" are represented by the same letter in writing) came into general use, but it seems that as the movement became more and more established, the word "kibbutz" gained increasing currency, even though *kvutza* continued to be used. Today *kvutza* is generally used for the early pioneer settlement and "kibbutz" for the later period of movement history.

The gradual development of the kibbutz movement was of course taking place in the context of the growth of Zionism and increasing Jewish immigration to Palestine. The success of the kibbutz movement, which was to become a dominant force in the later years of the Yishuv and the early years of the state (Israel was founded in 1948), cannot be understood without being placed in this context.

After the 1920s and the establishment of the federations, the kibbutz movement expanded more quickly than any other type of Jewish settlement in Palestine (Ben David 1964:50). Kibbutz population grew thirtyfold (from 1,190 in 1922 to 37,400 in 1945, and the number of settlements multiplied sixfold (from 19 in 1922 to 116 in 1945). They acquired ideological and political dominance, they developed a critical role in defense and they became the strongest sector of the rural economy. These developments were to have comprehensive influence on the character of the state after 1948 in economic, defense, political and ideological terms. The internal character of the kibbutz movement was to be colored by its role in the development of the state. As the settlements faced and resolved problems, they were shaping Palestinian Jewish society and the state to come and were, in turn, being shaped by it.

As more and more *kvutzot* and kibbutzim were founded, they followed precedents set by the experiences of the early settlers. From the beginning, there was great international interest in the young pioneers, especially in the Zionist movement which was by this time an organized political force in Europe. The Balfour Declaration of 1917 had proclaimed the British government's support for a Jewish National Home in Palestine and had given real hope for Zionist success. The kibbutz movement was therefore famous and was at the same time developing greater organizational coherence. This included liaison with Zionist youth groups in Europe, especially important, for it brought young immigrants to Palestine with some training for kibbutz life. By the 1920s, there were regulations, as much practical as ideological, for the type of immigrant required in the *kvutzot*/kibbutzim. For example, Hashomer Hatzair, insisted that the immigrant ". . . had to be seventeen years old . . . must have been a member of Hashomer Hatzair for a minimum of two years . . . must have learned to speak, read and write Hebrew . . . must have spent several summer vacations working in agricultural occupations" (Stern 1965:10). This move towards prepared immigrants was complemented by the crystallization of a more explicit philosophy (discussed below).

Consolidated ideological and organizational strength was not simply a result of the inherent qualities of the settlements, which were as much dependent on the JNF (for access to land), the Zionist movement as a whole (for manpower), and the Mandate authorities of 1918-1948 (both for land and as a target for resistance) as they were on their own resources (mainly manpower and ideas). The critical asset of the settlements was their ability to respond to circumstances in ways which turned out to be advantageous to their own development. Their responses proved increasingly beneficial to the Zionist endeavor and increasingly antipathetic to the Mandate government and the developing Arab nationalist movement.

To begin with, the *kvutzot*/kibbutzim had not found favor with the Zionist establishment. They had helped break its tight control over Jewish settlement in Palestine, which had previously deterred communal settlements in the first *aliya*. It is clear that the pioneers of Degania were very lucky to get land from the JNF. The Degania settlers had strongly protested the management of settlements by agents of European financiers (Baratz 1956, Stern 1965), arguing that both Jewish and Arab workers were being exploited. Once Degania and the later settlements had obtained land, however, the way was open for them to capitalize on their position.

In the Yishuv, the kibbutzim were predominantly agricultural. They saw their return to the soil as the first step in the rebirth of the Jewish people and valued rural settlement and agricultural labor particularly highly (Cohen 1970). Though there were a few urban kibbutzim, and Chever Hakvutzot at least was interested in them, the rural emphasis of the kibbutzim was at this stage overwhelming. Only recently have some large kibbutzim been likened to towns (Cohen 1976). Once a kibbutz was established, there was tremendous emphasis placed on progress in agricultural activity (Cohen 1966). Mechanization and intensification of agricultural production proceeded quickly, and kibbutz agriculture became the most efficient in the country (Cohen 1966:8). With the investment provided by the Zionist establishment, the kibbutzim had an advantage over the traditional farmers of Palestine (Zureik 1979). In their trained workforce committed to efficient production, they had assets which other Jewish rural settlements lacked. They were able to use the existing infrastructure of the country (e.g., markets and transport facilities) to their advantage. A variety of crops were tested to determine which ones were most suited to the communal organization. This progressive orientation enhanced their position in Jewish agriculture and resulted in further advantage.

The Zionist authorities, despite their initial characterizations of the kibbutz settlers as doubtful and rebellious communists, quickly saw the advantages of kibbutz settlement for the Zionist endeavor as a whole. There were two main economic advantages. A kibbutz required less capital investment than other forms of rural settlement, notably the *moshav*, a family farm cooperative (Kanovsky 1966). Also, land for Jewish settlement was in very short supply as time went on, and it became more and more important to try to guarantee that it would be successfully farmed. The progressive orientations and trained workforce of the kibbutzim therefore proved especially attractive.

Successful defensive operations were particularly significant for the rise of the kibbutzim in the Mandate period. In the first place, communes were relatively easily mobilized for defense, especially in comparison with the rather scattered family farm cooperatives (Kanovsky 1966). With increasing Arab (and later Mandate government) opposition to Jewish settlement, ready mobilization became more and more important to the Jews of Palestine. As the Mandate proceeded, the kibbutzim proved important bases and sources of recruitment for the Jewish underground resistance, especially the Palmach and the Haganah (Darin-Drabkin 1962). The kibbutzim developed their own method for establishing settlements in hostile regions; this was called the *choma vemigdal* (tower and stockade). Settlers would arrive in an area (often at night) with their defenses and houses in prefabricated sections loaded on lorries, and the settlement would be set up, complete with watchtower and surrounding fence, in a matter of a few hours, much to the surprise of the neighbors. The first such kibbutz was Nir David, set up in 1936 (Stern 1965). Finally, the defensive abilities of many kibbutzim were to be proven in the War of Independence in 1948, when they successfully held out against the advancing Arab armies. The settlers of Yad Mordechai for example held their kibbutz for six days against a mighty onslaught of Egyptian shells, giving the main Jewish forces time to prepare to repel the advance (Larkin 1963).

Yet another factor in the ascendancy of the kibbutzim was their role in the illegal immigration of Jews to Palestine. As the numbers of immigrants rose with anti-Semitism in Europe and as the Arab population became increasingly alarmed, the Mandate authorities tried to control immigration by imposing quotas in 1939. Kibbutzim were in large part responsible for the failure of the quota system to slow immigration to the required level. Illegal immigrants would be taken to kibbutzim, dressed in work clothes and set to labor in the fields. Mandate officials found it impossible to distinguish "legals" from "illegals," and the latter were able to move about undetected (Stern 1965).

During the Mandate then, the kibbutz movement became a dominant force in the Yishuv. The ideology of pioneering Zionism came to symbolize the Jewish settlement in Palestine, and today still does, especially to non-Israelis. The economic success of kibbutz agriculture made the kibbutzim the most productive and efficient sector of the rural economy; militarily, the kibbutzim were effective and prestigious. The proportion of kibbutz inhabitants in the Jewish population of Palestine peaked in 1947 at 7.5%, trebling in less than twenty years (Shur 1972). Davis (1977:27) notes that though the kibbutzim in recent times contain less than 3% of the Israeli Jewish population, they have maintained the elite position established during the Yishuv. They have contributed, he says, 25% of Israeli cabinet members, 22% (or more) of the middle and high military command, and an overwhelming majority of air force pilots, the elite fighting force. Elon (1972) says that when the kibbutz movement was at its height, the proportion of kibbutz members in positions of national importance was seven times greater than the proportion of kibbutz inhabitants in the population as a whole. Cohen (1970) shows how the early years of economic planning in the state were heavily influenced by the kibbutzim and argues that planning exhibited a bias towards rural settlement

which can only be attributed to kibbutz involvement in the planning process and
to kibbutz ascendancy in the Yishuv.

With the foundation of the state in 1948, the kibbutz environment changed
radically. The most far reaching change was in the character of immigrants:
European Jewry, including the youth movements which had been the main recruiting
grounds for the kibbutzim, were decimated during the war, and the early years
of the state saw a massive influx of immigrants from North Africa and Arabia
(Eisenstadt 1975). From the point of view of the kibbutzim, these "Oriental"
immigrants, were quite unsuitable as recruits. They were not, in many cases,
Zionists in the modern sense at all, they did not know Hebrew, they were not
socialists, they did not understand the importance of manual, agricultural labor.
Indeed, many of them wished to continue their old, urban way of life and traditional
occupations. They did not, in short, meet the requirements now expected by
kibbutzim of their recruits, and the kibbutzim were not prepared to accept them.
This is not to say that the kibbutzim took no part in the settlement of the Oriental
immigrants. Some offered them paid employment (Shatil 1966). Others refused
to do so on principle and thus remained isolated from the mainstream of post-
state immigration (Kanovsky 1966). Furthermore, between 1948 and 1953, one-
eighth of the veteran kibbutz members left their communities for government jobs,
becoming immediately involved in the processes of settlement and absorption of
immigrants.

In the field of defense, the role of the kibbutzim changed. After 1948, the army
was run by the state, and underground military activity based in kibbutzim was
no longer necessary. At the same time, the kibbutzim, easily defended and
ideologically committed to the state, retained their strategic advantages. Many post-
1948 kibbutzim were founded on borders and in other militarily sensitive areas
where they could provide a firm military presence (Talmon-Garber and Cohen
1964). In the mid-1950s, the army established a special unit called Nahal (a Hebrew
acronym for "fighting pioneering youth"), in which recruits spent part of their
army service working in kibbutzim. In more recent times, Nahal members have
participated in founding new kibbutzim in border areas. In its early years, Nahal
was especially important to the kibbutz movement as it helped prevent army service
from diverting potential recruits away from the kibbutzim; in fact, it even served
as a source of new recruits. It was strongly supported by the kibbutzim on these
grounds (Talmon-Garber and Cohen 1964).

With the increasing involvement of kibbutz members and ex-members in national
politics and administration, the kibbutz federations became more tied to political
parties, developing links which had been relatively weak during the Mandate period
(Ben David 1964). Party political involvement was a major factor in the splits which
developed in many kibbutzim in the 1950s (see above), and problems were increased
by disagreements in the Israeli political left — generally over Russian policies
towards the Jews. Once split, the kibbutzim became politically unified within
themselves and more firmly allied to the parties of the member's choice, allowing

the parties to be more confident in relying on "their" kibbutzim for support (Arian 1968). Views differ on the precise relationships established at this time between the kibbutz federations and the parties. Stern (1965) argues that the kibbutzim were and still are dominated by the parties; Kanovsky (1966) asserts that the kibbutzim dominated the parties. Whatever the relationship, it was certainly close and persists today. The kibbutz federations can take up to 6% of kibbutz members to work for them. These people are effectively full-time party workers, a steady, committed and reliable source of political manpower for the parties in question (Arian 1968).

As the most modernized sector of Israeli agriculture in the immediate post-state period, the kibbutzim were called upon to supply large amounts of food for the influx of immigrants (Stern 1965). This, combined with a lack of recruits, brought about a labor shortage in the kibbutzim (see Chapter 3). At the same time, Israel's borders with its neighbors were closed, trade ended (Rokach 1964) and the new state adopted the policy of increasing agricultural production as quickly as possible. This policy proved particularly favorable to the kibbutzim, as their inherent leanings towards mechanization and intensification of production could be rapidly satisfied by government sponsorship of efficient agriculture. Already more mechanized than other agricultural sectors in 1948, the kibbutzim maintained their advantage for several years (Kanovsky 1966). When a quota system was introduced in the 1950s to curtail what was now agricultural overproduction, the kibbutzim benefited yet again, as the system favored more established and efficient producers (cf. Abarbanel 1972). The kibbutzim were able to introduce economies of scale and to produce trained specialists, thus advancing further. The early 1950s saw the first industrial enterprises in kibbutzim (discussed in Chapter 3).

The efficiency and profitability of the kibbutzim in the early state period is represented by the relatively rapidly rising standard of living of kibbutz members, in comparison with other sectors of Israeli society (Kanovsky 1966, Shatil 1966, Stern 1965). All this was due, I have suggested, to the foundations laid by the movement in the pre-state period for its own subsequent development. The problems experienced in this period were primarily due to changes in the wider society, especially the new kinds of immigrants, and the relative lack of recruits for the kibbutzim.

## Kibbutz Ideology

The early pioneers developed a new way of life by, as I have said, "an almost pure process of trial and error" (Ben David 1964:47). It is very important to understand that there never was a fixed program for their activities and that their ideas firmed up only gradually as time went on. There is really no such thing as "kibbutz ideology," if by that we mean a clear set of principles and a detailed plan for a way of life. We are, in reality, talking about a historical process, a set

of ideas which have developed and changed with the kibbutzim and which continue
to do so today.

To begin with, it is hard to distinguish any clear set of ideas to which the early
pioneers subscribed. They were *against* many aspects of Jewish life in Europe
in the late nineteenth and early twentieth centuries. What they were *for* would
be clarified later as their communities developed. For example, they were firmly
opposed to the life of the *shtetl* (the Jewish community of Eastern Europe described
by Zborowski and Herzog 1962). They considered it closed, confined and artificial,
criticizing the ideal of a man as a scholar and a woman as a wife and mother
(Diamond 1957). They resented the restricted, family-centered life, with the father
dominating his wife and children. Most of them at this time were openly anti-
religious (Elon 1972, Frankel 1980). They criticized the occupations of Jews who
had joined the new bourgeois class as exploitative and inhuman (Hashomer Hatzair
1963). Inspired by the Zionist movement, they wanted to be in Palestine. Once
there, they were faced with new questions upon which they felt it was important
to have a principled stance; for example, they considered very carefully what kind
of employment they should take (Baratz 1954) and also thought at length about
their personal lives and personal relationships (Spiro 1972).

Once Degania was founded, the pioneers had decided, as a result of their
experiences so far in Palestine, that they wanted to be neither employers nor
employees, but to work for themselves. It is also clear that they now thought of
their activities as contributing to the regeneration of the Jewish people. At this
time, we can identify a number of individuals who provided the movement with
broad principles, which it was to build upon and adapt as time went on. Three
of the most important were A.D. Gordon, Ber Borochov and Martin Buber.

A.D. Gordon was, for a time, associated with Degania. Baratz (1954) describes
the great influence of his ideas about the importance of manual labor for the rebirth
of the Jewish people on the pioneers of Degania. He has been called the Tolstoy
of Palestine (Katzenelson-Rubashow 1976:111). Gordon said:

> A people that has become accustomed to every mode of life save the natural
> one — the life of self-conscious and self-supporting labour — such a people
> will never become a living natural labouring people unless it strains every
> fibre of its will to attain that goal. Labour is not merely the factor which
> establishes man's contact with the land and his claim to the land; it is the
> principal force in the building of a natural civilisation. Labour is a great human
> need for the future, and a great ideal is like the healing sun. We need fanatics
> of labour in the most exalted sense of the word. (quoted by Spiro 1972:13)

He also provided individual inspiration by example. Shifra Betzer, a woman pioneer
wrote:

> From the beginning, I conceived a deep affection for this old man. . . . Often,
> seeing me sit apart, completely exhausted, he would call out to me: 'Cheer
> up! Look at me, an old man, working as hard as the rest and always happy.'
> (Katzenelson-Rubashow 1976:28)

Borochov wrote widely on the relationship between socialism and Jewish nationalism. Studying European society, he realized that the Jews were concentrated in the middle class. As a minority group, they could not enter the ruling class, and for historical reasons associated with their minority status, they had no base in the proletariat. In his view, they were vulnerable because they were far removed from the economic core of society, its "basic branches of production" (Borochov 1948:45). When a national crisis threatened, the Jews, who serviced the economy and were a minority, could be made scapegoats. The way out of this position was Zionism, which would not only make the Jews a nation in their own right but would also allow them to participate in building socialism.

Martin Buber was a prominent Zionist thinker whose writings date from the early part of the twentieth century. He stressed the importance of the role of young people in building the nation, providing important support for the young pioneers. He was later to become an important advocate of the success of the kibbutzim (Buber 1949).

The pioneers' ideas then were gradually becoming firmer: they were able to build into their thoughts the philosophies of people like Gordon, Borochov and Buber. Some ranged more widely, looking to the work of Sigmund Freud especially for help with their personal relationships (Spiro 1972). Kibbutz ideology could and can be characterized as:

> . . . a heterogeneous system, composed of Socialism, Zionism, humanistic ethics and sometimes religion, which are integrated only in a most strenuous way. (Cohen 1966:3-4)

It was also inherently dynamic, partly because of the way it developed and partly because of its contents. Cohen (1966) gives a particularly clear example of this dynamism, by focusing on the twin values of progress and communality, which were and are central to kibbutz ideology. Communality was the basis of kibbutz socialism — sharing in all things, working and playing together, each person contributing to the best of his or her ability, and each being rewarded according to his or her needs. Progress referred to rebuilding the Jewish nation. The settlers returned to the land to work, to learn the value of physical labor, to regenerate and to rebuild. The "return to the soil" was the first rung on the ladder which would lead to a new socialist Jewish society. Cohen considers these two principles to have been contradictory, arguing for example that progress dictated a change from rotation of jobs to permanent jobs for all, which was no longer really communal. The problem with this interpretation is that it gives "communality" an absolute meaning it never had. Kibbutz people in fact saw permanent jobs for all as consistent with communality, a principle which therefore has to be understood as flexible. It could alter as progress, the fulfillment of another principle, occurred.

A further example of ideological reinterpretation can be found in the development of the principle of equality. One aspect of this is related to the field of consumption. In the early days, every kibbutz pioneer received the same goods for personal use. As Rosenfeld (1957) shows, such a system did not operate successfully for long and became especially problematic as the kibbutzim increased in size and diversity of population. With organizational consolidation, "norms of distribution" were developed (Rosenfeld 1957, Cohen 1976), involving a formally fixed notion of need. For example, people would receive only a certain amount of goods at specified intervals (perhaps one pair of workboots in two years).

When the kibbutzim became richer, there was more scope for the exercise of personal preferences in consumption, and "points systems" began to appear whereby, for example, a member would have a number of clothing points every year and could "spend" them as he or she wished. In some of the large, rich kibbutzim today, members have a personal allowance which covers all their consumption needs—clothes, books, furniture, shoes, etc.—and which they budget for themselves. As each alteration in consumption methods occurred, it was designed to maintain a principle of equality which, it is clear, was modified as time went on.

Such processes of reinterpretation characterize the development of kibbutz ideology, and many more examples will be given as the book goes on. We will see that, just as early ideological development involved interaction between ideas and practicalities, so the more recent ideological modifications result from the interaction of ideas and the current practicalities faced by the kibbutz movement. Historical precedents operate very strongly, and so the process of ideological development has become increasingly complicated.

## The Kibbutz Today

At present, there are about 275 kibbutzim in Israel, with a population of about 125 thousand. The kibbutz population forms just under 3% of the total Israeli Jewish population, and about 28% of the rural population (Central Bureau of Statistics 1986). They contribute about 12% of the Israeli Gross National Product. Just under one-third of the kibbutzim are affiliated to the Kibbutz Artzi federation (still the most left wing) and just under two-thirds of them to the large Takam federation resulting from the recent merger of the Ichud Hakvutzot Vehakibbutzim and Hakibbutz Hameuchad. There is also the small federation of religious kibbutzim, and a small number of kibbutzim are unaffiliated.

Apart from their federation affiliations, the kibbutzim can be divided into two major categories (Billis 1972, Cohen 1976), which broadly speaking are 1. kibbutzim founded before 1948; and 2. kibbutzim founded after 1948, that is, after radical changes in the environment of the kibbutzim. Billis (1972:246) outlines the major characteristics of each type: the older settlements generally have "a solid base of veterans, steady growth of membership and a continuous stream of children becoming members," and the post-state settlements generally "a mixture of population from many *Hashlamot* (population complements, groups of people sent to the kibbutz by the federation), cyclic membership growth, and a trickle of children becoming members." At the time of Billis' study, 39% of Kibbutz Artzi kibbutzim were in the second category, and about 42% of kibbutzim in Meuchad and Ichud (Billis 1972). With the foundation of new settlements, the proportion of post-1948 kibbutzim has increased since then. Generally, older kibbutzim are more stable, economically better off and industrialized, and their members are relatively satisfied with their way of life. The post-state kibbutzim have had great trouble in keeping recruits and in advancing economically, and suffer frequently from social problems arising from dissatisfaction among kibbutzim, their main strategy being to send them new recruits, from the youth movements particularly. Billis (1972) in his study of the Kibbutz Artzi federation found that most of these groups were being sent to the younger kibbutzim. The veteran settlements, which had formerly received groups of new members who had stayed, were now growing as the children of veterans and younger members stayed on. Kibbutzim which have failed to keep new members and become demographically, economically and socially consolidated are referred to by the federations as the "little kibbutzim" (*hakibbutzim haza'irim*).

Although the federations recognize the problems of this category of kibbutzim and devote considerable effort and resources to attempts to help them, it seems that they have not acknowledged the possibility that the twofold division of the kibbutz movement may continue for the foreseeable future. This is also true of some commentators on the history of the movement, who suggest that if only more people will join the little kibbutzim, they will recover, and develop to be more like the veteran settlements. Cohen (1976) for example divides kibbutzim historically into three types: the bund (characteristic of the early kibbutzim, a *kvutza* type), the commune (the mature small kibbutz) and the association (the mature large kibbutz). In suggesting that the development of the movement from a bund type to commune and association type settlements parallels that of the development of many individual kibbutzim, he notes that some kibbutzim have never reached the commune or association stage, but have remained "residual communes" or "sectoral communes," demographically depleted and internally divided. Provided that the federations continue their support for such settlements (the little kibbutzim), they will recover, Cohen feels, and continue their development towards commune or association. Billis (1972) considers this to be an unrealistic view, because of the long period over which the little kibbutzim have remained unstable, repeatedly failing to keep new members and repeatedly experiencing economic difficulties. He sees this as a self-reinforcing process, arguing for example that because new members will not stay, economic activity cannot be fully efficient. Thus, new members will leave because they see the kibbutz economy as unsatisfactory, and so on. The process is exacerbated by the existence of stable, profitable kibbutzim. People in the little kibbutzim inevitably compare their situations with those of the veterans and find the comparison unsatisfactory. Apparently, people who leave the little kibbutzim do not go to larger ones. Although this is difficult to establish firmly, my experience of Goshen suggests that they leave the movement altogether.

Cohen (1966) detects possible future problems for the kibbutz movement in the association type settlements — the large, rich kibbutzim. Although there are as yet no detailed studies of these, he is able to list a number of their characteristics which he feels threaten the autonomy and distinctiveness of the kibbutz movement. Included are an increasing tendency to identify with urban, middle class values and life-styles, weakening external boundaries due especially to extensive economic links outside the settlements, the development into a corporation type organization, and a "communication gap," which means that most members have little opportunity to participate in decision making in the community. It is possible, Cohen considers, that these characteristics may increasingly become those of the kibbutz movement as a whole. He warns against treating such change as anything like a "crisis" or a departure from "original values." He writes (1976:738):

> Whatever the conception of the kibbutz maintained by the "Founding Fathers" might have been, it is perfectly legitimate, within the framework of a secular conception of values, for members of successive generations to alter its values, goals and institutional arrangements. The only legitimate question about the future of the kibbutz, then, is the one relating to the kinds of alternatives which one could conceive of for its future development and the probabilities attached to each of them.

## Kibbutz Goshen: Introduction to the Case Study

The general perspective on the whole of the kibbutz movement will continue throughout the book to focus on different areas of institutional, organizational and ideological development. The basis of the account, however, is a detailed case study of the kibbutz I call Goshen. The real Goshen was the last "home" of the Jews in Egypt, before the exodus (Exodus VIII, 22; IX, 26). Kibbutz Goshen belongs to the Kibbutz Artzi federation and is a "little kibbutz." For many years, it was unable to raise its membership above one hundred, reaching this target only in the early 1970s after more than twenty years' existence. At the end of 1975, there were one hundred thirty-nine members and candidates for membership, not all of whom were committed to staying there. "Member" in the kibbutz is a formal status conferred by a vote in the General Assembly, a meeting of all who are already members. Candidates are people who have indicated a wish to become members and have been accepted for a trial period (normally a year) prior to the vote. Only adults are eligible to be members. The total population of Goshen, including children and various categories of temporary residents, fluctuated over the period of my fieldwork around the two hundred fifty mark.

ᐠ The pioneers of Goshen were three groups of young Egyptian Jews who went to Palestine with the intention of founding a kibbutz in 1945, 1946 and 1947. The total number was about forty-five members of Hashomer Hatzair, the youth movement attached to the Kibbutz Artzi federation. They came from the Egyptian middle class, were relatively well off, and many of them were extremely well educated. Though strictly Oriental immigrants, they were markedly different from the Oriental immigrants who went to Israel in vast numbers in the 1950s described earlier. Soon after they reached Palestine, the Egyptians were joined by a group of Hashomer Hatzair members from Western European countries, some of whom had been in Switzerland as refugees from the Nazis. They were allocated a little land near an already established kibbutz in Northern Palestine, where they began to live communally and to accustom themselves to manual labor by working in the veteran settlement. This "practice period" had been instigated as early as 1920 (Spiro 1972) and by the late 1940s had long been established as part of the training of kibbutz settlers. I was often told of the blisters and exhaustion which this unfamiliar work brought, descriptions which echoed those of the old pioneers (Amitai 1966, Baratz 1954, Katzenelson-Rubashow 1976, Maimon 1962). Land for Jewish settlement was in short supply at that time. The pioneers were briefly sent, in 1947, to the Negev Desert in the South to form a temporary defensive settlement, finally settling on their present site in 1949. Goshen is situated near the pre-1967 Jordanian border. Originally, it was located in the hills and fortified, but soon more permanent buildings were put on the lower ground where all the people now live. I was told that life was very hard in the beginning. The ground was very stony; earth to grow crops had to be carried from a nearby *wadi* (a dried up riverbed); water was collected every day in a trailer from a nearby town. At first, people lived in tents, then in wooden huts with three others. For the first few months, the settlers (joined by another group in 1949) were advised and assisted in their efforts by a veteran Kibbutz Artzi representative. The presence of this person is indicative of the degree of organizational consolidation of the movement at this time. Although the precedents offered by earlier settlers had always influenced new kibbutzim, by this time, they were being formally represented among a group of people who had already had movement training.

Once founded, Goshen started to receive population complements, *hashlamot* or groups of settlers allocated by the federation, (Cohen 1976), and very soon began to experience the problems characteristic of the little kibbutzim, that is, the new settlers did not stay. The table indicates the size of the problem.

## Table 1

Population complements to Kibbutz Goshen 1945-1971,
related to numbers remaining at the end of 1975

| Year of entry to kibbutz | Country of origin | Number in group | Number remaining | % who stayed | % who left |
|---|---|---|---|---|---|
| 1945-7 | Egypt | 45 | 14 | 31.1 | 68.9 |
| 1946 | Mixed European (see text) | 20 | 6 | 30.0 | 70.0 |
| 1949 | Israel and Europe | 40* | 23 | 57.5 | 42.5 |
| 1955 | 2 mixed youth groups | 23 | 9 | 39.1 | 60.9 |
| 1957 | Mixed youth group | 15 | 2 | 13.3 | 86.7 |
| 1959 | England | 20 | 1 | 5.0 | 95.0 |
| 1960 | Belgium | 20* | 1 | 5.0 | 95.0 |
| 1966 | Israel | 50 | 11 | 22.0 | 78.0 |
| 1967 | Morocco and France | 25 | 8 | 32.0 | 68.0 |
| 1971 | Israel | 20 | 6 | 30.0 | 70.0 |
| | **Total** | **278** | **81** | **29.1** | **70.9** |

*estimate

The latest groups could not, in 1975, be described as settled. Many of them did in fact leave Goshen in 1978, and the percentage of those who stayed thus declined. In 1975, for every member of Goshen who had gone there with a population complement, there were three ex-members. Kibbutz Degem by comparison had four ex-members for every member (Billis 1972). If members from sources other than population complements are included (see below), Goshen approaches this figure.

Interestingly, the folk view of the situation differed somewhat from reality. For example, I was often told that the Egyptians were the largest group of pioneers remaining and that there were between fifteen and twenty of them. Also, the 1966 group was frequently mentioned as having been very successful. The highest estimate here was that twenty-seven of them had stayed. There were many similar "mistaken views." Memories reflected either a very striking mass departure of a group as with the 1959 English group which was mentioned as the worst ever failure or the current participation of the group members in kibbutz life. The Egyptians and the 1966 group were particularly active when I was at Goshen. Other groups were barely remembered or simply not considered worthy of comment, notably the Belgian group of 1960. They seemingly had little impact on Goshen: neither leaving in the dramatic fashion of the English group nor participating in kibbutz life. They had simply drifted away from Goshen.

The most difficult period for Goshen was the late 1950s and early 1960s. This was a time of upheaval in the kibbutz movement generally and the Kibbutz Artzi in particular, and this upheaval seems to have reflected on Goshen. It was caused both by external political factors and factors internal to the federation. In 1955, the USSR started selling weapons to Egypt, a move which finally broke the once close identification of the Kibbutz Artzi with Russian socialism. This was also the period of political splits in the movement as a whole (Stern 1965, Viteles 1967 and see above). The aftermath of the turmoil resulted in the political affiliations of each kibbutz being firmly and more clearly defined. Until then, Goshen's future had been fair. It had begun to support itself economically and there was an active social and cultural life, but ideological uncertainty brought about the departure of some of the pioneers. The kibbutz lost its base, and the new groups arriving in the late 1950s found a community lacking direction. One group, the English, left *en masse*, and others left more slowly, one or two at a time.

Since then, Goshen's population problems have continued. In the end, the process has become self-reinforcing, as I noted before. People on Goshen often compared their kibbutz unfavorably with richer kibbutzim, in a way similar to that described for Degem by Billis (1972).

Population complements were not the only source of recruits to Goshen. At the end of 1975, twenty members had been born there, and thirty-eight others had joined the community as individuals. The origins of these individuals are given in Table 2.

**Table 2**

Origins of other members and candidates at the end of 1975

| Origin | Number |
|---|---|
| Volunteer workers (a) Married in | 4 |
| (b) Stayed on* | 7 |
| Marriage | 6 |
| Israeli urbanites** | 6 |
| Soldiers staying on (after Nahal) | 4 |
| Moroccans (friends of an existing member) | 4 |
| From other kibbutzim | 3 |
| Hired worker who became a member | 1 |
| Miscellaneous | 3 |
| **Total** | **38** |

* Includes two married couples
**three married couples

Many of these people, and many of those born on Goshen had only recently joined Goshen, and their continuation was not therefore guaranteed. The most common time for people to leave a kibbutz is after three to five years' membership (Kibbutz Artzi 1972:17). As many individuals had already come and gone, many children of Goshen had already left the kibbutz (some without becoming members at all) and because of the persistent population structure (see below), we should expect these people to become established members in approximately the same proportions as the population complements had done.

So at the end of 1975, there were one hundred thirty-nine members and candidates. The problems of keeping members had created a peculiar population structure. The majority of the members were aged between twenty and twenty-nine (the children of Goshen and the recent entrants) or over forty-five (the remaining pioneers). There were very few aged between thirty and forty-four. Table 3 compares this distribution with the population of other Kibbutz Artzi kibbutzim and shows the "generation gap" to be characteristic of kibbutzim generally. It is especially so of the little kibbutzim.

### Table 3

Age distribution of members of Kibbutz Goshen (1975)
and the Kibbutz Artzi federation (1971)

| | % Members | |
| Age | Kibbutz Goshen | Kibbutz Artzi |
|---|---|---|
| 19 | 1.4 | 6.0 |
| 20-24 | 17.3 | 19.3 |
| 20-29 | 34.5 | 14.8 |
| 30-34 | 2.2 | 9.7 |
| 35-39 | 5.8 | 8.4 |
| 40-44 | 3.6 | 7.5 |
| 45-49 | 17.3 | 7.9 |
| 50-54 | 15.1 | 6.7 |
| 55-59 | 1.4 | 11.3 |
| 60-64 | 1.4 | 6.0 |
| 65-69 | 0 | 1.9 |
| 70+ | 0 | 0.5 |
| | ——— | ——— |
| | 100.0 | 100.0 |

Source: (for Kibbutz Artzi figures) Kibbutz Artzi 1972:7

Table 4 shows that it was not general to the Israeli Jewish population.

**Table 4**

Percentage of Israeli population in age categories 19-70+ (1975)

| Age category | % total population |
|:---:|:---:|
| 19 | 9.0 |
| 20-24 | 15.3 |
| 25-29 | 9.9 |
| 30-34 | 8.5 |
| 35-39 | 8.3 |
| 40-44 | 8.2 |
| 45-49 | 8.6 |
| 50-54 | 7.0 |
| 55-59 | 7.8 |
| 60-64 | 6.8 |
| 65-69 | 4.6 |
| 70+ | 4.0 |

Source: Kibbutz Artzi 1972:7

The generation gap was responsible for many of the economic, social and political difficulties experienced by Goshen, and we shall be investigating these in later chapters. It was, I should add, immediately striking to the outsider (Bowes 1975).

When studying a kibbutz, it is tempting to focus exclusively on the members and candidates ("kibbutzniks") and possibly their children, as for example Spiro (1971, 1972) does. The temptation arises because these people are, in a sense, the kibbutz, for they run it, devote their lives to it, reap its benefits and suffer its losses. They certainly see themselves as such. As Shepher (1980) has argued, however, such a focus can be seriously misleading for three main reasons: 1. there are likely to be many nonmembers resident in the community; 2. there may be people working in the kibbutz who neither live there nor are members; 3. there may be members who do not work on the kibbutz and members may have links with outsiders, relatives, friends or workmates, who make their horizons broader.

On Goshen in 1975, there was a fluctuating population of volunteer workers, young foreigners who came to work there and to learn something of the kibbutz way of life. In return, they received board and lodging and a little pocket money (no wages). Between March 1975 and March 1976, more than a hundred volunteers stayed in Goshen for an average of three and a half months each. Over that period, their labor was equivalent to that of twenty-eight full-time workers. The presence of volunteers was explained by the members with reference to peak labor demands in the agricultural cycle of the kibbutz. They were said to fill excess labor requirements at difficult times of the year when the kibbutz workforce could not cope. In fact, they contributed something rather different, as I will show in Chapter 3 (and see Bowes 1980). Volunteers were a permanent feature of Goshen.

Some hired workers also lived on Goshen—a nurse and a kindergarten teacher—and others came to work from elsewhere on a permanent or temporary basis. These people were also said to be doing jobs which the members could not. Although this was certainly the case to some extent, again the presence of these people has a rather more complicated explanation (see below, Chapter 3).

Throughout my fieldwork, there were always at least four soldiers, weekday residents and workers in Goshen. They were Nahal members, sent to Goshen for part of their Army service. Four former Nahal members had become members of Goshen in the past, and these soldiers were looked upon as possible recruits by Goshen's members.

All these categories provided members with potential contacts outside the community, stretching world wide in the case of the volunteers. Young kibbutzniks on their travels would visit former volunteers who provided accommodation and meals—very valuable to rather poor travellers. Furthermore, many kibbutzniks had relatives and friends outside Goshen with whom they visited. Such people could be particularly helpful to anyone wanting to leave Goshen, providing money and contacts "in town," or they might simply be a source of outside stimuli of various kinds.

Some members of every kibbutz work outside the community in movement offices and enterprises. Four members of Goshen did this in 1975-6. Other members were given special permission to work outside. Four unmarried women in their thirties and forties were in this category primarily to afford them opportunities to meet marriageable men. These four, and one other woman whose husband had recently left her, worked for the movement. Others were permitted to work outside because of special skills which they could not develop in the kibbutz. There were two people of Goshen working as university lecturers.

The army provided further contacts outside. Most young people did army service: three years for men and two for unmarried women. This was, for most of them, their first experience of life outside the kibbutz. Many found their return to Goshen after army service a difficult period and would reflect long and hard before making the decision to apply for membership. Others found spouses in the army. Two Goshen women had done this, returning alone to the kibbutz with their children after their marriages to soldiers had broken up. After their three years in the army, men were required to serve reserve duty. In 1975-6, this was two months per year, until the age of fifty-six. Single women could also be called into the reserves, but this was very rare (Hazleton 1977) and happened only to one woman member during my fieldwork.

## Conclusion

In the rest of the book, I shall be concentrating mainly on the post-1948 period, over which Goshen has developed. The purpose of this chapter has been to set the scene and to give the reader a general appreciation of the historical and ideological background of the present day kibbutz movement generally and kibbutz Goshen in particular. In conclusion, I want to stress the main points which have emerged so far, and which form a crucial backdrop to the later chapters.

The kibbutz movement cannot be understood outside its context: the history of the Zionist movement and the development of Jewish settlement in Palestine/ Israel. This is also the case when we focus on one kibbutz. Its history and current character dovetail with those of the federation to which it belongs and the movement as a whole. The second major point cannot be overstressed, kibbutz ideology is not, and never has been, fixed. It has developed and continues to do so in interaction with practical historical experience as well as economic, political and social events. It is also important to recognize the extent to which a case study of one kibbutz can contribute to the understanding of the movement as a whole. This is clearly restricted by the category of kibbutz under study. In the case of Goshen (a little kibbutz), we are dealing with a community which is representative of one part of the kibbutz movement as described earlier. If we are to develop more general statements about the movement as a whole, then we should be clear how far the particular experience of the little kibbutzim differs from that of the communes or associations (Cohen 1976), or from very new kibbutzim which are still at the bund stage. Finally, care is required in delineating the boundaries of the kibbutz itself. I have suggested that we are looking at a population wider than that simply of members, candidates and their children.

# - 3 -

# Working on a Kibbutz

## Finding a Job

Talk to anyone who has been to a kibbutz as a volunteer, and you will be told about the work they did. They cleaned tables in the dining room where people's table manners left a lot to be desired; they fell off ladders in the orange groves stretching to reach the highest branches; they helped load chickens into baskets, hands full of the legs of six birds while the seventh ran away into the darkness; they were covered with scratches from head to toe after reaching for weeds between the rose bushes; and they got sunstroke hoeing weeds along endless rows of cotton plants in open, shadeless fields. All these were part of my own experience, and indicate the kind of work that kibbutz volunteers generally do, which is predominantly unskilled, manual, and very often seasonal. Work is allocated to volunteers on a kibbutz by the Labor Organizer, a kibbutz member who is elected every few months to match up labor shortages and available workers. In short, the organizer allocates people who can be moved between different branches of the kibbutz economy. Volunteers form one of the major categories of such people. On Goshen, they were at least 12% of the workforce (of about 165 people) throughout my fieldwork. There has been very little research on kibbutz volunteers, because they are generally considered outsiders and are therefore excluded from study, and there are few records which could be used for comparative purposes. Nevertheless, the figures which are available (Bowes 1980) suggest that volunteers were about 6% of the workforce of all kibbutzim in the mid-late 1970s. If such a figure is reasonable, then Goshen had more volunteers than the average. Goshen probably relied more heavily on volunteers because it had very few hired workers. Kibbutzim with fully developed industrial branches hired people in large numbers. Leviatan (1973) found that in the early 1970s, 55% of workers in such branches

**43**

were hired. Given the recent rapid development of kibbutz industry (Don 1977), it is likely that the figure has since increased. More hired laborers would make the percentage of volunteers look smaller, even though their numbers have recently increased (Bowes 1980).

Whatever the actual proportion of volunteers in any kibbutz workforce, they play an important role in the community. Ostensibly, according to the publicity which attracts them and the statements of members of the kibbutz movement, they go to the kibbutzim to fill labor shortages, particularly seasonal ones, which cannot be met by kibbutz members. Many of the jobs done by volunteers on Goshen were indeed seasonal—fruit-picking, chicken-loading, rose-weeding and cotton hoeing. When volunteers found themselves doing nonseasonal work like washing dishes or serving meals, they were told that they were relieving the members to work in the fields. The numbers of volunteers on Goshen during my fieldwork did not rise and fall with the need for labor (Bowes 1980). It became clear that their role was not quite as they thought.

To begin to explain what exactly the volunteers were doing for Goshen, it is necessary to look at the rest of the workforce which consisted of the members (numbering one hundred and thirty-nine), visiting soldiers and hired workers.

The soldiers' jobs were rather similar to those of the volunteers, although different in compensation. Whereas volunteers received their keep and a little pocket money, soldiers got their army pay plus their keep. Due to their ability to speak Hebrew, they also had access to what they (and the volunteers) thought were better jobs, particularly working in the children's houses, and they were entitled to attend kibbutz meetings which they could comprehend, whereas most volunteers could not. Most of them spent much longer on Goshen than volunteers did, staying about a year as compared with an average of three and a half months. They were accorded higher status than the volunteers, being Israelis and seen by the members as desirable potential recruits. Two ex-soldiers had married into the community and proved good members. Ex-volunteers who had done so had brought nothing but trouble in the eyes of many members. Soldiers on Goshen, who were members of Nahal, usually numbered three or four at a time, so that their presence was less significant than that of the volunteers.

In 1975-6, Goshen had six permanent hired workers, two of whom, an electrician and a kindergarten teacher, were recently hired. The others were a nurse and three manual workers who came from the nearby town to work in the hothouses, the chicken sheds and the factory. Only the nurse and the teacher actually lived on Goshen. They were not members and had no intention of becoming so (Rayman 1981 says this is commonly the case). Of the members of Goshen in 1975-6, only one was a former hired worker who had married into the community. Occasionally, workers would be taken on to do specialist jobs such as building or reroofing the hothouses, but there was no large, regular, hired workforce, such as existed on other kibbutzim (e.g., Rayman 1981), and there was considerable resistance among the members to its development. The presence of the permanent hired workers was justified by reference to the needs of the community; they had to be hired because none of the members were available for the jobs. In fact, among the members, there were a nurse and two electricians who were working elsewhere. It was not simply a question of whether or not people had the appropriate training which dictated the need to hire. As with the volunteers, the situation was more complicated than it first appeared.

Members formed by far the greater proportion of the workforce on Goshen. Most of them remained in the same jobs for years at a time, and many, particularly the men, had been trained in particular skills. As members, they were obliged to work for the kibbutz, either within the kibbutz economy or elsewhere, in which case their salary would go directly into the kibbutz coffers. They had the right to housing, furniture, clothing, food, care and education of their children, health care, in fact all their needs. There was also an entitlement to holidays and other luxuries. Anyone with special needs—such as music tuition, artist's materials, a special diet, care of a handicapped child—could have these supplied. Furthermore, all members were entitled to a say in running the kibbutz by participating in the General Assembly, the weekly meeting of all the members and the highest authority of the community, and by serving on committees, elected by the General Assembly and delegated tasks in the day to day running of the kibbutz. One of the most important tasks of this administrative structure was running the kibbutz economy, planning what crops would be grown in what quantity, organizing the process of production, marketing the produce, administering the kibbutz finances, organizing the service part of the economy and so on. It was therefore the members who collectively took on volunteers and hired any paid workers they considered necessary. Obviously, not all the members could know every detail of the workings of the kibbutz economy or all the technical aspects of running all the different branches, so there were some people with very detailed knowledge of one particular branch, others with particular expertise in accounting, and so on. Thus there was differentiation between the members in terms of administrative skills and technical knowledge, and when the time came for elections to committees, people with skill and experience would be chosen. Despite the differentiation and the resulting fact that not everyone was equally capable of holding office, it was possible for any member to have his or her say in running the economy. Within each branch, the situation was rather similar: the branch would be democratically run, with one person as its nominal manager— usually someone with years of experience in the work and extensive technical expertise whose job was to insure that production ran smoothly. The extent to which a branch manager exercised (or attempted to exercise) authority over his or her fellow workers varied. The cotton branch in Goshen ran very much on the basis of cooperative agreement between the workers, whereas the manager of the roses branch would try to give orders to the other workers (who would obey, disobey or answer back depending on whether or not they agreed with him). Generally though, it is important to understand that because both "manager" and "worker" among the kibbutz members had formally the same relationship to the means of production, divisions of assets and rewards between them were nonexistent and divisions of power and interest very limited. Differences arose from experience and technical knowledge which could be acquired, in theory, by any kibbutz member.

A crucial key to understanding the organization of labor in Goshen, or any other modern kibbutz, lies in the importance of permanent, skilled jobs for the members (cf. Shepher 1972, Blasi 1980, Rayman 1981). In the early days of the kibbutz movement, members would move around between jobs, taking their turns at cooking, washing clothes, etc. This was possible because there was little skill involved in the jobs which had to be done. However, the return to the soil was not an end in itself but the first stage in the rebirth of the Jewish people. The early kibbutz members felt they had to learn manual labor, to work for themselves and therefore avoid exploiting their fellow human beings, and to start building a progressive, modern, Jewish economy. As Cohen (1966) argues, they were orientated to both communality and progress. In order to make improvements in agriculture, to increase its efficiency by improved production methods and mechanization, it was necessary to acquire specialist knowledge, through training, which had to be paid for. It was thought inefficient for all kibbutz members to be trained in all skills needed to develop every branch of the economy, so individuals would train as experts in particular aspects. When they returned to the kibbutz, they would use their newly acquired skills by working in a particular branch for years at a time. Thus the kibbutz would get maximum return from its investment. Shepher (1972) has argued that this development had important repercussions for the working life of every kibbutz member. Clearly, if a few, trained individuals stayed in one branch, while everyone else continued to move about between jobs, then sharp differentiations between members would exist. Due to their orientation towards communality, the kibbutz members tried to divide the acquisition of skills among themselves so that everyone would have a share of skill. Since it had been expensively acquired, a worker would remain on one job for a long period. Shepher (1972) stresses that equality was therefore maintained; instead of everyone doing all the jobs, people became equally indispensable in particular jobs because of their training. Generally, the goal of a kibbutz member today is to acquire skills and hence a permanent job, which is seen as a sign of being well established in the community. Someone who cannot become so established is referred to by the derogatory term *p'kak*, a cork, who bobs about from one place to another.

Some vestiges of job rotation among members remained on Goshen (and other kibbutzim; see Blasi 1980, Rayman 1981), the most symbolic of which was the institution of *toranut* (duty or service). Every member gave a few days extra work to the community, helping in the kitchen or dining room on the Sabbath. Generally, this was treated as a great joke by all concerned, and the extra workers often proved more a hindrance than a help since they were unaccustomed to the routine of the more practiced workers, many of whom were volunteers. During slack periods, some people would spend a few weeks away from their permanent jobs doing less skilled work. Such times were also used for holidays or taking one's turn at guard duty (around the perimeter of the settlement for men, outside the children's houses for women). Although these intervals from one's usual occupation occurred regularly every year, they were not utilized systematically to funnel workers from slower branches into busier branches. Thus, they could not be interpreted as rotation of work in the sense of the early days of kibbutz settlement.

Young women in the process of having their families might also change jobs several times during the course of a pregnancy and the first few months of a baby's life. As the pregnancy proceeded, a woman would do less and less strenuous work, reducing the hours in her regular job or relinquishing it for lighter work such as sewing. Once the child was born, she would start to build up her work hours again. After some months, she might return to her original job. With the next baby, the process would repeat. These arrangements were due both to the prevailing ideas in the kibbutz about what pregnant women were capable of doing (light work) and the arrangements for the care of small babies. After the age of six weeks, babies spent much of their time in the "baby-house" in the care of a kibbutz woman who was trained as a children's nurse. Mothers would visit the house several times a day to feed their babies. While breast-feeding, women needed jobs which were physically close to the baby-house and which could be interrupted at regular intervals. Thus, an individual woman might change her job several times during her twenties and thirties. Her movements were not dictated by any principles of work rotation, but by the culturally defined imperatives of having children. Women, like men, aspired to the ideal of a permanent job and would invest considerable resources in trying to obtain one.

Permanent jobs for kibbutz members were not guaranteed but depended on a process of social interaction in which individuals would build careers by negotiating support in the community. Support of other members was needed to work in the branch of one's choice, to remain there, and to get the training and acquire the skills which would eventually make one indispensable. The process began when people first became members of the kibbutz. As mentioned earlier these members had either been born there, finished their army service and decided to stay as members, or had come from outside the community as applicants for membership (such people would spend at least a year as candidates before being voted members by the General Assembly). The first step was to find a branch of the economy in which one would be accepted by the other workers and where the work was satisfying. This was done by negotiation with the Labor Organizer and the various committees which dealt with labor allocation. Initially, a new worker's position in a branch could be precarious. Before a person became integrated into a branch, they could be treated as moveable labor and could find themselves suddenly allocated elsewhere. The way to avoid this was to get the other workers in the branch to insist that they needed *you* and nobody else. When it came to acquiring skills, the starting point was to learn from the workers already in the branch. If the training involved leaving the kibbutz, it was necessary to mobilize wider support. The General Assembly needed to approve the study leave and the financial support. One of the best ways to insure an affirmative vote was to gain support from the Secretariat, the most important committee, which could present an acceptable argument to the General Assembly. Once trained for a job, a member was in a good position to stay in the branch of his or her choice. Sometimes people might acquire skills through training and then decide they were not satisfied with their jobs. Leaving a branch could be achieved by a process of negotiation similar to that just described, but there were extra difficulties because of the investment the kibbutz had made. The process did not always run smoothly. The following examples highlight some possible problems.

Ivram was a hired worker on Goshen in the 1960s who met a kibbutz member he wished to marry. He was accepted as a member following the marriage in 1971. At first, he continued working in the dairy where he had originally been employed because of a shortage of young, male members who could do the hard physical work required. Before long, he complained that he could not get along with the other workers in the branch and requested a move. He sampled several agricultural branches. Each time he had the same complaint which was reciprocated by the other workers. By 1975, he was working permanently in the dining room where he was in charge of the volunteers assigned to that task. He was criticized for doing this work which was unskilled and considered especially demeaning for a young man who should be making a proper contribution to the kibbutz by working in the fields.

Ivram's problem was that he lacked the prerequisite for success as kibbutz member—support in the community. He had been a hired worker which connoted outsider and inferior. The members had paid little attention to him and would not normally have established any more than a passing acquaintance. He was accepted as a member primarily because the woman he married was considered a pathetic and lonely character who needed a companion and a husband. People hoped that marriage would help solve her problems. Ivram came from India and had no compatriots in Goshen. His main language was English, which he shared with his wife and almost no one else. His Hebrew was good, so he could at least communicate with the other members; his wife could not and his linguistic ability was supposed to help her. Once married, the couple became almost totally isolated from the other members. They were considered a problem family, especially when their baby son (born in 1973) proved to be very slow in his development. In his search for a job, Ivram found building contacts and support very difficult, particularly since his background differed so markedly from that of his fellow workers. Repeatedly, he met and responded with hostility. As his reputation as an unaccommodating character spread, things became increasingly difficult for him. In the dining room, he would complain constantly about the women who worked in the kitchen who "poached" his helpers, about those women's loud voices and penchant for quarrelling, about the table manners of the people who came to eat, about the lack of consideration in walking with muddy boots over the newly washed floor, about the fact that he was the only Socialist in the place whereas everyone else was selfish and materialistic. The other members had plenty of complaints about Ivram and his wife. Ivram was lazy and incompetent, he should not be working in the dining room, he spoiled their mealtimes by being surly and rude, his wife was stupid, his child defective, and all were a burden on the community.

While this was an extreme case, it illustrates how tensions in a small community like a kibbutz can become magnified. It illustrates graphically how a lack of support and a lack of ability to win support can make the acquisition of a skilled, permanent job extremely difficult. It also shows how failure at work often accompanies other kinds of failure. Ivram and his wife were outcasts who did not and could not participate in community social and political life. Later on, I will examine how it was that they were able to remain members and continue to live and work on Goshen. They were, in fact, useful to the community.

The second example is that of Irella, a young woman who was born on Goshen and had many friends and considerable support in the community. Despite this, she too had problems getting established in the job of her choice, because her support proved inferior to that of a rival. After finishing her army service, Irella started work in one of the children's houses. She enjoyed the work, and hoped that she could train as a *metapelet* (a children's nurse). In 1976, Irella got married. After the wedding, she left for a month's holiday in Europe. Meanwhile, Sheli, also a daughter of Goshen, had left school. Because she was about to be married, she was exempt from army service and therefore ready to start her work career in the kibbutz. She too was keen to work with the children. When Irella went away, Sheli replaced her with the support of her mother who was a trained *metapelet* and anxious to help her daughter. When Irella returned, she found Sheli doing what had been "her" job with no signs whatsoever of moving aside so that Irella could return. Irella's friends had seen this happening and had complained loudly and bitterly on her behalf that Sheli and her mother were playing a dirty trick. Irella was good at the job, older and more experienced than Sheli; therefore, they felt she had a prior claim. Despite her friends' efforts, Irella did not get her job back. Sheli's mother had campaigned on her daughter's behalf among her own contemporaries, the pioneer settlers of Goshen who formed a "mafia" (the term used by the younger generation) which could still control decisions in the community. Irella's friends were members of the second generation of Goshen, with little experience of getting decisions made in their favor. Her parents had left the kibbutz some years before, and she had no effective means of mobilizing pioneer support. Later, still trying to achieve her ambition, she applied for study leave for *metapelet* training. Even though her circle of friends canvassed vigorously on her behalf and collected as many votes in the General Assembly as they could, the decision went against her. Irella's failure shows that even when someone was quite well integrated into the community and had a number of supporters, that support varied in its effectiveness. In this particular case, Irella lacked the backing of the pioneers as opposed to Sheli who obtained that support through her mother. Although Irella's backers were unsuccessful in her case, in other instances such support would have been very valuable. Ivram, for example, would have benefitted from the support of his fellow workers.

Some individuals, even if they had training, did not stay in the branches where their skills could be exercised. Sometimes, this could be due to inability to exercise skills effectively. Goshen, as I mentioned, had a trained nurse who was not working in her profession. She had done so at one time but had broken the rules of gossip (Chapter 4) by revealing details of her consultations with patients. This unacceptable practice led to her being removed from the job by popular acclaim. I do not know precisely how this was done. Usually, it would have transpired subtly. For example, hints might be dropped that the work was too much for her delicate constitution. That message would have passed through the same gossip network in which she was so enthusiastically involved. In 1975 Goshen had a hired nurse; the community eagerly awaited the return from army service of one of its daughters who had nursing training and could take on the job.

It was also possible for people to choose not to practice their skills. Rachel, for example, had trained as a *metapelet* for small children at Goshen's expense. Disliking the work, she had worked with older children for some years. Later, she was able to use her training as a bargaining counter. In 1975 Goshen needed a *metapelet* for a group of toddlers, and Rachel was asked to go back to the work for which she had been trained. Amongst the toddlers was the apparently retarded son of Ivram. Rachel announced that she would take the job but only if that child was kept with other, smaller children. This was an outrageous suggestion, even in the context of the general attitude towards Ivram and his family, since it was a matter of principle that once a children's age group was established, its integrity should be respected and maintained. Any deviations from this pattern were regarded as damaging to the children by the kibbutz movement generally as well as Goshen specifically. Nevertheless, Rachel was needed and Rachel could not be forced to do the job. A compromise was reached, whereby the unfortunate child was allowed to stay with his age group but spent several hours each day with Ronit, a woman who was a candidate for membership and was herself having difficulties finding a suitable job. Rachel argued from a position of strength, not only because she had a much-needed skill but also because she was already well-established in a permanent job elsewhere and because she had plenty of supporters.

The rewards of establishment in the community through skill and indispensability could be considerable. Yaakov had been a pioneer of Goshen. During the early part of my fieldwork, he was the Secretary. In order to attain this major official position, one needed to be very firmly established in the community. Only through widely established links with other members could one hope to enjoy the flow of information about what was going on and to engender the support to facilitate effective decisions.

From the start, Yaakov had a number of advantages. As a pioneer, he had experience of Goshen, knew its history including who had come and gone, understood how relationships between people had developed, and how the economy had changed. He knew Hebrew very well, had excellent French and could therefore communicate well with the whole community. He also had several compatriots among the remaining Egyptian pioneers. In 1975, Yaakov was sixty years old and still moving irrigation pipes in the cotton fields every Summer. This was heavy work and all the other workers (in their twenties) called Yaakov "the Tiger," for he was the strongest of all. When the university was in session, Yaakov spent two days a week away from Goshen working as a lecturer. Thus, he had two full-time jobs, as Secretary and as a cotton worker or lecturer. As Secretary, he managed the day-to-day administration of the kibbutz, attended committee meetings, conducted the weekly General Assembly, visited federation headquarters in the city for frequent consultations, and dealt with the regular crises of Goshen including quarrels between members and personal difficulties. He was always ready to take on extra work. In 1975, this included participation in a federation committee, helping out in branches of the economy which needed extra labor and, for a time, running the kibbutz store when the manager was called away unexpectedly and a regular replacement could not immediately be found. Yaakov was universally acknowledged to be an excellent secretary (a position he had occupied several times since Goshen's foundation), even though he was not especially popular with all the members. His success in the office derived from his position as a well established member of the community, skilled and useful in all his jobs, and the fact that he had a wide variety of links with other people in the community which helped him keep in touch with events. In the view of the younger members, he was part of "the mafia" which ran the kibbutz, and they would marvel at his ability to know everything about everybody without apparently seeking out such knowledge.

All these cases illustrate the general importance of permanent jobs for members, the strategies which could be employed to acquire both jobs and skills, and the reasons for failure in these strategies. In all of them, the process of social interaction had to be carefully and sensitively managed by an individual who was to succeed in his or her objectives. The consequences of failure could be disastrous, not only in terms of one's job but also in terms of one's wider social and political relationships within the community.

## Division of Labor

The various jobs done by volunteers, soldiers, hired workers and members, and the attempts by members to find permanent jobs formed a structure which is common to all but the very newest kibbutzim. The workforce as a whole was divided in various ways; examining these divisions helps us see the structure as a whole.

Members and nonmembers had markedly different jobs, roles and statuses in the community. Members collectively controlled the kibbutz economy and had all the more skilled jobs in which they were permanently employed. Unpaid workers were the volunteers and soldiers who did less skilled work for short periods and were under member control. Paid workers (hired laborers who happened to be few in numbers on Goshen but were common on other kibbutzim) were employees of the members, also subject to their control. The stated purpose of all this nonmember labor was to fill labor shortages. In fact the "shortages" were only in specific areas primarily those jobs which were unskilled and therefore not desirable for members developing their careers. Volunteers on Goshen were essential to the kibbutz. By doing the most menial jobs, they were allowing members to work on their careers. Similarly, the soldiers were doing menial work. Since there were so few of them, they formed only a very minor additional labor force. However, they were afforded a higher status than the volunteers and were seen as an important source of potential marriage partners for young kibbutz members as well as potential recruits to the kibbutz.

In the case of Goshen, the hired workers were also filling labor shortages of a particular type. The three manual workers, like the volunteers, did unskilled work which could otherwise hinder members' careers. The kindergarten teacher was needed because at that time there were more children of kindergarten age than available skilled members could deal with. The hired nurse and the electrician, however, were there because of the particularities of social interaction on Goshen. The trained member nurse had been found unsuitable for the job, and both the electricians had decided they preferred not to exercise their skills.

In kibbutzim where the hired labor force is much larger, most of the people concerned will be found doing unskilled work, particularly in kibbutz factories where the management will consist of kibbutz members. It is likely that in any kibbutz factory, the majority (in some cases all or nearly all) of the shopfloor workers will be hired. One way to explain the existence of these very large hired labor forces is to say that (like the volunteers, soldiers and hired manual workers on Goshen) they help the members acquire permanent jobs. Up to a point, this is certainly the case. Many kibbutz members have become very skilled managers of kibbutz industry. The question of hired labor in the kibbutzim has been a bone of contention since the foundation of the Israeli state. To explain the situation fully, it will be necessary to look more generally at the development of kibbutz economies. First other aspects of the division of labor need examining.

The second major axis of differentiation between workers on Goshen and on other kibbutzim was gender. Recently, gender divisions in the kibbutz have generated much discussion, both within the kibbutz movement (Leon 1964, Rosner 1967, Mednick 1975) and among academics (Tiger and Shepher 1975, Bowes 1978, 1986, Spiro 1979). I will be looking at the question in much more detail in Chapter 5. Here it is necessary to note that among the members of the kibbutzim generally, 90% of the women work in the service branches of the kibbutz economies (child care, food preparation, laundry and so on). In the kibbutzim, this work is referred to as "unproductive," a classification applied to all work which does not directly produce revenue. "Productive work" by contrast is revenue producing work, and most kibbutz members who do it are men. Productive work is more prestigious and those members performing it have higher status than those who do not. The fact that nearly all women members do unproductive work is, not surprisingly, associated with a generally lower status for them than male members (though as members, they still have higher status than nonmembers, whatever work they may do). Kibbutz women generally then have little or no experience with the "productive" branches of the kibbutz economy and are therefore less able than men to participate fully in the decision making processes involved in its management. Furthermore, as I have mentioned, women may change their jobs several times during their childbearing years. Thus, finding and becoming established in a permanent job is much more difficult for women than for men. Given the importance of permanent jobs, women's failure in this area reflects on their status and often on their ability to function as full members of the community. Because "unproductive" work is considered a necessary evil, rather few resources have been allocated to improving conditions of work, technological innovation, training and so on. This has insured that much of the work has remained menial, monotonous and unpleasant. The progress orientation I discussed before has applied mainly to productive work. Even if women manage to get permanent jobs, it is not easy for them to become skilled and indispensable.

This general picture was reproduced on Goshen. Nearly all the women members worked in the service branches of the economy, and many were dissatisfied with their work. The greatest demand among the women members was for work in the children's houses, where at least some opportunities existed to become established and get trained. Some older women, in their late forties and fifties, had permanent jobs in the kitchen and the *communa*. For younger women in their twenties and early thirties, there were problems (the generation gap meant there were very few aged between thirty and forty-five). In this age group, the women moved about between jobs. My field data provide many cases illustrating the difficulties faced by such women in their work.

Maya finished her army service in 1974 having served as a soldier in the Yom Kippur war. Although not eager, she returned to Goshen (her birthplace) because she saw no real alternative. She was assigned to the kitchen as a cook's helper. At that time, the kitchen was small and dark, the equipment was very old, and working conditions were extremely unpleasant. Maya hated the work. Although she preferred to be somewhere else (anywhere else, on her worst days), she explained that there was no other job for her on Goshen. At the time, Maya was in the process of deciding what to do with her life; remaining on Goshen as a member was only one of the possibilities. Her experience in the kitchen tipped the balance. She saw that the future on Goshen for her would entail a hard struggle to find a job, and there was no guarantee that she would succeed. By the end of the summer, she had decided to go for training as a dental nurse and had persuaded Goshen to allow her to go. After this training, there was a possibility for her to return to the kibbutz and work, at least part-time, with the dentist who visited every week. Maya had no real intention of returning and has still (1987) not done so.

Maya was not married and had no children, so her problems were not increased by the necessity of moving in and out of jobs. Nevertheless, her case illustrates some of the difficulties faced by a young woman starting a career on the kibbutz; they were sufficient to drive her away.

Vreni, a Swiss volunteer who had married a member of Goshen, had firmer ties with the community. In 1975, her husband, (an immigrant from Morocco) was doing army service. She had nowhere to go but Goshen, and was expecting her first baby in the early summer. Until very late in her pregnancy, she worked in the kitchen. The work became increasingly taxing; finally, she was allocated to the *communa* to do sewing. She did not get along with the other women in the *communa* and was relieved to get away from them when the baby was finally born. When he was six weeks old, she went back to the *communa* to work the four-hour day customary for a nursing mother. Very quickly, her relationship with the other workers worsened; they resented former volunteers marrying into the community and vented their resentment on Vreni. Soon, things were so bad that Vreni asked for a different job. This posed a problem for the Labor Organizer because there was really no other job except *communa* work considered suitable for a new mother. The administrative officers of the community manufactured a job for her—visiting two bed-ridden old people, taking them their meals, providing some companionship, etc. This had previously been done by female members of the old people's families who had left their own work for an hour or two every day. When Vreni's baby was older, her "job" reverted to the relatives and she returned to kitchen work.

This case is important not only because it illustrates the difficulty faced by a woman with very young children in establishing a permanent vocation but also because it exemplifies characteristic kibbutz attitudes towards women's work. Vreni had to work once the child was more than six weeks old. In the kibbutz context, there was no alternative. So a job had to be found, yet since she was a woman, it could be "unproductive." Her "work" was manufactured for her and ceased to exist when she no longer qualified for special hours. No such manufacturing would have been done for a man. Furthermore, male members of the invalids' families would not have left their work to visit them. All this is indicative of the general view that women's work in the kibbutz was not only unproductive but also unimportant.

Thus the division of labor by sex in Goshen was part of the more general low evaluation of women and their work. From an analytical point of view, the women and their work were clearly essential to the smooth running of the kibbutz economy. Few of them worked directly in "productive" activity, but no one would have been able to do so if the women had not prepared the food, kept the clothing supplied, clean and mended, and looked after the children. The attitude which demeaned womens' work caused considerable dissatisfaction among the women on Goshen. Within the kibbutz movement in general, "the problem of the woman" (Leon 1964) had caused and continues to cause considerable concern. Examples like Maya, who left her community because of the lack of opportunity, represent the economic consequences suffered by the entire community.

The third division in Goshen's labor force related to age. As soon as they were capable of doing so, small children began their training for work. Five and six year olds would "help" the *metapelet* in their children's house straighten up and set the table. As time progressed, they would start to do such things independently. School children had duties, and during their final year of schooling would spend one day per week working on the kibbutz in an adult job. This was a time when they could start thinking about their careers in the kibbutz. They could prepare for their return from the army (boys served for three years; two years for unmarried girls), and lucky ones had help from their parents. This preparation for work was an integral part of the kibbutz educational curriculum which, as well as cultivating academic skills, was designed to groom the pupils for life as kibbutz members.

After the army, those who opted to become members would return to the kibbutz and build their careers as described earlier. Aside from the differences between men and women I have outlined, if people managed to become established, they would stay in the same job for years at a time. If their physical abilities began to fail, they would move to less strenuous work. For example, the manager of the hothouse roses branch in Goshen in 1974 was in his late fifties and was beginning to find the work too strenuous. He was transferred to the new factory to work as a traveller negotiating contracts. Another man, the father of two of the members, was working two or three hours a day doing light jobs in the shed where the cut roses were graded and packed. In his younger days, he had worked as a roadbuilder with the old pioneers of Palestine.

Kibbutzim generally are proud of the special provision they have made for the old. The general principle of this is that work confers dignity on the human being and that none should be arbitrarily deprived of that dignity by retiring when they reach a certain age. Old people in kibbutzim can stay at work as long as they feel capable. One factor in planning the industrial branches was a hope that they might provide sitting-down jobs for old people who could no longer be on their feet all day (Wershow 1973). When people can no longer work, they are cared for, at home, by members of the community. There is no thought of their being sent away because they cannot work any more.

The importance of the special provisions for schoolchildren and the old is that they illustrate particularly clearly how work organization and the management of kibbutz economies are not dictated purely by considerations of economic efficiency, but are influenced by other ideological factors. Both the kibbutz economies and the distinctive ideological considerations which apply can be understood by examining their development. The interaction of ideas and action can be clearly seen, offering an explanation for the structure just outlined and placing the cases in their full context. Both the ideological and the action components have changed considerably since the early days of the kibbutz movement, if sometimes in rather unexpected ways.

## Development of the Kibbutz Economy

As I described in Chapter 2, the kibbutz economies have been very successful in terms of increasing efficient production and contributing very significantly to the national agricultural, and more recently, industrial economy. They are not and never have been independent of or isolated from this wider economy. The management of their relationship with the national economy has been crucial to the economic success of the kibbutz and the increasing prosperity of members. Within the kibbutz movement, changes have occurred in ideology and social relationships. The interaction between the demands of participation in a wider, nonkibbutz structure and the dictates of maintaining a semi-autonomous, communal way of life have precipitated adjustments. In examining these changes, we must remember that the kibbutzim have always been outward-looking, seeing themselves as contributing to a wider, national effort. Also, kibbutz movement ideology has never been a rigid plan for a singular way of life.

I have said here that one of the most significant developments in the kibbutzim has been the importance of permanent, skilled jobs for kibbutz members. This resulted, as I explained, from the efficiency orientation of the kibbutz movement. One of its effects was to deter kibbutz members (for whom a permanent job became a marker of success in the community) from certain routine, menial jobs which were performed by volunteer workers from outside the community. Thus it can be said that the efficiency orientation, by increasing the importance for members of skilled, permanent work, had brought about a kind of labor shortage which could not be filled by members themselves. The existence of hired labor can be partly explained in a similar way. Hired workers do jobs which members cannot do without endangering their position in the community, but other explanatory factors must also be considered.

As individual workers have become more specialized over the years, so has each kibbutz economy. In the early years, each kibbutz grew many different crops. A mixed farm was viewed as a means of equalizing labor requirements over the year and allowing workers to move between jobs while being occupied throughout the year (R. Cohen, 1972). This practice was not considered efficient, however. Some crops, such as vegetables, offered a small return for a large amount of investment in labor. In any case, not all parts of the country were equally suitable for the necessary variety of crops. The principle of the mixed farm had been largely abandoned by the 1950s, and kibbutz economies concentrated on a few crops which could be grown well and efficiently in their areas. Once widely mixed farming was abandoned, so was the possibility of keeping all members occupied all the time by moving them between branches. Of course, they were less and less inclined to do so anyway because of their commitment to permanent jobs. Mechanizing agriculture helped to keep down labor requirements, but the tendency of kibbutzim to concentrate on fewer crops generally created seasonal shortages of labor. The shortages were made more serious by the fact that by the 1950s, when they were being strongly felt, new recruitment of members into the kibbutz movement started to tail off. European Jewry, formerly the main source of recruits, had been almost destroyed. The new immigrants coming from the countries of North Africa and the Middle East were not thought suitable "kibbutz material" by the kibbutz movement (it is extremely doubtful in any case whether they would have wanted to join kibbutzim, even if they had been given the chance). So it was not possible to recruit new members to do the work.

Kibbutz industrial branches started to appear in the 1950s (Don 1977), as part of the drive towards modernization and to aid the national goal of population dispersal. Like other aspects of kibbutz economic activity, these branches had to be large enough to be effectively competitive in the country-wide economy. The optimum sizes, as it turned out, were larger than the kibbutz workforces could fill; therefore, hired labor started to be used extensively at this time. Its use continues today, filling labor shortages actually created by the principles of efficiency and progress.

Hired labor however was and still is a highly contentious issue in the kibbutz movement. It seemed in the 1950s that the movement's commitment to progress was taking it directly into conflict with another basic principle, that of self-labor. For the early pioneers, self-labor was seen as a way of creating a Jewish proletariat and, for some at least, a Jewish economy. It meant that Jewish people would work for themselves—neither as employers nor employees—creating a solid foundation for the economic development of their nation. The importance of the principle in the early days is clear. One of the major immediate stimuli for the foundation of Degania, the first kibbutz, was the settlers' rejection of hired labor and foreign management. It was never possible, however, for the kibbutzim to pursue the principle of self-labor in isolation. As Zureik (1979) points out, the Yishuv settlers were largely dependent on the existing infrastructures of Palestine. After 1948, as I have explained, the kibbutzim were part of the wider Israeli economy.

When kibbutzim first started to hire people, this was reconciled with the potentially compromised principle of self-labor by referring to national duty. In the early 1950s there was a food shortage in Israel, and many new immigrants looking for work (the Oriental immigrants, not potential kibbutz members, but still Jewish workers). All kibbutzim tried to contribute to food production, and some saw it as their national duty to provide jobs for the immigrants (Shatil 1966), thus finding a convenient and ideologically acceptable means of solving their own labor problems. Some kibbutzim, especially of the Kibbutz Artzi federation, refused to hire people, stating that whatever "national duty" might be, it could not include exploitation by hiring (Kanovsky 1966).

To this day, the question of hired labor in kibbutzim arouses the passions of kibbutz members and critics of the movement alike. Members of Goshen were vehemently opposed to it. However, as I have shown, they were prepared to take people on when jobs would simply not otherwise have been done. As the industrial branch was still in its very early stages and volunteers were doing much of the more routine work on Goshen, the members had not yet faced the dilemma which has confronted other kibbutzim of reconciling for the long term the two principles of progress and self-labor. On Goshen, hired workers were seen as a temporary expedient to be taken on in emergencies. Very little has been written on hired laborers in kibbutzim, partly because the kibbutz movements find the whole question very embarrassing. It is difficult to be sure how the matter will be resolved, if indeed it ever will. There are some indications in the literature (Stern 1965, Don 1977) that even on kibbutzim where there is a large, longstanding hired labor force, this is also seen as temporary, to be phased out when the community recruits new members. More recently, some kibbutzim have started to reexamine the whole question of hired labor, especially in industry, and to consider altering the nature of the branches with a view to reducing the embarrassingly high numbers of hired workers. Generally, it is fair to say that in the matter of hired labor, the kibbutzim have lived with ideological contradiction for many years. This is one instance in which it would be particularly inaccurate to talk about "compromised principle" or "decline" in the movement. In the first place, the principles concerned have always been somewhat contradictory, as are the principles of many peoples of the world today. In the second place, the kibbutzim have been working at the problem for many years and continue to do so. There is no intrinsic reason why they, or anyone else, should come up with the solutions which satisfy any outsider's conception of what a kibbutz, or any other society, should be like.

In regional cooperation, there is interplay between the kibbutzim and their environment, and the kibbutzim have not always acceded to environmental demands. This area too is somewhat embarrassing for the kibbutz movement and has seldom been studied. Cooperation between kibbutzim on a regional basis is longstanding and well established. Goshen sent its children to a regional high school, was involved with kibbutz-run, regionally-based, processing plants and in 1975-6 was negotiating with a neighboring kibbutz about sharing the running of the new factory. Such arrangements are today commonplace for kibbutzim (Rayman 1981 gives another, detailed example). Particularly successful are the longer established ones (Cohen and Leshem 1969). However, cooperation between kibbutzim and other types of rural settlement has been much less successful. Cohen (1970) describes how after 1948, settlement planning in Israel showed a rural bias, brought about by the dominance of cooperative movement representatives in government and administration. One result of this bias was an attempt to create a "hierarchy of settlements," particularly by establishing small towns which would fill the gap between large cities and small rural villages (the already existing kibbutzim and moshavim). These small towns or "development towns" were intended to be regional centers and were simply planted between the villages. They proved, however, to be "foreign bodies" (Cohen 1970) resented by the surrounding kibbutzim and moshavim. Kibbutzim, which already had a degree of regional organization of their own, either ignored the towns altogether or used them simply as sources of hired labor (Cohen and Leshem 1969, Cohen 1970). The towns acquired reputations as miserable dumps, and only those people with no other choice remained there (Cohen 1970, Deshen 1970, Berler 1972). Only when given specific tasks independent of the villages in the late 1960s and 1970s did the towns improve. The embarrassment for the kibbutzim arises here from their failure to participate in the national effort, their aloofness from the new immigrants, and their failure even to try and cooperate with the towns, despite their own influence in setting them up in the first place.

A central value for the kibbutz pioneers and for kibbutz members today was and is manual labor, the practical side of building a Jewish workforce. Here, as I described in Chapter 2, A.D. Gordon's ideas about *dat haavodah*, the religion of labor, were especially influential. Historically, the most valued kind of manual labor has been what is today referred to as "productive" labor—work in field and factory which directly produces revenue. Such work, as I have shown here, is still more highly valued than its counterpart, "unproductive work"—work in the services in which most female kibbutz members are involved. The fact that women are relegated to service work undoubtedly reflects on their roles and statuses in the kibbutz generally. We can therefore say that the high value accorded to manual work has helped subordinate women in the kibbutzim.

In the early days of the kibbutz movement, there were very few women and no children involved. If a young Jewish man left home for Palestine, that was sufficiently radical. For a young woman to do so was immeasurably more so. When they arrived in Palestine, the women worked alongside the men (Maimon 1962, Katzenelson-Rubashow 1976), partly because they too wanted to participate in manual labor, building the proletariat and so on, but also because the traditional women's work of the *shtetl* (the Jewish small town community of Eastern Europe) simply did not exist. With living conditions in a primitive state, there was minimal housework and children were not yet born. In working alongside the men, they developed their own commitment to equality between the sexes, struggling to be allowed to do the new men's jobs. As Maimon (1962) shows, the men were not always sympathetic, and the women went to the lengths of establishing their own training farms, where they could get over the blister and backache stage and develop the muscles which would win them respect among the men. However, as living conditions improved, and as children were born, the women took on the work involved. Although they had shared men's work, the men had not done this "women's work," nor had anyone considered that they should. The equality had been asymmetrical in that women strove to be equal with men, but men strove only to be better men. By their efforts, the women had, paradoxically, devalued themselves by devaluing their traditional work. Later on, State sexism, as I will show in Chapter 5, reinforced the division of labor by sex in the kibbutz. All this, I want to emphasize, has no demonstrable connection with the nature of women, but arises from the nature and development of the kibbutz.

The economic roles and status of women have consequences for other aspects of their lives in the kibbutz since economic values are intertwined with social and political ones. Such a combination of values is also apparent in the case of the division of labor by age. I have shown that training for work begins early, not so much out of a demand for labor (although High School children can be very useful) as out of a demand for appropriately socialized kibbutz members. Old people continue to work because of the notion that work brings self-respect.

It should be clear that an understanding of the kibbutz economy is basic to an understanding of the kibbutz, revealing as it does much of the community's *raison d'etre*, the various divisions of roles, statuses and interests within it, many of its ideological contradictions, and many ways in which it is influenced by and influences the environment in which it exists. But in the kibbutz, economic strategies, relationships and history are bound up with other factors—social relationships, political activity, values—which reflect upon the economic dimension, and are, in the last analysis, inseparable from it.

# - 4 -

# Controlling the Community

## Gossiping

Work in the *communa* on Goshen began at 6:30 a.m. with tea for all the women working there that day. Then the pressing machine, the sewing machine and the iron would be switched on, and the daily conversation which always accompanied the work would begin. A typical day's talk might go something like this. A new volunteer might come in to pick out some work clothes from the store left behind by previous volunteers. Rivka, a pioneer who sat all day at the sewing machine, would ask the volunteer ironing shirts "Who is he? Where does he come from? Has he a girlfriend? How long is he going to be here?" Having gleaned the information, she would turn to the woman doing the hand sewing. "Another American — we haven't had one since last year, that group who made a lot of noise and didn't work. Terrible they were." For a few minutes, the conversation would turn on volunteers, what a nuisance they were, and how they might be kept under control. Then Rivka might notice that Miriam had not appeared. "Where is she now? She's always late. It's that baby, you know, he's not normal. And neither's she nor her husband." This topic too would be fully aired, until Miriam turned up. "I'm sorry I'm late. I had to see to the baby," she would say in halting Hebrew, a language which did not come easily to her. Esther, the *communa* organizer would mockingly repeat, "I'm sorry I'm late. I had to see to the baby. Well, there's a pile of sheets to be seen to now, and it's nearly breakfast time already." At breakfast, the women did not generally sit together. They might join their husbands if they came to the dining room at the same time or sit with friends. The talk would continue. "There's so-and-so. He looks so miserable these days. I think perhaps marriage doesn't suit him after all. And she doesn't look too bright today either. You know she came back at two this morning after that outing with the others

**61**

from the hothouses. Far too late for a pregnant woman to be out. My daughter wouldn't have done it. But mind you, when I was young, we worked in the fields until the last minute. I nearly had my second baby in a ditch. Anyway, how does that lot in the hothouses get an outing when we don't?" Breakfast encounters would fuel the rest of the morning's conversation, which would also involve people who visited the *communa*, bringing their washing, collecting clean clothes and linen, and trying on new clothes. After the visit of a young man, a member of Goshen: "He's such a nice boy. It's time he got married and settled down." "He had a Dutch girlfriend, you know." "Yes, but these affairs with foreigners never work out, and the girls take them away from the kibbutz. What he wants is a nice Israeli girl, like Dvora who was in here the other day. She's a good girl, doesn't sleep around like those Dutch ones." "She's applying for a room with Avri you know. We'll have another wedding this year, you'll see." The volunteer organizer might come in. "I see there's a new American volunteer. They're nothing but trouble you know. I hope he won't be noisy. My husband hardly slept last summer with their campfires going on all night." "Well, I've got a Swiss group due any day now. . . ." The details would be elicited and discussed, then selected visitors would be told the news, with accompanying comments on "problem volunteers" and their effects on the kibbutz. After lunch, there would be coffee. "My husband went to the General Assembly last week. He says we're getting instant coffee on our allowance now instead of paying for it." "That's a bit unfair isn't it? I can't bear instant coffee. I must have real coffee, and that costs money." "Well there are cigarettes on the allowance too, and lots of people don't smoke, and even those who do seem to pay for the better ones." "But it shouldn't have been passed. The next thing will be television sets all round. And we know they're only for anti-social people with rich relatives abroad" (here, she would look pointedly at Miriam). At this point, Heidi, a former volunteer who had married then divorced a young man of Goshen, might come in and say to Miriam "Oh I've got a television too now. My boyfriend brought it from Belgium. But we don't get a very good picture." Miriam might say "Neither did we at first, but Ivram's got the knack of tuning it now. I'll ask him to come and look at yours too." Soon, work would be over for the day, and the women would disperse to their family homes and their afternoon activities, keeping a sharp lookout for items for conversation the next day.

In a paper on gossip, Max Gluckman wrote (1963:314):

> . . . the Greek lexicon defines 'an anthropologist' not as 'anthropos plus logos,' a student of man, but only as a scandalmonger.

He argued in the paper that scandalmongering is a social duty in all societies and the major occupation of an anthropologist. Though terms like scandalmongering and gossip carry with them notions of triviality and unimportance, perhaps even malice, many anthropologists have argued, with Gluckman, that understanding of and participation in such processes is crucial to learning about an unfamiliar society. To an outsider, people of Goshen appeared to gossip all the time. To borrow from Paine (1967), they constantly talked "of personalities and their involvement in events of the community" and would attempt to induce their fellows to join in talking this way. Their gossip was not trivial and not random but an activity in which people consciously engaged, with the full knowledge that what they said, how, when and to whom, would affect relationships in the community in certain ways. The account of a day's gossip in the *communa* I have just given includes many elements which start to show how gossiping was done on Goshen, and how it affected the lives of different people in the community.

Rivka asked the volunteer about the new American. She knew very well that as soon as a new volunteer arrived, particularly one who came alone as this one had, he or she would be surrounded by the others who would seek precisely the information Rivka wanted. All this was part of the volunteers' own "community life," somewhat separate from the members', as I have described. Rivka also knew that the ironing volunteer would give the information she wanted, partly out of deference and politeness and possibly pride that she was actually being addressed by a pioneer of Goshen. Also, the volunteer would regard the information as quite harmless and innocent. Rivka's subsequent comments to the sewing woman indicate that this was not quite the case. Having reminded her audience of a troublesome group of volunteers, she then quite deliberately turned the conversation to the problems of volunteers generally, which at the time was a topic of heated debate on Goshen. She was able to give her own views on the matter, to elicit those of her fellow workers, and to try to persuade them of her own anti-volunteer opinion. I should mention that although carried out well within earshot of the ironing volunteer, the discussion would be conducted in Hebrew, of which the volunteer was presumed ignorant. This was an assumption members of Goshen frequently made about volunteers and was part of the stereotype of such people.

Rivka's remark about Miriam's lateness was common. Miriam was often late because her little boy was indeed somewhat backward for his age and could be a handful for the *metapelet* (children's nurse) in the morning rush to get the children out of bed, cleaned up and breakfasted. Miriam would visit the children's house before work and would sometimes stay to help. The extended comments on Miriam and her family were part of the process of exclusion I described in Chapter 3. The *communa* workers were united in their disapproval and spent much time reinforcing one another's opinions and communicating them to visitors during the day. Esther, who mocked Miriam and ordered her to start work, publicly demonstrated her agreement with Rivka and insured that Miriam was again reminded of her place in the community.

At breakfast, the women looked around at what was happening on Goshen. They made what, to outsiders, seemed to be "personal remarks" about people in the dining room, hoping to elicit further information of possible future relevance from their fellow breakfasters. As they made their remarks, they were already relating them to wider issues of kibbutz life such as the type of activity appropriate for pregnant women, changes in the position of women, or the rivalry and struggle for equality between the different branches of the kibbutz economy.

As other people visited the *communa* during the course of the day, the women continued to collect and disseminate information. In the discussion about the young man, the most recent news was collected, comments were made about the importance of marriage for such a person, the problems of foreign volunteers were reiterated focusing now on the female, and who qualified as a "good girl." Then the women made their views about volunteers explicit to the volunteer organizer, suggesting it was his responsibility to control them more firmly. Later, these views and the news of the new volunteer group were passed on to others who visited the *communa*.

At coffee, proceedings in the General Assembly (the weekly meeting of all the members of Goshen and the governing body of the kibbutz) were reported. The *communa* women rarely attended the meetings and learned of the content through reports from others. They would discuss agenda items beforehand and decisions afterwards; they were capable, using their gossip strategies, of influencing the proceedings of the meetings. After discussing the adjustments of allowances, they began to attack Miriam again. She had rich relatives who had bought her a television, and she and her husband spent most evenings watching it. The implied criticism was that they were acting in an inegalitarian manner. However, when Heidi came in and started talking to Miriam about her set, more varied attitudes were shown. Heidi clearly thought having a television set quite acceptable and was prepared to discuss it in public. As a former volunteer who had "caused trouble" in Goshen, she belonged to a category of people the *communa* women did not like. Although regarded by them as undesirable, she was not outcast as firmly as Miriam and her husband were. The other women did not confront Heidi with having committed an anti-social act; she was more of a match for them. In fact both she and Miriam were pioneers in a process of innovation likely to result eventually in private television sets for all the members (this will be discussed fully later on).

Thus a day's gossip in the *communa* was conscious, controlled, systematic and linked, often in complex ways, to the process of social relations in Goshen. Of course, the women in the *communa* were not the only people who gossiped, although the place was well-known as a gossip center or information exchange. Now, we can look at gossip more generally and at the patterns and regularities of gossiping on Goshen. It is very likely that these apply on other kibbutzim too, although there is very little literature which would allow proper comparison.

## Patterns of Gossip

Almost everyone in Goshen was known to be involved in gossip. The well-known abstainers were considered odd. Talking with and about other people was seen as an important way of keeping oneself informed about what was happening, and if you were after any particular piece of information, you would approach certain key individuals known to be well informed. Gossip could also be used to discover the tenor of public opinion, perhaps to sound out in advance the likely response to some action, or to get people's support for it by persuading them to your point of view. Certain sets of people were known to spend much time gossiping together, some messages could be passed to individuals with a guarantee as to where and how they would be passed on. Some groups were known to be powerful and to use gossip to maintain their position, both by collecting maximum information and by passing out messages warning others of their opinions and possible actions. The major power center was the so-called "mafia," the pioneers of Goshen, whose strengths were wide experience and knowledge of the community and access to information from many other subgroups within it. The importance of gossip to the mafia's position was well known and understood by other community members, except perhaps the newest volunteers (they would soon learn). Those outside the mafia also knew that they needed a network of contacts to be accepted and integrated into Goshen. Without it, they would be outcasts and would find life in the community very difficult. Everyone knew that contacts were largely made and principally maintained through gossip. Generally then, the process of gossip was evaluated fairly positively and recognized as important for the position of the individual in the community.

However, there were cases in which gossiping was regarded more negatively: excessive, avid collection of information (usually for the mafia) and overstepping the boundaries of acceptable behavior. Newcomers, and sometimes old hands as well, would be warned to take care with the first. The major example of the second had been the nurse, described in Chapter 3, who was removed from her job for gossiping in an uncontrolled way.

The fact that boundaries marking how far people could go in gossiping existed is our first definite indication that gossip on Goshen was a controlled process. The boundaries suggested to the people of Goshen both the need for special care in passing information to certain persons and a limit on the extent of gossip considered acceptable. They were not absolute, rigid boundaries, and seemed to vary to some extent with individual cases. For example, almost anything could be said about an outcast. However, gossip about an integrated member of the community required more caution, perhaps because they had the means to reply and the resources in the form of other people's support to retaliate in kind.

There were patterns too in the comments people used when they gossiped. Some statements would occur with marked regularity. One example was that a particular person was "in the mafia," another that someone "did not work." These were simply shorthand ways of remarking on quite complicated sets of social relationships, which only insiders could understand. The statement about the mafia has already been explained. It referred to someone with access to the centre of community power who could be particularly supportive or particularly dangerous, depending on the circumstances. The comment that someone "did not work" was a code of criticism (Bowes 1977). It bore very little relationship to the amount of work people actually did, but referred to someone guilty of a socially defined misdemeanor which might simply be unpopularity or something more serious. Given that manual work was a major value in kibbutz ideology, someone who really did not work would be committing a serious moral violation. The accusation usually indicated some sort of social pariah—someone who was not a good kibbutznik—notions related to day-to-day social relationships as well as moral standards.

The content of gossip was very much concerned with the reputations of individuals in Goshen, especially pioneers and sabras (those born on Goshen). Someone's reputation resulted partly from their own activities and personality and partly from those of their associates, especially kin and age-mates, or in the case of sabras, more especially their parents. For nonmembers, especially volunteers, stereotypes provided an equivalent to the reputations of members; these were in evidence in the day's gossiping in the *communa*. Groups of volunteers were accorded characteristics depending on nationality. Americans were considered riotous, Swiss kept themselves to themselves, and so on. Those who came as individuals were considered dangerous until proved otherwise. They were in fact more "dangerous" to Goshen than the groups because it was easier for them to make contacts with kibbutz members, and they deliberately sought to do so. Some members felt very much hampered by their reputations. Maya's (the trainee dental nurse's) rather odd family and difficult childhood dogged her in her search for a job in Goshen. People were wary of her and did not, she felt, make their best efforts to ensure her happiness. The stereotypes helped control the volunteers, bolstering the member/nonmember boundary and clarifying for members who volunteers were and how they should interact (or not interact) with them.

The content of any particular item of gossip was dictated by considerations of information management. What was passed on through the gossip network depended on the desired effect, such as mobilizing support or attack on an individual or set of individuals. Some items of gossip therefore might be very restricted in circulation while others would be passed on, even elaborated, with alacrity.

There were regularities in participation in gossip. Within the community wide network of gossip in which nearly everyone was involved, sets of people who regularly gossiped together in "gossip cells" (West 1945) could be identified. One example was the mafia, another the women of the *communa* whom we have already met. Within the gossip cells, there would be one or two people who acted as gossip brokers, making it their business to specialize in information collecting or passing messages. In the *communa*, Rivka acted in both capacities, and the mafia had a number of brokers (young members of Goshen called them "spies"). If an individual was used as a starting point for studying the mechanisms of gossip, we would find that s/he had a unique gossip network overlapping with those of other individuals, and s/he might be involved in one or more gossip cells. Of those who did not participate in gossip, some were deliberate abstainers, opposed to what they saw as petty politicking and personal bickering, others were outcasts, people who did not participate above the bare minimum in kibbutz life (going to work every day, receiving their livelihood from the community, and otherwise withdrawing into family life).

When gossiping, people would take into account both the targets of gossip and the audience present. What could be said about whom varied, as I have already described, and those who heard could be guaranteed to pass on certain items of information to certain others. Information therefore was carefully couched in appropriate terms and dealt out with an eye to its next destination. Sometimes it was necessary not to say things, other times to change to a different language comprehensible only to some of those present.

There were regular occasions on which gossip could occur, and to some extent, these influenced the type and flow of gossip and the opportunities for individuals to develop particular positions in the gossip network. For some people, the workplace was an important gossip center, provided they were working close to others and there was not too much noise. The *communa* in particular was well known as a gossip center, with, as we have seen, the added advantage of a constant, daily stream of visitors. Elsewhere, in noisy places like the factory or where the workers were spread out in the fields, continuous gossip was impossible. Conversation was restricted to coffee and meal breaks. Outside working hours, gossip went on as people visited their friends in their homes, or at mealtimes or social events, and between neighbors sharing communal gardens. Such interactions were open to more choice than those in the workplace, so that some people barely spoke to their neighbors, while others spent every afternoon with them.

## The Importance of Gossip

So far then, gossip now appears to be a deliberate, patterned activity relating to issues of kibbutz life, particularly social interaction. The next questions, difficult ones, are how important was gossip, and how precisely did it work? To begin to answer this, it is necessary to look into some of the literature about kibbutzim.

Schwartz (1954) compares a moshav (an Israeli family farm cooperative) and a kibbutz arguing that the moshav had "distinctly legal institutions." That is, there were formal agencies specifically designed to keep order and settle disputes (in sociological jargon, for social control) including a Judicial Committee whose purpose was to deal with internal disputes which might be brought directly to it or referred by the moshav governing body, the General Assembly. In the kibbutzim such "distinctly legal institutions" did not exist, and order was maintained through the exercise of public opinion expressed in gossip. In Schwartz's opinion, the kibbutz could do without "distinctly legal institutions" because it was a primary group (i.e., people had many and varied links with one another) whereas the moshav needed them because the moshav members were much less intimate with one another. He felt that public opinion could be effective in the kibbutz because of the strict selection procedures, the intimacy and comradeship among the members, the fact that they all identified with the kibbutz as such, and the generality of kibbutz ideals. In the moshav, all these factors were much more limited or missing altogether. Schwartz concludes (1954:491) that legal controls ("distinctly legal institutions") develop where control cannot be informally achieved.

Shapiro (1976) questions Schwartz's conclusion that informal controls cannot operate in nonprimary groups. Since the late 1940s and early 1950s when Schwartz did his study, Shapiro finds that the kibbutzim have changed. Many of the conditions Schwartz thought essential for informal controls no longer exist. But, he finds,the kibbutzim have not developed "distinctly legal institutions," and informal controls still operate. Schwartz's predictions have therefore remained unfulfilled. Despite this however, Shapiro argues that there are institutions in the contemporary kibbutz which perform "judicial functions" even if they are not "distinctly legal." He describes cases in which the General Assembly (the weekly meeting of the members and candidates and the highest authority of the kibbutz) and the Education Committee (a subcommittee of the General Assembly with delegated powers) dealt with disputes and misdemeanors. What caused this to happen clearly varied with the circumstances. In one case, Shapiro shows, the failure of public opinion to have any effect led to formal adjudication, and in another, the General Assembly formally and impersonally denounced behavior which public opinion had defined as unacceptable.

Shapiro also questions Schwartz's assertion of a common starting point — no law — for both moshav and kibbutz. Examining the history of Degania, the first kibbutz, Shapiro finds a distinctly anti-legal ideology. The people deliberately tried to avoid creating legal institutions in the kibbutz, whereas the moshav was more formally constituted and provided for (although did not necessarily use) legal institutions from the start. Finally, although there was a general anti-legal ideology, Shapiro shows that neither this nor other aspects of the ideology were as clear-cut as Schwartz suggested when he described the agreements among kibbutz members. Shapiro writes (1976:431):

> . . . there was never a time in which rules were entirely unambiguous, nor
> when their interpretation and application did not require the institutionalised
> weighing of competing principles.

Schwartz and Shapiro, although they disagree, both refer to the same level of social reality, that is, to the kibbutz as a collectivity and to very general features of its social life. By contrast, Evens (1975, 1980) looks at the question of control from the starting point of person-to-person interaction. He examines the exclusion from a kibbutz he calls Timem of a young man, a son of Timem, who wanted to marry a woman the other members thought was not suitable to become a kibbutz member. As Evens sees it, their objection to the prospective wife was actually just a surface expression of their objection to the man who was a social outcast. While unmarried, he could be tolerated and ostracized, but marriage would create ties with the community (he would be "settling down") which the others did not want him to have. People focused their criticism on the woman because the man was a product of Timem. They were in some way responsible for what he was, and if they criticized him, they criticized themselves. Evens interprets the situation like this (1980:2055):

> In alienating . . . [the man] . . . , the community was symbolically casting out its own essential faultiness, thus reanimating the kibbutz version, renewing the conviction in its own meaningfulness.

Evens is able to analyse the particular case much more effectively than either Schwartz or Shapiro, but he does not give as clear a picture of the community-wide mechanisms of control as they attempt to do. It therefore looks as if we need to examine both the general and the particular aspects of control, and we can use these three studies to suggest how this might be done. Schwartz (1954, 1976) insists that informal means of control are particularly important, but concedes that they can only operate under particular conditions. Shapiro (1976), who finds the anti-legal philosophy and the lack of purely legal institutions, nevertheless feels that social control in the kibbutz is and always has been more formal than Schwartz suggests. He also asks whether everyone in the kibbutz really agrees on ideology and raises the important question of change. On the subject of gossip, Schwartz considers it the main agent of social control and Shapiro shows that it does act as such, but only in certain contexts. Evens' work raises two more points. Although ideology is flexible, as we have established earlier on, it is not infinitely so. Shapiro appears to be correct in his insistence on the ambiguity of rules, whereas Schwartz (1954) is also correct to argue that there is a degree of consensus about them. Evens also shows that kibbutz rules may not necessarily be explicit but may take the form of unspoken agreements. Evens' work emphasizes the importance of looking at social interaction which enables him to show how gossip can operate as a means of social control.

From the example of gossip in the *communa* I gave earlier on, we can see how the women there were taking part in the process of control. They made general moral statements about right and wrong: especially about the question of volunteers, about the position of women and how they should behave, about the importance of marriage and so on. In this, they were contributing to the process of ideological interpretation which, as we have seen, has always been part of kibbutz history. It was not necessary for them to say exactly what they were doing. The underlying principles remained unspoken as Evens (1975, 1980) suggests they often do. They also used gossip to test the opinions and possible activities of others. The volunteer organizer knew that mentioning the new Swiss (by definition, less troublesome) volunteers, he would provide some comfort to the women, and at the same time implicitly indicated that he understood their complaint about riotous volunteers.

He was answering what underlay their actual comments, which was "lots of people here really object to these volunteers. What are you going to do about it?" There were also examples of attempts to control the activities of particular individuals. Miriam was attacked more than once for being late and for having a television set. For some members of Goshen, such attacks would have brought them back into line, but for Miriam, they merely indicated again the fact that she and her family were outcasts.

The questions of television sets *per se* and the discussion about supplies from the store move us into a slightly different area. In some respects, all the matters discussed in the *communa* were "political" if we take one of the standard anthropological definitions of the political process, in that they were all concerned with:

> . . . determining and implementing public goals and . . . the differential achievement and use of power by the members of the group concerned with those goals. (Schwartz, Turner and Tuden 1966:7)

However, the questions of television sets and instant coffee were not only considered in gossip. Instant coffee had already been discussed in the General Assembly, and the acquisition by members of the community of consumer goods others did not have would come to the General Assembly in the end. It would be a serious mistake not to see gossip as part of the political process on a kibbutz. To understand how it operated, we have to look at the way the political process has been institutionalized and to look at the interaction between gossip and other methods of politicking.

## Formal and Informal Politics

In Goshen, as in other kibbutzim, there were two "arenas" of politics. The formal arena consisted of all the institutions specifically designed to make political decisions, including the General Assembly, the Secretariat (elected administrative officials), and a series of small committees set up to deal with particular matters like education, health, security, economic planning, entertainment, etc. All these were answerable to the General Assembly. The informal arena consisted of political activity which took place in gossip and everyday social interaction; it was vitally important to the political process in the kibbutz. In principle, each kibbutz of the Kibbutz Artzi federation decided as a community how to organize itself. In reality, there was general ideological consensus in the original movement and later kibbutzim were founded on precedents set by earlier ones thus most contemporary kibbutzim in the federation are similarly organized.

The arenas in Goshen were interlocked with one another. Sometimes a decision reached informally might be "rubber stamped" in the formal arena. Items for informal discussion and decision came from the General Assembly; people might "vote with their feet" by attending or staying away from General Assembly meetings. When meetings did come to a vote, the result was, more often than not, predictable from informal discussions which had gone on beforehand. Some political matters, we should note, remained altogether outside the formal arena.

All members of Goshen could attend and contribute to the General Assembly meetings and could be elected to serve on the committees. As was well known for other kibbutzim as well, participation in formal politics tended to be limited to certain people. On Goshen, whether people took part or not depended on their sex, their age, and their general position in the community, and the same factors dictated their informal politicking too. Generally, formal politics tended to be a male preserve and informal politics a female one. Two factors seem to explain this. "Important" issues in Goshen tended to relate to economic planning, production, and the continuing battle to make a profit. Since most men worked in the productive branches, with which women had little experience, they were directly concerned with and able to comment usefully upon the topics which came up. Secondly, women working in the services had opportunities to talk with one another during the day; they came into contact with others as they worked and were therefore in a position to do informal politicking.

In kibbutzim like Goshen (a "little kibbutz"), there was a tendency for the community pioneers ("the mafia") to dominate politics, primarily because of the generation gap in the population. In Goshen in 1975-6, the second generation was just at the stage of becoming members and had just started to take part in formal politics. It proved difficult for them to have much effect, as the pioneers had the situation well under control with their knowledge and experience, their established ways of doing things and so on. In 1975, a young man was elected Secretary (the most important administrative position) but found the job virtually impossible because of the power of the pioneer generation which extended through formal and informal politics alike.

To be a successful kibbutz politician in either or both political arenas, it was necessary to have a wide circle of reliable contacts in the community for support and information collection and distribution. This was due to the fact that making decisions and implementing them required a majority opinion. Someone with plenty of reliable contacts and access to all the different categories of people in Goshen could do well in politics and exercise considerable influence over community affairs. The young Secretary of 1975 was forceful and clever but did not have the right contacts. Indeed, it is quite likely that people voted for him knowing well that he would not prove effective. By contrast, the pioneer who preceded him had quite a limited circle of contacts, but they were extremely reliable and gave him indirect access to all corners of the kibbutz. He was a most effective and influential Secretary. The contacts that an individual could develop depended partly on his or her career in the kibbutz and partly on the history of the kibbutz as a whole. Those who had come to Goshen from the Hashomer Hatzair youth movement (58.3% of the members) or who had been born on Goshen and brought up in peer groups which developed strong identities (14.4% of the members) had ready-made contacts when they began their political careers. Members of youth groups and peer groups were expected to and generally did interact. Over time, the strength of these ready-made links might fade as people developed other contacts, particularly less formal ones like work relationships, neighborliness and friendship. People who had come to Goshen as individuals (27.3% of members) had to build contacts from scratch. Generally, the more recently someone had come to Goshen, the more significant the ready-made contacts were. They could give someone a start in politics; the lack of them meant hard work was necessary before they could start politicking.

## Politics in Action

The best way to see how politics operated in Goshen is to look at some examples of how the two arenas worked together and the way gossip fed into the process.

### Case 1: Work in the Cotton Fields

By 1975-6, the cotton branch of Goshen had proved profitable and was expanding, taking over new fields both that year and the next. Since the beginning there had been problems getting enough workers to do seasonal jobs like hoeing weeds and pressing the harvested cotton into bales (something like climbing through a warm snowdrift). In June 1975, there were not enough people available for the hoeing. Several possible solutions to the problem were discussed. One possibility was to take on more volunteers, but members decided against this informally in the context of the current problems with volunteers which I have already outlined. The solution voted for in the General Assembly was "mobilization": everyone took a turn at hoeing in addition to their usual work, going out to the fields in the afternoon and on weekends. But their efforts, though enthusiastic, did not solve the problem. The third possible solution was to hire workers. As previously described, Goshen was not in the habit of hiring workers except when absolutely necessary as a stopgap measure.

The permanent cotton workers informally passed round their opinion that things were so bad that hired labor was essential. Many other members were outraged at the very idea. They argued loudly and in public that *their* kibbutz was not going to exploit people by hiring them—especially not Arabs (the only people likely to be available for casual work at short notice); they were not going to become a bourgeois class of capitalists.

The problem was put on the agenda for the next General Assembly meeting which happened to coincide with an international basketball game on television (Israel was doing well that year, and members of Goshen were fervent supporters of their national team). Very few of those so violently opposed to hired labor attended the meeting; they watched the match instead. Thus, the cotton workers were able to hire people without opposition and get the hoeing under way. After the meeting, the objectors continued to protest and to complain that they would have gone to the meeting if they had known the question was coming up.

Actually, the agenda had been well publicized in the usual manner, and the coincidence with the match was accidental. So why did the objectors stay away from the meeting? The effect of their doing so was to separate matters of principle (against hired labor) and practicalities (the need to get the cotton hoed) and to allow the practical problem to be solved for the time being. Given the need for the hoeing and the high status and recognized expertise of the cotton workers, the objectors were perhaps saved some embarrassment by the choice of activities that evening. The matter was an extremely delicate one, and this is indicated by the objectors' attempts to save face after the meeting by making allegations of dirty dealing. After some days (and some hoeing) another meeting rescinded the decision, and decided for more mobilization, this time including school children. The 1975 cotton crop was saved.

The interesting point about this case is that the kibbutz was faced with a dilemma—how to assure its profit and yet remain uncompromised on the principle of not hiring labor. This was done by keeping the principle out of the formal political arena until the immediate problem had been solved. The dilemma itself remained unsolved. The case shows how important it was to have support in the General Assembly to get measures passed, and that such support might be tacit (the objectors were supporting the decision by not attending the meetings, whatever they claimed the situation to be). We also see an example of the interaction of the two political arenas, and in this particular case, careful attention being paid to what was discussed where.

## Case 2: Innovation

As mentioned previously, Miriam and Ivram and Heidi, the former Swiss volunteer, had television sets in their flats; Miriam and Ivram, in particular, were heavily and openly criticized for this privilege. The vast majority of people on Goshen, if they wanted to see television, had to go to one of the two communal sets in the *moadon* (clubhouse) or one of the air-raid shelters. The only people officially permitted a private set were the aged parents, one of whom was bed-ridden, of two members. It was not simply that Miriam, Ivram and Heidi had violated a general understanding that private television sets were not allowed, but they had also accepted gifts from relatives outside Goshen, which should have been handed over to the community as a whole. Criticism of them, although fierce, remained informal, passing back and forth through the gossip network in tandem with the criticism of their other misdemeanors. It is notable that neither Miriam and Ivram nor Heidi, showed any inclination to dispose of their sets. If the criticism was intended to persuade them to do so, it was very clearly having little effect. In fact, things were not quite what they seemed. Members of Goshen knew from past experience that the two private television sets had started a process of innovation which would eventually lead to sets all round. Previously a few people, then a few more, had acquired kettles for their flats, refrigerators, or stereo equipment. After several occurrences of private acquisition, the matter was discussed in the General Assembly. By this time, enough people recognized possible advantages and voted for proposals that would allocate money from the kibbutz budget for every family to purchase the article in question. This convoluted process provided a way out of the dilemma of how to raise the kibbutz standard of living without explicitly being overmaterialistic.

Now we can see how Miriam and Ivram and lesser outcasts were useful to Goshen. Better integrated members of the community quite simply could not have taken the radical step of acquiring a television. It was necessary to criticize Miriam and Ivram for having done so. We can be quite sure that critics knew how innovation worked, and also that they knew Miriam and Ivram would not dispose of the set. At any time, the problem could have been taken to the General Assembly for a formal ruling, but it was not. Already a less marginal individual, Heidi, had also acquired a set. The criticism continued, but the acceptance process was well under way. The *communa* women did not attack Heidi, even when she sided with Miriam in public.

Here again, great care was exercised over the arena where a political issue was discussed. In this case, the issue would be decided informally before reaching the formal arena. Informal discussions took place in the context of, and made use of general aspects of social relations in Goshen.

## Case 3: A Kibbutz Politician

Batsheva immigrated to Palestine before the Second World War, as a refugee from Germany and joined Goshen in 1949. In 1975, she was forty-eight years old and still working in the hothouses. She was the only woman her age working outside the services. She had a forthright tongue, and many people were afraid of attracting her formidable disapproval. Since joining Goshen, she had taken part in formal politics by attending the General Assembly and by serving on a number of committees. In fact, she once stood for election as Secretary—highly unusual for a woman. Although fearsome, she was much respected, popular, and admired for her acute perception of community affairs as well as for her emancipation as a pioneer woman doing productive work.

Batsheva was a clever politician in the formal arena and an important member of the mafia. She could also be effective informally, although she was not as keen a gossip as many other pioneer women. Her specialty was to expose the community's raw nerves by publicly making explicit points which many others preferred not to discuss.

In late October 1975, a change of Labor Organizer was due. The post required someone to leave his/her permanent job for three months. The first suggestion for the position was the cook. Batsheva commented that if the cook left the kitchen, there would be no food for her dog. This was partly a comment on the cooking since dogs were fed on the plentiful leftovers. Batsheva was also pointing out that if the cook left the kitchen to be replaced, even temporarily, by a better one, something would have to be done about the many dogs on Goshen and people were unwilling to agree to anything which might threaten their pets.

The second nomination was a young man who was working in the dairy, and was known to be unhappy with the job. Batsheva's objection this time was that if this man became Labor Organizer, he would be able to leave the dairy. She was accusing him of trying to shirk his responsibilities: strong young men capable of heavy dairy work were in short supply on Goshen. If the man did leave the dairy, he would be difficult to replace. Those present at the General Assembly were equally aware of the problem. Batsheva explicitly expressed their doubts, and the young man was rejected. Finally, the builder was elected to the post, which would keep him busy over the slack Winter period.

Batsheva was influential in the formal arena through the pertinence and originality of her comments. Others would make the same speech over and over again, and would be ignored. Generally, people tried to avoid unpleasantness during General Assembly meetings. Batsheva operated by pushing the meeting to the point where unpleasantness (such as a public accusation of shirking one's duty) threatened to emerge. This could rapidly persuade people to vote for her point of view. Through the force of her personality, she represented the collective interests of the kibbutz as interpreted by the pioneers and helped maintain the mafia's power.

As mentioned earlier, she could also be influential in the informal arena. When a young couple applied to move to a vacant flat next to hers, she let it be known that she did not want them as neighbors. The young couple, as Batsheva intended, soon heard this, and withdrew their application. She had defended the interests of senior kibbutz members who had formally-defined priority in housing, a principle which the ambitious youngsters had threatened. Batsheva's action was subtly executed. If she had complained formally, she would most likely have been offered a new flat elsewhere, which would have embarrassed her since she did not want to move. The informal complaint therefore served Batsheva's own interests, as well as those of senior members generally.

Batsheva's case is to some extent unique because of the importance of her personality in her political actions. However, her status derived from values quite general to the community; her point of view expressed and defended the interests of the mafia and her effectiveness derived in large part from reliable information from good contacts. The case demonstrates very clearly the importance of the attributes of particular individuals for their successful (or unsuccessful) political careers.

## Case 4: Power Through Gossip

The *communa*, where this chapter began, was the center of greatest informal influence in Goshen. This was partially due to the nature of the work — quiet, enclosed, and numerous visitors providing much information. In giving out information, the *communa* women could be selective and, to a large extent, control of the development of public opinion. For example, they originally raised the question of volunteers and had, by doling out specific information, ensured that the kibbutz member/volunteer boundary was strengthened and maintained. They were largely responsible for the exclusion of Miriam and Ivram from community life.

Miriam and Ivram's inability to make friends or to find suitable jobs, their reputation for being stupid and difficult (respectively), and their unfortunate, backward child could not be grounds for them to be expelled from the community. Such action would have been an exceptionally serious measure; Goshen had only once expelled a member. Twenty years after that case, many people still argued that the expulsion should never have taken place. The gossip network, centered in the *communa*, reinforced Miriam and Ivram's isolation by criticizing them and their behavior at every opportunity. At one point in 1975, Rivka, the ringleader, approached the old Secretary (the pioneer) to suggest formal expulsion. He pointed out firmly that this was a matter for the General Assembly which could not approve it because Miriam and Ivram's unpopularity was not grounds for expulsion. It would, he said, be totally against movement principles for people to be expelled from a kibbutz simply because people did not like them. The issue thus remained in the informal arena. Rivka knew that she could not get General Assembly support. Indeed, her suggestion to the Secretary was more likely a message to him not to treat Miriam and Ivram favorably. The couple's "crimes" were defined, tried and punished by public opinion. For reasons already explained, the television set was not brought up in the discussion; there were far too many other members of Goshen accepting gifts from relatives for this matter to be brought into the open.

It is significant that the prime movers in the rejection of Miriam and Ivram were women. In general, women did their politicking informally. The formal arena, represented here by a male pioneer, was actually hostile to the conclusions reached informally. Such hostility did not alter the effectiveness of the *communa* women. Thus, the two arenas did not necessarily reach matched or even complementary conclusions.

# The Arena of Control

All the processes described so far were internal to Goshen. We have seen how the various dimensions and mechanisms of control interacted to cover a wide variety of community issues. These should now be placed in the context of community boundaries which controlled who was and was not involved in kibbutz affairs and limited the effects of the various internal controls discussed here.

Within Israeli society, a Kibbutz Artzi kibbutz is a fairly clearly bounded social entity when members, candidates for membership and their children are considered. Members and candidates (children are not members) are clearly differentiated from other residents, and workers, and outsiders by their formal commitment to the status of member. Members must complete at least one year as an approved candidate before being formally accepted as members by a vote in the General Assembly. Many will have been in the youth movement which trains people ideologically and practically for kibbutz membership. The older the kibbutz, the more members born there who passed through the collective education system and training for kibbutz life. Others, as seen on Goshen, arrive through marriage or after service as a volunteer.

The process of recruitment of candidates and members is controlled by formal rules and, perhaps more importantly, by people who are already members. During 1975-6, there were several cases of nonacceptance of candidates for Goshen. Some prospective candidates left Goshen having realized they were unlikely to be accepted as members. The person likely to be rejected as a candidate generally had some undesirable (from Goshen's point of view) personal characteristic. They might be the wrong age or sex (unmarried, mature women were particularly unwelcome on Goshen), or their children might have personality defects (a violent man was rejected as a candidate). Such undesirable traits would be revealed early. Others might leave later in the process. These people usually were unable to form relationships with others.

All this means that the membership of Goshen and any other kibbutz was reciprocally selected. The individual candidate made a conscious and deliberate choice to try to join; members with the power to reject carefully scrutinized possible candidates. Many successful candidates for membership had been trained.

It is useful to think of a kibbutz as what Durkheim (1964:70) called a "society of saints." Paraphrased, this means a community marked off from the wider society by its own rule boundaries while still firmly part of that wider society. Within the "society of saints," rules operate which are, according to Durkheim, in some way stricter than those outside. The kibbutz is differentiated from Israeli society by movement values and by its own special institutions. In addition, each kibbutz exercises specific control over who is to be admitted to membership.

Within the kibbutz, the values and the formal institutions cannot by themselves ensure social control or allow public decisions to be made. The values are open to interpretation, and the formal rules and institutions do not in themselves cover every possible eventuality. Where values are ambiguous and where rules are not easily applied, gossip comes into play. For example, the volunteers, whose position was ambiguous in that they worked for Goshen without membership benefits or pay, were controlled through gossip. Innovation could be achieved by back-door methods; labor could be hired in the cotton fields; Ivram and Miriam could be informally outcast.

For an individual in Goshen, gossip was vital. A candidate had to participate in gossip to make contacts and to establish a good reputation if she/he was to be accepted as a member. Once accepted, a "good kibbutznik" (a "saint") carried on gossip, understanding that this was essential for influencing decision making, getting support, resisting power groups, becoming powerful and so on. The importance of gossip for an individual is illustrated by the fact that his or her admission to the "society of saints" was controlled informally, depending on whether other members would supply contact and support. We could say that gossip set community boundaries in the most basic way, by deciding who could be let inside. The extreme rarity of formal expulsion, one of the powers of the General Assembly, has been stressed by other writers (for example: Spiro 1970, Evens 1980, Shapiro 1976). Seldom is more than one case in the history of the kibbutz studied cited, including Degania, the oldest kibbutz (Shapiro 1976). As we have seen in Goshen, it was much more likely that people would be informally pressured to leave. There was no guarantee that the pressure would work and, in fact, some doubt as to whether people actually wanted it to given the usefulness of outcasts.

## Country-wide Control

Despite the boundaries, kibbutzim remain linked with Israeli society through participation in the national economy and direct ties through the federations with political parties, usually the Israeli Labor Party or one of its coalition partners. Goshen, as a Kibbutz Artzi kibbutz, was affiliated with Mapam, a small party to the left of the ILP but generally united with it. Until recently, the kibbutzim were viewed as living representatives of the old pioneering ideology, part of Israeli mythology. In fact, the connection is so strong that settlements of the Gush Emunim ("Bloc of the Faithful," actually right wing religious extremists) are often mistaken for kibbutzim.

As an integral part of Israeli society, a kibbutz is subject to the laws of the land, even though the federations and the kibbutzim themselves are predominantly self-governing. In terms of national crime statistics, the kibbutzim have a very low crime rate; very few kibbutz members find their way into the statistics. In 1975-6, no members of Goshen were accused; the police came to the kibbutz once to pick up a visiting soldier who was suspected of handling stolen property. The low crime rate does not mean that no one in the kibbutzim ever breaks the laws of the land. The characteristics of kibbutz organization decrease the likelihood that anyone will be brought to the attention of law enforcement agencies. First, the scope for crime on the kibbutz is narrow. There is little money and no banks, there are no deserted places to mug people, no one has access to funds long enough to embezzle them, drug addiction is expensive, etc. Since everyone knows everyone else, secret plotting would be very difficult. Secondly, the kibbutzim are very jealous of their autonomy and reputation. One way to protect this is to deal with possible criminal activities internally and, more often than not, informally. On Goshen, petty thefts, cases of vandalism, minor assaults and a "peeping Tom" were dealt with internally. The property was returned, the vandalism repaired, the quarrels patched up, and women were warned about the harmless "peeping Tom" and simply drew the curtains before undressing.

Saltman (1981) gives further evidence of kibbutzim protecting their members by dealing internally with certain "crimes." Particularly, he notes that kibbutzim have developed their own methods of dealing with drug abuse, using suspension and, ultimately, expulsion as punishments. However, Saltman also points out that the kibbutzim remain subject to Israel's law and some of their autonomy is being threatened by court decisions. For example, when a member leaves a kibbutz for a new life, a kibbutz is now obliged to give financial support following a court decision that national labor laws must apply (Saltman 1981:144). The extent of such outside control appears likely to increase, but, in the meantime, a considerable degree of autonomy remains.

Politics had clearer and more direct influence over Goshen's affairs. Administrative officials of Goshen travelled regularly to the city for consultation with federation officials. They would get advice on dealing with community matters (such as the complexities of economic planning) and information about the federation's current and developing policies. This information helped the officials to be more effective in Goshen. They could claim superior information and, of course, most of them were members of the mafia. Access to the federation and experience dealing with it provided another means for the mafia to maintain control. Some members of Goshen worked full or part time for the federation either as administrative officials or serving on committees. For example, the pioneer Secretary of 1975 was a member of the higher education committee. These people had their fingers on the pulse of power, and they were more senior members of Goshen. There were also influences operating through the federation's links with Mapam. In some respects, federation workers were party workers (especially during elections). Many commentators (e.g., Arian 1968, Sherman 1980) have noted that the fates of the Labor government and the kibbutzim have been inextricably linked. During the time of my fieldwork, the Labor government was in power, and the kibbutzim enjoyed what many people in Israel were soon to decide was disproportionately favorable treatment and high status deriving from their virtual monopoly of the pioneering ideology at that time. Even then, however, they were conscious that their position was not as solid as it once had been and they carefully guarded their autonomy and reputation.

The election of 1977, described as an "earthquake" (Peretz 1977) or an "upheaval" (Sherman 1980) was a blow to the Israeli labor movement. The victory of Begin's right wing coalition threatened the position of the kibbutzim by removing one of the main pillars of their ascendency — the Labor government, which had held power since 1948. There was, as Sherman (1980) reports, an anti-kibbutz backlash. Resources were diverted from the kibbutzim to organizations like the Gush Emunim (a right wing settlement movement). Kibbutz politicians were characterized as intruders in urban (majority) affairs. The prestige of pioneering shifted toward settlers on the West Bank with their religious ideology and away from the socialist kibbutzim.

It is not possible to predict what the long term effects of the change of government on the kibbutzim will be. Certainly, the kibbutzim have been put on the defensive and are likely to remain so, even if a new Labor government is elected. The old pioneers, the guardians of the old ideology, cannot last forever. Whatever happens, it is likely that *internal* kibbutz politics will continue and that gossip will remain the duty of a good kibbutznik. Gossip in the kibbutz has a pattern and a momentum of its own.

# - 5 -

# Women and Men

## Some Kibbutz Women

In the early years of Goshen, women did what was seen as men's work; in the fields, clearing the land, helping to start the buildings, organizing the water supply, and so on. Living conditions were rugged and experienced equally by men and women. The pioneer women of Goshen remembered how hard they worked to build the kibbutz. They explained to me that their land was covered with rocks which had to be removed, that fields were created with earth transported from a nearby *wadi* (a dry river bed), and that when the rain came, the site became a quagmire. These memories were an important part of the notion that Goshen was theirs; they had shared in the early hard work. It was clear that they saw their efforts equally as important at the men's. There were some stories about the incompetence and bad behavior of some of the men at the time. These were told to me in the spirit of showing that men, although they seemed to think they ruled the world, were not as wonderful as all that. One of these stories was about a male pioneer who had since left Goshen. One day he refused to drive the tanker to the nearby town to collect the water supply stating that it was too muddy and the tanker would get bogged down. This was a bogus excuse used to disguise the fact that the man simply could not be bothered to go. The storyteller related, "And I was disgusted. We had to have the water. He would take the water away from the babies from sheer laziness. To think he claimed to be a Socialist." Similar behavior, she went on to explain, could now be seen in the man's son, still a member of Goshen. Another story, told with laughter, went back to the time when the pioneers lived in tents. The "hero" of this one was a man who in 1975-6 was regarded by many as an ideal kibbutz member who contributed to kibbutz life unusually fully. He was an intellectual and had brought many books to Goshen

**81**

with him. To keep them out of the mud, he had tried to build a bookshelf in the tent. The repeated collapse of the bookshelf and the great hilarity this provoked were, it seemed, a sign of incompetence, showing that even the most accomplished of men had failings. When the same man insisted upon wiring a plug for my radio, the wires came loose almost immediately. I had to reconnect them myself, and this story too entered the repertoire.

The stories referred to the past but also related to contemporary kibbutz life. The women were indicating both how they valued their own work in founding Goshen and how they perceived some of the men's failings, past and present. The tanker driver's son was said to have inherited a character from his father; the new story was added to that of the failed carpenter. In the past then, women on Goshen had worked equally with the men. In talking about those times and the present day, they would tell stories enhancing their own efforts and contributions while diminishing those of men.

The pioneer women of Goshen worked with the men for only a short time. Along with other kibbutz women of their generation, they moved quickly into service work (already classified as unproductive) as the general conditions of life improved and as more babies were born. In Goshen, such developments were seen as completely natural. As on the veteran kibbutzim, the tendency of women to work in the services and the method of child care were already well established. By 1975-6, all the pioneer women except one (Batsheva, the politician) were working in the services. Their daughters and the other young women of Goshen were following in their footsteps. Indeed by this time, as described in Chapter 3, there were very few opportunities for young women to work outside the services. Most of the younger women therefore lacked even the limited experience of productive work the female pioneers had. This was one of the factors that led their outlooks on life to differ quite radically from those of the pioneers. We can see these differences by looking at some women of Goshen in 1975-6.

Elissa, a pioneer, had two daughters, one aged twenty-five and the other twenty-two. She had come to Goshen through the youth movement where she met her husband who was to become a highly respected member of Goshen. She had worked in the fields with other pioneer women, toiling hard all day. She had also been very much involved with the ideological and political sides of community life, with a firm commitment to socialism and to the reconciliation of Jew and Arab. She had participated in community politics and kept well in touch with events and relationships in Goshen. When her children were born, she had gone into service work, in the kitchen, losing direct touch with the "productive" side of the kibbutz and with formal political activity. She kept herself informed of these matters, as did many women of her generation, through her husband's accounts of meetings. Later still, she took a teaching job outside Goshen, lessening her contact with the service branches and with other women too. Although still a member in 1975-6, she was by then very peripheral to community events and activities. Elissa did not see herself as peripheral; she still thought of herself as an important person in Goshen, still valued her past and continuing life as a pioneer, and still commented on contemporary community events frequently and at length to her contacts in the community. For this, her family criticized her. "How do you know?" they would ask, "How can you say that when you never see what's happening?"

Elissa's daughters' experiences and activities were quite different. Both born and brought up on the kibbutz, they shared none of their mother's experience of pioneering. For them, Goshen was not a community of their own construction but a place they inhabited by accident of birth. The elder daughter, Sarah, had married during her army service. Soon after the birth of her first child, she returned to Goshen with the baby. Her divorce was finalized in 1975. Reflecting on her marriage, she explained that she had been very innocent in her relationships with men, very trusting and romantically inclined, and had entered into a bad marriage without realizing what she was doing. She saw her innocence as a result of her upbringing where kibbutz boys were like brothers to her and the only potential marriage partners seemed to be outside Goshen. Too late, she had learned that outsiders were not good, kind and trustworthy, as she had assumed. Returning to Goshen was her only option if she wanted to leave her husband. She simply had no resources to survive anywhere else alone with her baby; that is, she had no money, no home and no job. In 1975-6, she was working as a teacher in the primary school on Goshen but did not see herself as settled there permanently. Frequently expressing pride in the kibbutz way of life generally, she complained that Goshen was a bad kibbutz. In her opinion, many people were lazy and quarrelsome, and therefore not good members. Working in the services, she, like other women, lacked access to the kind of information needed to be an effective politician. Without a husband, it was more difficult for her to keep in touch with events in the productive branches. Despite these handicaps, she kept in touch through talking to her father and attempted to participate in formal politics by attending meetings. In common with other members of her generation, however, she found that attempted political activity frequently proved ineffective because "the mafia" would close ranks against any measure they saw as radical. Her comments on the more general position of women on Goshen were complex, and this was a topic which concerned her greatly. She pointed out that women in the kibbutz were much better off than women elsewhere, having greater freedom including the right to take part in community decision making and greater opportunities, particularly in the workfield. At the same time, she saw women's roles in the kibbutz as less than ideal, particularly given their concentration in the services. She was critical of some of her female contemporaries for their failure to challenge the position of women. She was particularly scathing about two of them who stated that their ambition was to be housewives. She felt that many people, especially men, in Goshen did not respect women and did not bother to think about their position. During my fieldwork, she was reading European and American feminist literature and was eager to hear about the women's movement in Britain. For her, it was new and exciting, and she felt the kibbutz could benefit from more concern with the position of women.

Elissa's younger daughter, Caramit, also complained of Goshen as a bad kibbutz. She had left after her army service, although she continued contact with the community through visits to her family. She described Goshen as "the worst kibbutz I have ever come across," referring to what she saw as people's (particularly men's) laziness and the chaotic way she thought the community was run. By keeping in touch with her family, she kept up with current events in Goshen and would comment on particular cases as examples of the community's general character. In 1975, a couple who had been part of an earlier *garin* (a "nucleus" or group of young people intended as future members) returned to Goshen to try living there again. They were married on Goshen with a rabbi coming to the kibbutz to perform the ceremony. There were many guests at the wedding. Soon afterwards, the couple were both to enroll as university students. They would live on Goshen while they studied, working there only on weekends and during vacations. To Caramit, the whole affair was an "absolutely disgusting" example of the depths to which Goshen had sunk, a corrupt attempt to gain members at any price. The wedding, in her view, had been too large and extravagant, much more elaborate than other weddings, even those for sons and daughters of Goshen. The rabbi should not have been allowed in the atheist kibbutz. Although required by law, that part of the proceedings should have taken place quietly in town. Worst of all, the couple should not have been permitted to begin study immediately when other new members were required to work on Goshen for at least a year before their application to study would even be considered.

Caramit was less interested in discussing the role of women than was her sister, but she too was developing her ideas and starting to criticize attitudes toward women in the world outside the kibbutz. Reading Simone de Beauvoir for the first time, she was surprised and shocked to learn of the Jewish man's daily prayer thanking God he had not been born a woman. She looked critically at the relationships between her kibbutz agemates and their boyfriends. One in particular came under attack for addressing her boyfriend as *ish* (man), as if to emphasize his masculinity. Caramit felt this demeaned the woman concerned.

None of these three women was particularly satisfied with life on Goshen. Elissa had her own life rather separate from the rest of the community, although some pride in her pioneer status remained despite her family's criticisms of her activities. Sarah was secure on Goshen in the sense that she had a home and a job and could bring up her son without any great struggle, but she was very ambivalent about kibbutz life in general and Goshen in particular. Caramit had given up her membership of Goshen and did not plan to return. Their particular activities and attitudes were partially due to their individual personalities. However, each of them faced a number of freedoms and constraints basic to the lives of all kibbutz women which dictated what their opportunities were both within and outside Goshen.

In terms of status, there can be no doubt that in Goshen, and in the kibbutz movement generally, women have lower status than men. I have already explained how this is connected with the kind of work most valued in the kibbutz and the fact that this work is done primarily by men. Women who had once done such work (the pioneers and the one female pioneer, Batsheva, who continued to do it) had higher status on Goshen. It is difficult to say whether this actually derived from the work or from pioneering itself with its associated ideological kudos and greater experience. Women's lower status is also connected with more diffuse ideas about men and women, particularly regarding marriage. On Goshen, and I have no reason to suppose other kibbutzim are any different, it was thought much more important for a woman to be married than for a man. Lifelong bachelors were thought a little odd, perhaps, but a woman heading for lifelong spinsterhood was a figure of, alternately, pity and fun. One woman of Goshen had been the mistress of a (married) man for years. Finally, in 1975, she met another man and planned to marry him. Comments were in the vein of "at last — now she'll have a husband of her own."

Elissa had the status of having been a pioneer, even though she did not work on Goshen. Sarah had married very young and had clearly, at the time, attached great importance to doing so as soon as possible. One important aspect of her ambivalence about Goshen was that she was unlikely to find another husband there, something she hoped to do eventually. She resisted being drawn too tightly into the web of life on Goshen, refusing for example to become a formal assistant to the head teacher in the primary school. Caramit had had few relationships with men in her life, and this failure would not have enhanced her status had she remained on Goshen. It is extremely doubtful whether she would have found any of the work available there to be satisfying and probably would have had trouble finding a permanent place. At least Sarah's job was skilled, and she, unlike the majority of women on Goshen, was indispensable in it.

Despite having lower status than men, kibbutz women have certain freedoms not available to women in many other societies. No kibbutz woman is dependent on one particular man; she can be sure that her children will have adequate food, clothing, shelter and education no matter what happens to her or their father. She herself is assured of housing and the necessities of life including a job. Conversely, there is little choice of a job, formal right to participation in community decision making is restricted, and there are practical problems for a woman on her own. In the examples I have given, both sides of the situation are shown most clearly in Sarah's case. Her return to the kibbutz with her baby gave both of them a safe refuge and meant that she need not worry about being able to raise her child. She was not, on the whole, dissatisfied with her job, although she resisted becoming entrenched in it. Her attempts to take part in decision making were restricted not only because she was a woman but also because she faced opposition from "the mafia" (as did others of her generation). Being without a husband meant she lacked contact with the economic and political activities of men, even though her father provided her with a degree of this. She also complained that there was no one to do small jobs around the house that men on Goshen normally did, particularly things like wiring plugs, mending fuses and fixing washers. When she wanted something done, she had to find the electrician or the plumber and persuade them to come to her flat, a process which could take days or weeks. She would not approach her neighbors to do these jobs. This would be interpreted by other people, she said, as an invitation to more than repair job, and would be morally compromising for her. "I would be suggesting I was available," she explained, "and I'm not."

## Some Kibbutz Men

Male pioneers on Goshen had high prestige deriving from pioneering itself, as did the women. Most of them had done productive work throughout their lives on the kibbutz and were much more active in formal politics than women, even pioneer women. They enjoyed what were generally seen as all the advantages of kibbutz life and few of the disadvantages.

Reuven, a pioneer of Goshen, had survived a Nazi concentration camp. In common with other such survivors on Goshen, he did not talk about his experiences there, although he would sometimes say that his survival had been a matter of luck. Reuven's history would sometimes be mentioned by others to explain some outrageous behavior, but this was done only when Reuven had acted in what was seen as a particularly extreme way. Usually when explaining his behavior, people would refer jokingly to his marriage to Batsheva (the very forceful woman we have already met) contrasting his weakness with her strength.

Reuven often looked back to the early days of Goshen expressing his pride as a pioneer, the hard work he had done, and the harshness of the living conditions. He described himself as "the head of Goshen's Rumanian community" (of three). Goshen as a new community he had helped to build had great significance for him.

In 1975-6, Reuven was working as both a truck driver and volunteer organizer. Although defined in the kibbutz account as service work, truck driving did not have the usual negative connotations of such work. It involved helping to load the lorry, Reuven's pride and job, and driving the produce away for sale or processing. According to Goshen's folk wisdom, this was important and essential work. As volunteer organizer, Reuven was entrusted with the vital work of maintaining the boundaries of who belonged to Goshen, as defined by "the mafia." He performed this task with great success. He was able to ensure that he was the principal medium of communication between the volunteers and the kibbutz. It was extremely rare for volunteers to approach a mafia member other than Reuven with any problems they might have. Volunteers might complain to younger kibbutz members but since younger people had little influence, they were unlikely to get anything done. Reuven, the go-between for mafia and volunteers, had considerable influence and could get things done—or do them himself, if he wanted to.

From the volunteers' point of view, Reuven's activities and way of operating often seemed arbitrary. Some volunteers were permitted to stay on Goshen for months; others would find themselves constantly bothered by Reuven asking when they were leaving, suggesting he needed their rooms for someone else, or saying that soon there would be no more work for them. Also, Reuven seemed to make trouble over the equipment volunteers needed in their houses. If a lock were broken, he would sometimes simply replace it. Other times, volunteers would be lectured loudly and at length on vandalism and threatened with reports to the Secretary. In these activities, however, Reuven's way of doing things actually reflected the fact that he was keeping the boundary intact. Volunteers whom he harassed were those the mafia had identified as dangerous to the integrity of the boundary such as young women with apparent designs on kibbutz men or people who were simply too friendly with certain kibbutz members and were thought likely to unsettle them. Reuven's ability to control the volunteers—his "messages" usually had the desired result—was vital to the nature of his job. "The mafia" was most concerned with that aspect. His good performance ensured he had permanent work and was considered indispensable to it. Politically, too, he was effective. He had to keep his finger on the pulse of mafia opinion and did this both formally and informally. He also paid attention to his own position in the mafia and would, for example, make savings on the volunteer budget whenever he could, knowing the approval this would bring.

Reuven subscribed firmly to the central ideology of kibbutz life, as defined by the pioneers and developed through kibbutz history. Though not a great intellectual, his conversation with volunteers and with fellow members frequently referred to the tenets of communalism. He also discussed distinctions between members' work and unproductive work, sometimes more explicitly than other members would have preferred. Comments like "If you only sew, you don't eat" were greeted with shock, resulting not so much from Reuven's idea that sewing was unproductive work as from the very bold and explicit way he had expressed it.

Generally, Reuven enjoyed life on Goshen. He liked his jobs, had a comfortable standard of living and plenty of good conversation—one of his favorite pastimes. He was a fully integrated member.

Reuven's son, Ya'ir, was twenty-two years old. He was much less happy with Goshen than his father, complaining that it was not a good kibbutz. Nevertheless, he was proud to be a kibbutznik and proud of his youth and strength. During 1976, he took a job outside Goshen to save money for a trip abroad, saying "We kibbutzniks are the best; they want to employ us because we are strong and we know how to work." He also stood firmly on what he saw as the principles of kibbutz life and the main areas of Goshen's failing. For example, he saw opportunities to travel abroad as luxuries and privileges which should be offered to kibbutz members on a rotational and equal basis. However, because Goshen

was "a bad kibbutz," he had devised the scheme whereby he would work outside
to earn money to finance his trip. "I knew they would accept it because they don't
think about principles, so I take advantage of them. I am a good kibbutznik living
on a bad kibbutz."

Ya'ir had his problems. He had an affair with a foreign volunteer and the
prospective trip abroad was partly to visit her. Other members of Goshen were
worried by this. For the pioneer generation, it suggested that he might be lost
to Goshen. For younger people who knew the woman concerned, an innocent
kibbutznik had been seduced by a sophisticated and callous foreigner. There were
repeated attempts during my fieldwork to get Ya'ir involved with someone else
and to enlighten him as to the foreigner's character. None of the attempts were
particularly successful until news was received that she had married at home. As
gossip phrased it, she had "ditched" Ya'ir. A more minor problem related to Ya'ir's
work. During the Summer of 1975, he worked in the cotton fields, enjoying the
physical effort of moving irrigation pipes. Ya'ir loved children, however, and asked
if he could work in the children's houses in the Winter. This request was considered
preposterous because Ya'ir was a man. Men could certainly love children, but
working in the children's houses was a woman's job. It would be ludicrous, never
mind wasteful, for a man to do it. Ya'ir's application was unsuccessful.

Compared to the women I described earlier, Reuven and Ya'ir were much happier
with kibbutz life. Again, this was partly a result of individual character but also
attributable to the general character of the kibbutz as a community. As with the
women, there were generationally-based differences between Reuven and Ya'ir
resulting from pioneering experience or the lack of it. Reuven was fiercely loyal
to and identified very closely with Goshen as the kibbutz he had helped to build.
Ya'ir subscribed to what he saw as the more general values of the kibbutz movement
as a whole; he was critical of Goshen yet ready to use its resources if they were
available to him. His application to work in the children's houses revealed that
he had not fully understood all the historical implications of "general kibbutz
values" or at least that he did not follow them as his father did. He saw an
opportunity to satisfy his own feelings about work and children. For those who
emphasized the "productive/unproductive" work distinction, and its respective
associations with men and women, it was simply inconceivable. In any case, there
were other opportunities for Ya'ir to do work he enjoyed.

Reuven and Elissa illustrate the general differences between pioneer men and
pioneer women on Goshen. For both of them, pioneering had been an important
experience—a sign that Goshen was really theirs. By 1975-6 however, Reuven
was in work considered vital to Goshen and involved directly in kibbutz political
life. Elissa had virtually no direct contact with Goshen's economic affairs and
politics, having rejected the options taken by other women of her generation to
work in the service branches and to be involved in informal politics. Both Reuven
and Elissa had seen the changes in men's and women's roles occur as Goshen
had developed. Reuven was not greatly concerned by this. Indeed, he could belittle

women's work and, by implication, women themselves. Elissa, despite encouraging her daughters to read feminist literature and discussing the position of women in a very general way, did not often comment specifically on the position of women in Goshen. She did participate in telling stories about men's incompetence, however, and it was clear that she did not see women as necessarily subordinate to men.

Differences between the generations arose primarily from the experience of having been a pioneer. The younger people were more openly critical of Goshen than their parents were and there was variation in their responses. Of courses, it is important to remember that the pioneers who still lived on Goshen were those who had chosen to remain there. Many other pioneers left the community in the years since its foundation. In 1975-6, the second generation were making up their minds whether to stay or not. Caramit had already gone; Sarah and Ya'ir said they planned to stay for the foreseeable future. It is, nevertheless, a well attested fact that marriage and children make it more likely that kibbutz members generally will stay. The prevalent idea in the movement is that children need a stable environment in which to grow up. We should bear in mind that the roles and attitudes of the second generation were in a process of formation during my fieldwork. In itself, this may account for some of the variation. We can say generally that the pioneers saw the future of the kibbutz in their children's hands, whereas the children themselves were looking to their personal futures with the kibbutz as only one possibility.

It is important that all three young people were primarily preoccupied with work and marriage. Caramit had no interest in the work available on the kibbutz and was building her career outside. She was not, at that time, looking towards marriage as a possible future but was instead concentrating on getting her degree. Sarah had work on Goshen but felt she had been forced into it and did not want to be forced any further. She was interested in another marriage, but was concerned that there were no possible partners for her on Goshen. Unlike the women, Ya'ir was happy with his work, even though he would have liked to try something else. He too was looking for a marriage partner, although this was not generally thought as urgent for him as for the women.

In seeing work and marriage as important for their future, the three were representative of their generation. Many young women were dissatisfied with the work opportunities open to them, as well as being anxious to find husbands. Not all of them reacted to the position of women on Goshen as did Sarah and Caramit. Although there was general criticism, the possible solutions varied. Some women wanted to be housewives or wanted to defer to men. Generally, young men enjoyed kibbutz work, although they also saw their roles in different ways. They were not all prepared to use Goshen's "badness" in the way Ya'ir was. Men too looked forward to marriage, although they rarely discussed it explicitly.

## Relationships

Within a kibbutz marriage on Goshen, there was a prevalent accepted and expected division of labor. Tasks in the couple's flat were particularly delineated, and the behavior was observable in all age groups. According to this domestic division of labor, women were primarily responsible for keeping the flat clean and tidy, for baking cakes for afternoon snacks (not all women did this, but no men did), and usually for collecting food from the dining hall should the family wish to eat supper at home. Small maintenance jobs such as wiring plugs or minor plumbing were considered men's work. Some of the flats had flower gardens in which the division of labor was less clear. Men generally did any heavy work; maintenance would be the responsibility of either or both spouses. The division of labor was quite strictly observed. Men might reprimand their wives for leaving the flat messy, and there was an informal suggestion during the year that women might be given an hour or so off work on Friday afternoons to tidy up for the weekend. Women generally could not and did not try to do the men's jobs. Sarah was a case in point of this, as we have seen.

Parents generally spent equal time with their children, except when they were small. Women would visit their young babies in the baby house several times a day to feed them. Until the children started school, their mothers visited them every morning for an hour set aside from work especially for that purpose. This time is called *sha'at ahava*, the hour of love. Married couples were expected to spend their nonwork time together and to go on outings and holidays together. Couples who did not observe these conventions were rare and regarded with some suspicion. "Don't they like one another?" "Are they splitting up?" When possible, they would eat meals together, although this was sometimes difficult for meals taken during work hours, i.e., breakfast and lunch. There were no cases of husband and wife working together, so couples were separated at work.

Sexual relationships were by no means confined to married couples. All those who married on Goshen during 1975-6 had lived together, often for months and sometimes for years before the actual ceremony. This was common practice, officially recognized by the kibbutz which would allocate double flats to unmarried couples. Where such flats were allocated, it was generally expected that the couple would marry sooner or later. Indeed this happened in the cases I observed. If a relationship was going to end, it had done so before the stage of an application for a double flat. In the early stages, couples would live together unofficially while retaining separate flats.

In premarital sexual relationships, there was a very clear code of conduct, somewhat different for women and men. Women were criticized very heavily if they "slept around," but not if they had a long-standing relationship with one man. In contrast, a man who had many affairs was thought of as something of a hero, particularly by younger men. Such a man would have most of his affairs with women volunteers not with kibbutz women, who either viewed him as a brother or knew the damage their reputations would suffer from a casual affair.

Extramarital sexual relationships were thought scandalous, although they certainly occurred. Generally, they would go on for months in secret. When suddenly revealed, everyone would know very quickly and lengthy discussions would take place in private. Exceptions to this were a few long-standing affairs which were known about but excused, usually on the basis of the problems of the people concerned. These were not considered threats to the marriage or marriages involved, whereas the first type were and usually proved to be so.

Married couples, as I have said, normally spent most of their free time together. Older, unmarried people led rather lonely lives outside work. Amongst younger people, however, there was a good deal of socializing outside work in mixed sex groups often based on the peer groups in which people had come to Goshen. Those who interacted in peer groups explained that their relationships were "like those of brothers and sisters," and indeed they were very free and easy with one another, both sexes taking part equally in the activity and conversation. They did not look at one another as potential sexual partners. In the nationality groups, there were more likely to be relationships involving or leading to sexual activity, and when young people interacted with volunteers, sexual undertones and overtones were nearly always present. Generally, this meant interaction was much less relaxed than it was in the peer groups. Except within the peer groups, a man and a woman with an obviously close friendship were assumed to be sleeping together. Close male-female relationships without a sexual element were extremely rare. One man who liked to have women as friends but not lovers complained that he had a reputation for having a wild and promiscuous sex life just because of this.

Outside work hours, single sex groups were quite rare, although they did occur. Single women might visit one another for coffee in the afternoons; men would not necessarily be excluded from such occasions. Single men occasionally met together to play sports from which women were excluded. On at least one occasion during my fieldwork, some men met to view pornographic films (this shocked many young people, both male and female). There were no formally constituted all male or all female meetings.

At work, all male and all female groups were the most common, as might be expected from the division of labor. Sometimes there might be one member of the other sex in a predominantly single sex group. For example, a man did heavier chores and operated the dishwasher in the kitchen where all the other workers were women. In the factory, a woman did the office work and men did all the other jobs. The hothouses were the only branches where the workforce consisted of both men and women during "the Season" (the Winter) when the roses were cut and packed for export. Volunteers were more likely to work in mixed sex groups, doing work that members did only occasionally.

All male work groups were characterized by boisterous comraderie during breaks in the working day. Women working together had more opportunity and quiet time to talk during work, and the gossip network could be observed in action in their work places as described in Chapter 4. Certain women, particularly those pioneers who worked permanently in the kitchen, had reputations for hot temperedness, and shouting. This behavior was explained as symptomatic of the awfulness of the work they had to do. Many women were known to gossip extensively at work.

As well as being the only branch in which men and women regularly worked together, the hothouses afforded women one of the very few opportunities they had to work in a productive branch. At work, there was an atmosphere of relaxed banter, expressed in jokes and teasing fellow workers. For example, when I first started work, the "boss" (the branch manager) welcomed me to the branch with the remark "Ah! English. I want to learn English — you can help me." Another worker retorted "Only God can help you!" to the general amusement of everyone else. Underneath this friendly joking, however, work relationships were not quite as they first appeared. The men clearly saw themselves as equals. Even though one of them was formally branch manager and liked to give orders, the others would argue every point with him on the basis of equal knowledge of and experience in the branch. Certain tasks, such as dealing with the agency to which the flowers were sent, they saw as their own preserve and would involve the women only as a last resort. For example, the agency sent reports in English on the flowers we had sent. The men would argue for hours about the meaning of the reports and only in desperation would they ask any of the women to help interpret them. Usually after the arguments had been resolved, we would simply be told the comments in the form of orders. "Not so many bent stems, please." "Don't tie up the packets so tightly." "Put the string lower down." Sometimes the orders were contradictory. "Don't throw these out, they're only a bit bent. You can put them in the middle of the bunches." "Tie them up properly or the box will be full too soon." "Move the string up, the flowers will get damaged." Sometimes we felt we could do nothing right, especially when there was a big flush of flowers, and we were almost overwhelmed with them. The work was long and arduous and needed considerable skill as the flowers had to be exactly matched in each packet of twenty by stem length, color, size and shape of flower. Sorting the flowers was women's work. Here, although the joking carried on, the women were far from equal in what they did. The lowliest and least skilled (usually volunteers), sorted the flowers according to stem length. Moving up the hierarchy, women sorted different types of blooms and the larger (more valuable) flowers according to their years of experience. Batsheva, the senior woman, began the day sorting the longest, largest red roses. Women with fewer years of service would begin with the smaller ones. Then Batsheva would start on the next superior category, the others moving down accordingly. Junior women competed for places in the hierarchy below Batsheva. This competitiveness can be related, I think, to the problems women had getting into and staying in productive work on Goshen. If their skill was acknowledged such that they could be entrusted regularly with the most valuable flowers, they had succeeded in establishing their indispensability in the branch. They could therefore be confident that they would return to a respected job after an absence such as having a baby. They did not have to fear being called away to kitchen work.

## Attitudes

Young men on Goshen, especially those who had come there as adult immigrants, enjoyed discussing the attractiveness and potential sexual availability of young women, particularly volunteers. This would be done unashamedly and in public. It was quite separate from the search for wives by the same men. The sort of woman they would marry would not have had casual affairs. Once married, she would be considered theirs, once and for all. Men guarded their wives vigorously from the advances of other men and were unwilling to let the women go outside Goshen alone.

These attitudes were condemned by many older men and by many of the younger men who had been brought up on Goshen. They considered women more as equals than as sex objects or property. This attitude did not, as we have seen, relate to the status of women working on the contemporary kibbutz. It was commonly stated that women already had equality, and that the kibbutz was the one place where women really had an opportunity to express themselves. One particularly interesting view was voiced by a pioneer at a public meeting for representatives of the whole kibbutz movement. He argued that a true socialist society would bring full emancipation with it. The kibbutz movement should work towards socialism nationally and internationally. The modern Western women's movement was not only bourgeois but also diversionary.

I was present at that meeting, and commented afterwards to Elissa on what the man had said. She responded "Oh, take no notice of him; he's always had verbal diarrhea!" This is another example of the attitudes of women towards men mentioned earlier, showing the tendency to expose what was seen as weakness whenever possible. In turn, this is part of a more general lack of passivity among kibbutz women concerning their roles and status in the community. We have already seen (Chapter 4) that although women's participation in formal politics was restricted, they were very active informally and could influence community affairs quite significantly that way.

In the field of work and more general daily activity, women on Goshen were involved in other changes affecting the kibbutz movement as a whole. One of these is the so-called "return to familism" where kibbutz women are spending more and more time with their children. In Goshen in the 1950s, when the first generation of children were small, mothers visited the children's houses infrequently and at strictly regulated times. "We didn't dare go in—the nurses were so strict," they told me. By contrast, the young mothers of the 1970s visited their children whenever they had a moment to spare during work hours and made full use of the "hour of love." In some kibbutzim (none in the Kibbutz Artzi federation in 1975-6), extra rooms have been built onto the flats, at considerable expense, where the children spend the night. Another aspect of the "return to familism" is the popularity among women of work in the children's houses. On Goshen, as we have seen, there was great competition for the jobs. Women valued this so-called "unproductive" work very highly, as they valued being mothers and having as much contact with their children as possible. I see these moves by women as a fight back against the subordination imposed on them by the structure of the kibbutz. Women are organizing and securing a niche in the kibbutz which has value and is not in the dust bin category "unproductive work." Why this particular niche was chosen is a matter of some debate, as I will show later on.

Young women on Goshen were radically questioning their roles and statuses. As I showed in the case studies earlier, there were two ways of doing this. A minority wanted a very "traditional" role as "housewife." They wanted to marry a nonkibbutz man and to spend their lives looking after home and husband outside Goshen. They attributed this attitude to the "awful work" they had to do on Goshen. Another, although larger, minority found these suggestions totally unacceptable, saying they would bring inequality and domination to the women's lives. They argued unsuccessfully with the prospective housewives. This group sought to develop thinking in Goshen about the roles and statuses of women in more general ways. They would write articles for the kibbutz newspaper and would argue forcefully against any suggestion that women were, or should be, inferior or subservient to men in any way. Some of these women knew about the women's movement in Europe and America and imported ideas for their arguments. At the same time, they were very much aware that the kibbutz was supposed to be one place where women could be independent; they were somewhat bewildered by the contradictions they found.

## Comparisons and Context

It is not difficult to find parallels between the situations and attitudes of women and men in Goshen and in other kibbutzim. Tiger and Shepher (1975) used census data from the three kibbutz federations. They supplemented that data with intensive questionnaire surveys of two veteran and two younger kibbutzim and lengthy interviewing of selected kibbutz members. They found all kibbutzim to be similar to Goshen concerning the generalities of women's and men's roles. They found (1975:262-3) that all kibbutzim had developed similarly from relative equality in work towards a very consistent division of labor like that in Goshen, becoming more pronounced in later generations. They found that women did not take part in formal politics or hold offices to any great extent. When they did, they were involved in social and personal issues rather than economic ones. Women tended to prefer working with male bosses; they achieved less at school; in the army, they did service jobs; they were the main instigators of the "return to familism."

When men were called away from the kibbutzim to serve in the Yom Kippur war, there was only a temporary change in roles. The study concluded that the kibbutzim aimed in principle at equality and that the federations had long been concerned with the so-called "problem of the woman." A similar general picture is reflected in case studies of particular kibbutzim such as Spiro's (1979) restudy of Kiryat Yedidim, Blasi's (1980) study of Vatik, and Rayman's (1981) of Har.

Leon (1964) gives an extended account of the Kibbutz Artzi federation's concern, and his personal concern as a kibbutz member, with "the problem of the women." This "problem" is said to lie in the fact that kibbutz women do not seem to participate in kibbutz life as fully as men do. They express (in various ways, as we have seen) dissatisfaction with the kibbutz and the opportunities it offers or fails to offer them. As early as 1958, the General Council of the Kibbutz Artzi, consisting of representatives from each kibbutz in the federation, was trying to change women's roles and status. It asked for more discussion of the situation, improvements in women's work through training, and a change in attitudes towards women as being suited only for service work (Viteles 1967:331ff). These were recommendations to the kibbutzim which the General Council could not enforce; the subsequent history of the federation shows that the question was discussed repeatedly and similar measures were proposed again and again with little effect, as the more recent data on the kibbutzim has shown. This is not as surprising as it may first appear. Representatives to the General Council are unusual kibbutzniks; men (as are most formal politicians) who have the time, inclination and commitment to be concerned with affairs wider than those of their own communities. The information for its discussion comes from a special research department. Ordinary kibbutz members have little concern with and less knowledge of either the research or the discussions. A cynical kibbutz veteran on Goshen complained that the researchers, mainly sociologists, had become the new ideologists of the movement. "What do they know about our real lives? They are obsessed with their surveys and think they can solve the problems just by doing more and more silly MAs. Where are the activists now?" In these comments, he expressed the very real gap between federation concerns and the concerns of the ordinary kibbutz member. The fact remains, however, that existing roles are a very practical problem for the kibbutzim, because they have brought dissatisfaction among women who, whatever their ascribed status, are essential to the continuing viability of the movement.

How did the present state of affairs occur? Why has the apparent commitment to equality in principle not been achieved in practice? Why does the contemporary kibbutz seem to be a man's world? To begin answering these questions, we have to look back at the history of the kibbutz movement and the history of Israeli society and how these have interacted (cf. Bowes 1978, 1986).

In the early stages, women were a tiny minority among kibbutz pioneers. This is not really surprising when we consider the very subservient and wholly domestic role of women in the *shtetl* (the Jewish community of Eastern Europe) (Zborowski and Herzog 1962). For a young man to migrate to Palestine from the *shtetl* was radical enough; for a woman to do so was revolutionary and even more difficult since women's lives were greatly restricted. The women who did leave for Palestine were exceptional indeed and rejected everything that was expected of them. Their rejection of the assigned role for women was not, however, a focus of attention for the movement in these early years. In the 1920s however, women's efforts became more deliberate, directed towards attaining a pioneering role alongside and equal to men. Women formed their own work teams, farms, and training centers to show the men they were equal to the pioneering task (Maimon 1962, Katzenelson-Rubashow 1976, Rein 1980). The men's responses were sometimes hostile, sometimes tolerant. In general men were not very concerned or enthusiastic for change in traditional gender roles. At that time, women's roles seemed to be an issue mainly for women themselves.

The pioneer women apparently believed that socialism should bring about their emancipation; they sought to be equal members of the new Jewish proletariat by doing the same work as men. This notion is important because it meant that they were aiming, as Mednick (1975:3) stated, to "take on the occupations, attributes and goals of men." I have called this "asymmetrical equality" (Bowes 1978) because it was a one-way change. The male pioneers had changed from the traditional sedentary and scholarly pursuits of the *shtetl* to become manual laborers; the women also aimed to do the manual labor regarded as central to building the country. In the meantime, women in the *shtetl* had done other jobs: cooking, cleaning and child care. These did not figure largely in the early pioneers' efforts when living conditions had been very basic and there were no children. When living conditions improved and children were born, the work involved was seen as necessary but "unproductive," not for "real" pioneers. Men simply did not take on the work, it was still thought of as women's work, so women did it. The paradox, at least to the outsider, is that by wanting to be like men and by valuing manual labor above all else, the women themselves had contributed towards devaluing what had once been their traditional tasks. In the *shtetl*, women had been subordinate but their homemaking and child care had been seen as valuable work (Zborowski and Herzog 1962, Diamond 1957). In the kibbutz, it was devalued.

The "asymmetrical equality" of the pioneering movement formed the basis for women's roles and status in the contemporary kibbutz. Women are concentrated in the services as we have seen, and service work is of low value. The lack of participation in formal politics, the difficulties in finding permanent jobs and therefore being good kibbutzniks follow from these early developments. During the evolution of the kibbutz movement since those early days, the experience of the women pioneers has been repeated with the foundation of one kibbutz after another. Thirty years after the first pioneer women had started as manual laborers and then gone into the services, women of Goshen did the same thing.

Dissatisfaction among kibbutz women has a long history. We may ask why women seem to have repeated practices which would make them unhappy and which undoubtedly threatened the movement as a whole. The early pioneer women were very radical, after all. A modern feminist might forgive them for failing to anticipate the results of asymmetrical equality. It is more difficult to understand why the later pioneers repeated the pattern. To appreciate this, it is necessary to look beyond the kibbutz movement into the Zionist movement and the wider Israeli society.

In Chapter 2, I described how closely the kibbutz movement was tied into the Zionist movement. As time went on, the kibbutzim became part of the Zionist establishment. They were important symbolically as representatives of pioneering Zionism. They also had great practical significance since their representatives held high political and military offices. Recent writers on Israeli women like Hazleton (1977) and Rein (1980) have argued that the position of Jewish women in modern Israel, including the kibbutz movement, has been directly conditioned by the role of fighting forces in the genesis of the State as well as today (cf. Bowes 1986). Rein (1980:47) writes about the 1930s:

> At this critical time for the Jews of Palestine, the establishment of a viable fighting force created a basis for the nation-state. While the British Mandate ruled elsewhere, the growth of a serious fighting force became a symbol of potency for the aspiring nation. At last, Jews were showing their strength and power. The men who had come from generations of emasculated manhood were at last fulfilling their deepest needs to assert themselves and gain recognition.

She goes on to explain that this view of things was so strong that women were squeezed out of the fighting force, away from the front line. Rein explains that although many women did fight (particularly in the Palmach), their contribution was systematically undervalued. Women were progressively moved into service jobs such as nursing, wireless operating, administrative positions, and secretarial work. This process also happened to women in the kibbutz movement, where "productive work" was man's work. As Hazleton (1977) shows, both army and kibbutz began by appearing to emancipate women but very soon became vehicles for their "imposed and accepted regression into the feminine stereotype" (1977:137). The army reinforced the kibbutz making any resistance by women increasingly difficult.

Once the State was founded in 1948, the ideology of manhood identified by Rein (1980) permeated all its major institutions. The kibbutz representatives and the Labor Party with which the kibbutz federations were affiliated participated directly in this process. The law, the judiciary, the army and the religious institutions all treat women primarily as wives and mothers, only secondly as independent individuals (Lahav 1977). The influence of religion is particularly important for defining male and female roles and enshrining them in law. Often in Israel's history, religious parties have held a balance of power in the Knesset (the Israeli parliament).

Successive Labor Party coalitions have made concessions to them to stay in power. This means that through their representatives in government, the kibbutzim have voted for inequality between men and women in the country as a whole and thus in the kibbutzim as well. Issues concerning founding the State and continued power for the Labor Party were considered more important than changing gender roles. This attitude was paralleled within the kibbutzim; getting productive work done was more important than changing gender roles.

Thus, it seems, there was never very much hope that women in the kibbutz movement would be fully emancipated as they once tried to be. The obstacles were too great. Not only did they face deeply entrenched attitudes from the male pioneers, about what women were fit to do, but they were also to see their efforts at equality obstructed further and further in the later years of the Zionist movement and, subsequently, in the State. It seems their unhappiness is not important enough for State or federation to take any really effective action. Now we can see how the "return to familism" might be explained. If kibbutz women want their work and themselves to be valued in the movement, it is clear that only they are going to be able to do anything about it. They appear to be staging a takeover of the child care niche: raising the value of work in the children's houses and working for more time with and more direct control over their own children. In doing this, they are capitalizing on the ideological importance of children to the kibbutz, thereby seizing one of the few openings available to them given the enormity of opposition to radical emancipation in the kibbutz movement and the State. The "return to familism" can therefore be seen as the latest stage in kibbutz women's struggle for what they see as a deservedly important role in kibbutz life. It is linked to the other ways of arguing for women's equality and the criticisms of men that we observed in Goshen. Undoubtedly, it is entrenching the kibbutz division of labor and division of attitudes still further. Women pioneers fought to be the same as men and therefore equal. Now, their aim appears to be "different, therefore equal."

## Implications

Once upon a time, an anthropologist studying an exotic society needed only to observe the fact of a division of labor to establish that the important work was done by men, that important decisions were made by men and that males were regarded as superior to females. Monographs would then portray the society predominantly through men's activities and men's affairs. Quite recently, feminist anthropologists have started to challenge this kind of work. We have argued that since "women hold up half the sky," it is simply ridiculous to suggest that studies of societies which virtually ignore us can even approach validity. In kibbutz studies, a body of literature (e.g., Rosner 1967, Tiger and Shepher 1975, Spiro 1979) apparently sets out to show that the kibbutz proves that women have a natural proclivity for motherhood, child care and housework. This is done by asserting that equality between women and men in the kibbutz has been tried out and has failed because people's natural instincts have dominated. Looking at the contemporary kibbutz, some writers conclude that phenomena such as the division of labor, the differences in status of women and men and the work they do, and power differences between women and men result from human nature. If this is correct, then it is a very important argument with implications for women everywhere. It would suggest by implication that my teaching in a university and writing this book is unnatural as are my female readers.

There is, however, strong evidence to suggest that the argument is incorrect, certainly enough to show that it is not proven. The major problem of the studies is that they rest on a number of assumptions which are invalid. A common and typical assumption is that women and men once were equal in the kibbutz. This is very questionable in view of the asymmetrical equality I described which existed in the early pioneering period when there was very little traditional women's work to be done. A further assumption is that both female and male pioneers actively sought equality. As I have shown, women tried to be like men and probably wanted to change gender roles further, but there is very little evidence that men were helpful in this or committed to it. Then there is the problem of what "equality" means. Tiger and Shepher (1975) in particular appear to consider that it means men and women are the same in every way. Given the basic biological differences between men and women in reproductive terms, this is impossible. We are discussing social equality which means different things to different people; it is mischievous of Tiger and Shepher to set up an absolute standard. Furthermore, if there are such things as natural predispositions to certain social roles, then it seems to me that they could only be shown to operate where there were many possible options open and instincts could have a truly free rein. In fact, the choices open to kibbutz women have been very much restricted by developments internal to their communities as well as by the wider historical context. If a woman wanted to do something other than be a mother, work in the services, and leave the "important" decisions to men, she would find this extremely difficult.

Agassi (1980) noted the argument frequently put forward in the movement that the kibbutz contains all the preconditions for women's emancipation. The argument maintains that because relations of production within the kibbutz are non-capitalist, because women are not dependent on their husbands for survival, because they all have work and the right to participate in community decision making, they are free to choose what they want in life. Therefore, their concentration in the services and all the other aspects of their lives I have examined here are a result of free choice. Agassi (1980) considers this view to be complacent and basically wrong, and her views support the interpretations I have put forward here. In the first place, there are strong elements of capitalist relations even within the communities which are further linked into a wider, fundamentally capitalist structure. Among these elements are the profit motive, the accumulation of capital for consumption and reinvestment, the employment of labor, and the use of the volunteer workforce. The last items in particular create a distinction between those who control the means of production and those who do not. These features alone call the argument into question, and its problems are increased if we examine, as I have done here, the constraints on women's choices. Agassi (1980) suggests that another reason for the failure of the kibbutz federations to work for equality in gender roles is their conviction (a kibbutz sociologist's-ideologist's conviction) that it is already there, if only people would appreciate it.

So the kibbutz does not prove either that its male and female roles are natural or that socialism brings equality. The lessons it offers are not as clear-cut as some commentators would like to assert. If we are interested in gender roles, we find the kibbutz raises some interesting questions. For example, it challenges us to consider what we mean by equality. It warns us that attitudes towards men and women are very deeply entrenched. It shows us that if one gender works for change, the other does not necessarily do so, and it demands that we look much more carefully at the reality of the choices and opportunities men and women are offered.

# - 6 -

# New Generations

## Being Four

The children's nurse (*metapelet*, pl. *metaplot*) came to the children's houses at about 6:00 a.m. Usually, the children were beginning to wake; some were already up and playing. During the night, they had been watched over by a woman guard, stationed near the babies' house with an intercom so that she could hear any crying or commotion. Now and then, she had checked all the children's houses to make sure that everyone was all right. When the *metapelet* came to work, the guard would go home to sleep, probably dropping in on her own children first to say good morning.

In the house, there would then be a great rush to wash and dress all the children. There were seven four-year-olds on Goshen in 1975, and one *metapelet* and a young assistant looked after them during the day. Food for breakfast was collected from the kibbutz kitchen at about seven. There would be fresh bread, milk, cheeses, and salads prepared by kitchen workers who dealt only with children's food. The finishing touches would be put to the meal in the children's house. The *metapelet* might cook scrambled eggs, the table would be set, and breakfast would begin at about 7:30. Afterwards, the children had jobs to do: helping to clear away dishes or tidying the house. Their responsibilities would change from one week to the next.

For most of the group, the morning was spent at play. Often, they would be taken for a walk around the kibbutz to visit their parents' workplaces or to see all the different animals and crops. Each would have their particular favorite place. One liked the dairy, one the carpark where the lorry ("the Scania") could be seen, another the chicken houses, another the tractors in the fields, and so on. Some

101

days there would be special events such as a camping day at another kibbutz or preparation for a kibbutz festival.

Two children in the group were old enough to begin lessons, particularly reading and writing. Soon, they would all join in. In the meantime, the kindergarten teacher (a hired worker) came to the house to give lessons to the two older children while the others carried on with their play.

At about 11:00 a.m., the children's mothers would come and visit briefly. Those with only one child might stay an hour; those with more could not stay as long since they had to visit other houses. Some fathers would come too although their work was usually too distant for a short visit to be worthwhile. These morning visits were known as the "hour of love" (*sha'at ahava*) and were treasured by mothers who would race through their morning work to be sure to have time to see their children. The mothers' visits gave the children's house workers a welcome break too for a cup of tea or for a visit to their own children.

Lunch (in special containers) was collected from the kitchens by the workers. It was a hot meal accompanied by bread, a little salad, and some fresh or stewed fruit. Often, there would be something a little extra for the children such as a special vegetable or some extra good fruit.

After lunch, there was a nap for the children then all would be washed and spruced up ready for 4:00 p.m. The *metapelet* was relieved by someone else for the afternoon; she would return later on. At 4:00 p.m., the children's parents came to collect them and families would spend the rest of the afternoon together. The four-year-olds saw their brothers and sisters at this time, and a few of them also had grandparents who were members of Goshen. They were among the first children of Goshen to belong to three generation families and to have aunts, uncles and cousins. Extended families often met together in the afternoons. Whatever arrangements there were, this was a time for parents to devote themselves to their children, and vice versa. Each child had toys at the parents' flat. The parents would play with their children, read them stories, listen to music, go for walks, go swimming (in summer) and so on. Most would have an afternoon snack of juice and cake or biscuits. Some mothers baked their own cakes using special tins; others used the kibbutz store to get biscuits.

The children normally returned to their house for supper at about 6:30 p.m. Supper was usually salads, cheeses, bread, yogurt, sometimes eggs, or sliced sausage. If it was anyone's birthday, there would be a cake baked by the kibbutz kitchen designed especially for the child. One particularly memorable one was shaped as a lorry. There would be songs chosen by the children, a candle-blowing ceremony, and presents. Each child in the house would give a small gift and the group as a whole would give a larger one selected by the metapelet. On Thursday evenings, the children would have supper in the kibbutz dining room with their parents. This was Goshen's "Oriental evening," a weekly reminder of the Oriental origins of the kibbutz symbolically represented in the food. There were *pittot* (flat, Oriental bread), falafel (cooked, crushed chickpeas made into balls with spices and deep fried), and an extra variety of salads including hot pickles. For four-year-olds, this event was a highspot of the week, and they would talk grandly about Thursdays, "The day when I eat with *you*" stressed one of them to his mother.

Bedtime followed upon supper. The children would be prepared for bed by the *metapelet*, then parents would return to tuck their children into bed and kiss them goodnight. Some stayed until the children were asleep, most did not. When the children were settled for the night, they would be left alone, and the night guard would take over from *metapelet* and parents.

Only on Shabbat (Saturday) and festivals did the routine differ. Then, children would spend most of the day with their parents who generally had the day off. Children would return to their houses at suppertime. Such days would normally be spent on Goshen. People had no means of going on trips, since there were no private cars on the kibbutz and no public transport anywhere on Shabbat. On festival days, there would be community ceremonies for everyone, but an ordinary Shabbat was considered a time for families to be together.

## Growing Up

On Goshen in the mid-1970s, children were being brought up for kibbutz life in a system of rearing and education unique to the kibbutz movement. In kibbutzim belonging to the Kibbutz Artzi federation the process took its most radical form. There was much more collectivism apparent in Kibbutz Artzi practice than in the other two federations. Members of Goshen felt that in the other federations the principles of the system were being compromised by the practice of building extra rooms onto parents' accommodations so that families spent the night in the same house.

On Goshen, babies of six weeks old began to spend most of their time in a communal baby house. At this stage, their mothers would spend several hours a day there too, feeding their babies and playing with them. As the children grew older and their mothers gradually returned to full-time work in the kibbutz economy, mother and child spent more hours apart each day. The mothers' return to work was reasonably flexible, but certainly they were expected to be back full-time by the time their babies were about six months old. Women who fussed about their babies or "couldn't stay away from the baby house" were often said to be not fully committed to the kibbutz. Some people, particularly veteran members, saw the "hour of love" (the midmorning visit which was a relatively recent development) as a threat to the communal system.

Older children, including the four-year-olds whose day I have described, lived in larger communal houses according to age. An age group would eventually include all children within an eighteen month age span. At first, the groups would be smaller and cover a shorter span. The fully-fledged group would have its own name, and children would start to identify themselves as members of "my group."

Children in a group were encouraged to live and work together communally; they became very close to one another emotionally. Members of Goshen stressed the importance of these groups which they saw as a key component in training for communal kibbutz life. They were particularly concerned with this issue because there had been a period when few children were born on Goshen in the late 1960s. As a result, there were only three seven-year-olds on the kibbutz during my fieldwork. Too young to join an older group, too old to join a younger one, and too few to form a group themselves, these three were considered very unfortunate. Their living quarters and their classrooms had been shifted several times until their parents and teachers decided the situation was simply impossible. They insisted that the children have a stable way of life, and that they must join a group with which to forge an identity and prepare for kibbutz life. The solution was for these children to join a group of children of a similar age from another small kibbutz located nearby. This was not thought an ideal solution since the three would be joining an already existing group and would have to travel away from Goshen frequently. It was considered preferable to a lack of group identity and an unstable life-style.

Children of primary school age on Goshen had schoolrooms attached to their living quarters where they had daily lessons from kibbutz members who had trained and qualified as teachers. There were two schoolhouses and two teachers who alternatively taught classes in each house while being primarily responsible for one of the groups. During the day, a few children from a neighboring kibbutz came to share lessons and meals, but they returned to their own houses after school every day.

Teaching in the school was arranged mainly through projects. For example, the children might work on the geography of Israel, study Bible stories and history connected with the places they had learned about, and eventually take a trip to the area. The teachers explained that the children were given options so that they could respond to the work in ways that best suited each individual child. One might collect pictures and make an album or poster with captions, another might prefer to write stories, another to draw pictures, and so on. They deliberately tried to avoid having a classroom of children arranged in rows with a teacher directing them from the front. Rather, the arrangement of the schoolroom was completely fluid; furniture was continually rearranged. Each classroom had one corner set aside with comfortable chairs and cushions and a small library. Children who were tired of studying or who wanted to be away from the class commotion for awhile could go there to sit and read quietly whenever they wanted to.

The classrooms were filled with wallcharts and displays done by teachers and children. Often there were nature study exhibitions. One classroom had an ant city, the other a transparent beehive attached to the window. Each day, the children entered their observations of these items in a special notebook. The children's work would be on display for their parents at regular meetings between parents and teachers or at special events. At the end of the school year in Summer 1975, the children acted in two plays. One was presented in Hebrew and the other in English. The English play was very much admired since the children had only been studying the language for a year.

Arrangements in the children's houses reflected communal living. There was a dining room where meals were taken and a kitchen area for warming food, making tea and coffee, and washing dishes. Meals were prepared in the main kibbutz kitchen. Bedrooms accommodated four, boys and girls together until about ten years old. On Goshen, children took communal showers until they decided otherwise for themselves. The eleven year old girls asked to shower separately from the boys in 1975, saying they were fed up with the boys throwing water about. Some of the girls were already well into puberty. Their physical maturation did not seem to be a source of shame, nor was such an attitude encouraged.

Goshen was too small to run its own high school. Children from the age of twelve attended a regional high school situated on another kibbutz. They spent most of their time away from Goshen living in houses attached to the high school. Each group from Goshen was joined with several groups from other kibbutzim to make a school class. Classes were run like the primary school with an emphasis on informality, project work, and encouraging pupils to respond to studies in their own way. Collectivism in these larger groups was encouraged through discussion of the affairs of the school and concerning kibbutz and Israeli life. High school children were kept in touch with life on their home kibbutzim by working there regularly. Those in their last year spent an entire day each week working in a branch of their home kibbutz. They also returned to Goshen one weekday night, at weekends, festivals and school holidays. Their accommodations on these occasions were somewhat makeshift. Younger children slept on couches in their parents' flats; some of the older ones occupied the wooden huts which remained from Goshen's earliest phase of building.

Upon leaving school at seventeen pupils had no formal qualifications and took no examinations. While waiting for army service to begin at age eighteen, they worked full-time on Goshen. Many described this as a frustrating period. Nothing was happening and they felt they were just marking time.

Two years in the army for girls and three for boys meant more time away from home, new experiences, meeting people from different backgrounds, and moving into an environment where kibbutz life was an oddity rather than a common experience. Those doing their army service in 1975-6 were rarely seen on Goshen; they would be away from the kibbutz and from their fellow group members for many weeks.

After army service, there were decisions to be made. Those who wanted to train for careers or go on to higher education had to persuade the kibbutz to support their decisions. Members of Goshen considering applications for study support looked more favorably at those whose proposed training would make them useful workers for the kibbutz afterwards. To gain admission to some courses, people had to complete another year of "school" and pass state examinations. There was a special kibbutz movement college for this. Other options for army graduates were army careers, early marriage, travel outside the kibbutz and Israel, and working on Goshen. Of Goshen's children at the decision stage in 1975-6, none had chosen an army career. A few had married, many had travelled abroad or were trying to do so, and a few had simply carried on working on Goshen. The majority had opted for further study and planned careers which Goshen considered would be useful although the option of working elsewhere was always a possibility.

The most important decision was whether or not to become a member of Goshen. Being born on Goshen (or, indeed, any kibbutz) did not automatically confer membership. Kibbutz children had to apply, complete a period of candidacy, and then be voted in as members by a General Assembly meeting. No child of Goshen had been refused membership. Indeed, a kibbutz child becoming a member was a cause of great rejoicing. For the pioneers, such an occasion signified the realization of their dreams and of their emotional and practical investment in their children. Goshen was having some problems keeping its children as members and had tried to encourage them to stay by being very generous with study leave, travel facilities, and length of time to decide. However, in 1975-6, some members were beginning to doubt this generous strategy, and arrangements were tightened up during the year so that army graduates would be expected to work one year on Goshen. This period was "owed" to the kibbutz. After this, they could apply for study leave, travel, or whatever and could give some indication of their feelings regarding commitment to membership.

## Experiences of Childhood

In 1975-6, Goshen's first generation of children had grown up. Two groups had completed the decision-making process, and ten people had become members. During my fieldwork, the third group was in the process of deciding what to do. The accounts given by these people of their childhood on Goshen not only show what it felt like to be a kibbutz child in the decades beginning with 1950, 1960 and 1970, but also begin to indicate how the methods of child-rearing in a kibbutz have developed over time, enabling us to identify continuities and changes in the system.

Goshen's first children were born in the late 1940s through the early 1950s, soon after the pioneers of the community had settled in their permanent home. They came into a kibbutz world which had already developed its distinctive methods of child upbringing and education. The terms "collective" or "communal" were used to describe these methods. They entered, says Spiro (1971:49), a "child-oriented community *par excellence*" where "one cannot escape the conclusion that children are prized above all else, and that no sacrifice is too great to make for them." Children were the future of the community. When they became members, the kibbutz really would have become a new way of life. Veteran kibbutzim already had their own children as members, and the pioneers of Goshen hoped to repeat this experience.

Almost from birth, the children were placed in groups of age mates, and began to spend most of their time in special houses separate from their parents'. The fact that Goshen's "baby-house" was among the first, permanent, concrete buildings to be erected on the kibbutz site emphasizes the importance attached to children and their welfare in kibbutzim at this time. This had not always been the case, as we will see. The new baby-house was designed specifically for baby care, and a trained nurse was there permanently caring for a number of babies. Nursing mothers would visit at feeding times. The mothers of Goshen's first babies told me that they were afraid to visit at times other than those prescribed, so strict was the regime. There was none of the flexibility which characterized baby care in the 1970s. In part, this reflected European and American methods of the time, with regular feeding schedules and strictly regulated days (Hardyment 1984), but it also embodied a strong commitment to and insistence on a particular view of communalism in the kibbutz movement of the immediate post-state period. The emphasis at this time was on the greatest possible degree of sharing and a strong leaning towards the idea that equality entailed "the same" for everyone.

After the baby-house, there was the toddlers' house where the children went, as a group, after their first birthday. Soon, a permanent toddlers' house would be built. The first toddlers moved into a wooden hut with a stone floor which was somewhat better than the living quarters of some of their parents who were still living in tents. In the toddlers' house, there was a timetable for sleeping and waking, eating and playing. They were cared for by a trained *metapelet*, a woman member of Goshen who had been trained for the job at a kibbutz movement college. A *metapelet* at this time in movement development was not just a children's nurse, but a *kibbutz* children's nurse. Special training supervised by the movement and guided by the principles of the time was required. The toddlers' house was the children's home where they spent most of their time including nighttime. They remained there throughout their parents' working days until about 4:00 p.m. The parents would then collect them to spend the hours until suppertime (about 7:00 p.m.) at the parents' room. Then they would go back to the toddlers' house in time for supper and bedtime.

From toddlerhood, the time spent each day with the parents followed this daily routine except on Shabbat (Saturdays) and festival days when families would be together all day. Some outsiders (particularly western middle-class ones in my experience) are shocked to hear how little time even very small children in the kibbutz spent with their parents each day. To develop a more balanced view on this, it is important to realize that when these children were with their parents, they received undivided attention. The afternoon was the time for the children. There was no evening meal to prepare, no laundry, no lawn mowing or any of the other household tasks which might distract attention from the children; no one brought work home with them. "My parents didn't even have a kettle" explained one of Goshen's first children. "Everyone took their afternoon snack together in the dining room." When in the children's house, these children were in the care of trained personnel who were also able to give total attention to their task. There were no worries about whether there was time to race to the supermarket, or whether there was any cat food left, or any of the other matters that complicate western home life. Thus the type of contact with parents and other carers cannot be directly compared with that in the stereotypical western family.

Kindergarten, the earliest phase of schooling, began for Goshen's first children at about four years old when small toddler groups were merged to produce groups of about a dozen boys and girls. These groups continued to live and work together until army service began at eighteen. Members of such groups continued to speak of one another as "brothers and sisters" until well into their twenties. In describing their relationships, they emphasized intimacy and asexuality. A favorite comment was "We sat on the potty together." Such relationships encouraged in childhood proved a source of disappointment to their parents since the brother-sister type relationship precluded marriage for the children of Goshen. Their views seemed to be widespread in the kibbutz movement. Shepher (1971) surveyed nearly three thousand second generation kibbutz marriages and found none between members of the same peer group. He also failed to find any cases of heterosexual relationships within groups. The possible existence of any homosexual relationships has not, to my knowledge, been considered by researchers and is consistently denied by the kibbutz movement itself. Spiro (1965) points out that where small children are concerned, it is difficult to decide what actually constitutes "sexual" behavior. He observed much heterosexual, homosexual and autosexual play among kibbutz children, particularly young ones, but still no recorded cases of sexual intercourse between peer group members and no intra-peer group marriages.

An important part of the children's education was training for work. By the time Goshen's children were born, this was well established as a principle of child-rearing. From kindergarten age, they began to follow a duty rotation in their house taking turns to tidy up, set tables, clear away after meals, and so on. Work demands increased as they grew up. In the 1950s, demands for children to do productive work in the kibbutz economy were quite extensive. Almost no hired labor was taken on by Goshen at this time, and there were no volunteer workers. Children helped fill seasonal labor shortages which were already beginning to appear. In a new, poor kibbutz like Goshen, production was relatively unmechanized; many extra hands were needed for jobs like cottonpicking, later to be done by machines. "We really worked hard," said one daughter of Goshen, and she and others expressed pride at having done highly valued manual work for the kibbutz.

From kindergarten, the children went on to primary school, moving to a larger children's house with bigger furniture and more suitable equipment. For the older children, wooden huts with stone floors were still the normal accommodation. The more permanent and comfortable houses were built for the younger ones first. At primary school, children continued to follow a curriculum standardized for all children of the Kibbutz Artzi. There was great stress on independent study and on allowing them to develop at their own pace.

The stress on communalism of an "everyone the same" type continued. The sabras (term used for people born in Israel) recalled how they had all, boys and girls, been dressed the same until well into high school, when the girls were finally allowed to wear skirts. They remembered their weekly chocolate ration, meticulously divided into equal (very small) pieces by the *metapelet*. Like the children of Kiryat Yedidim (Spiro 1965), they shared bedrooms and showers until well into high school. Again, this contrasts with the more relaxed regime of the 1970s. By this time, the allocation of resources to families had changed from direct grants of clothes, shoes, etc. to a system which gave people greater choice. For children's things, parents could choose from a range of items available on Goshen. If they did not like any of these, they could have vouchers to take to certain shops in town. Some mothers liked to knit jumpers and cardigans for their children, and these were the most individual clothes of all. Similarly, treats like chocolate were not only more plentiful but also less standardized. Shared bedrooms and showers were no longer compulsory. The children of the 1970s were allowed to choose if and when they wanted to give these up.

High school for Goshen's first children began at about twelve years of age. Goshen had never had its own high school, so all its children went to the regional high school on a nearby, longer-established kibbutz. Some members of Goshen were teachers in the High School. They had received most of their education outside the kibbutz movement in their countries of origin. Like many other aspects of their former lives, they had rejected "traditional" education (of whatever sort) in favor of a specific commitment to kibbutz education. They had received a little training in kibbutz educational methods. The movement had well-developed ways of educating new pioneers in kibbutz life, and this training was supported by more general ideological training and commitment. None of these people were still teaching high school in the mid-1970s. Some had left Goshen, as could be expected of the early members of a post-state kibbutz. Others did not see themselves teaching long-term. The general consensus in Goshen and the movement as a whole was that people should not work permanently away from their home communities. Daily absence would lead people to lose touch and inhibit their ability to participate in communal life. So a new generation of teachers, with more kibbutz training, worked in the high school in the 1970s.

Remembering their high school days, Goshen's first children explained that their studies emphasized education for kibbutz life, focusing on the ideological principles and how to put them into practice. For example, one young woman had been particularly impressed by the study topic "What would be your ideal society, and how would you bring it about?" For her, this topic encapsulated both the ideological and practical ways of doing things. In high school, children continued to make a real contribution to the economy of their home kibbutz. In doing so they came to see the kibbutz way of working, stressing teamwork and collective achievement.

One incident from my fieldwork will serve to illustrate. On Goshen in the 1970s, weeds in the cotton fields were hoed by teams of temporary workers. This was a job that Goshen's first children had known first hand. In the 1970s, the teams were shown the field then left to get on with it. One day, a team, including myself, was joined by a pioneer of Goshen who was taking one of his turns at manual work (*toranut* described in Chapter 3). As usual, we began at one end of the field, each working on a line of plants. In the center of the field, there was one patch thick with weeds. People working there began to fall behind quickly. The pioneer saw this and told them to leave that section and carry one with another part of the row where they could keep up with the rest of the team. When the rest of the field was finished, he called us all to work on the hard patch which we finished quickly. This approach impressed me. The work was done without anyone being left behind or feeling they had pulled the short straw. I told one of Goshen's children about it later that day. "Oh, yes," she said, "That's the old way of doing things. That's how kibbutz work should be done.

At high school, groups of Goshen's children were joined with groups from other kibbutzim to form a class of about thirty. Within the classes, however, the groups continued to be cohesive. Goshen's first children remembered boasting of the merits of their kibbutz over others represented in their class. For its pupils, the high school was in many ways a self-contained world on its own. Children spent most of their time there, visiting their home kibbutz once or twice a week. They no longer had special lodging at home and would spend nights on sofas in their parents' houses. All their meals, laundry, etc. were provided for at school. There was also a lively program of social and cultural events, much of which the children organized for themselves.

Ideological training was reinforced by children's experiences in the Youth Movement (Hashomer Hatzair) which they joined at about twelve years of age. Youth Movement activities were something like those of European and American scouts, or the Pioneers of the USSR. There were regular meetings, ceremonies, special tasks to complete and a program of camps and hikes. The Youth Movement for kibbutz children was a direct descendant of the Youth Movement abroad and also offered training for kibbutz life. Memories of Youth Movement activities were generally positive. Many had albums of photographs of camping trips and torchlight ceremonies which they remembered happily and showed proudly.

## Continuity and Change

Between Goshen's pioneering days and the 1970s, changes in the collective education system had been few. However, when the system was seen by Goshen's members in the 1970s to be under threat in the kibbutz movement as a whole, people discussed even superficial changes very thoroughly.

The strongest and most basic continuity was the emphasis on child-rearing and education as principally reflecting principles of kibbutz life and secondly training children for their own lives as kibbutz members. The system was therefore strongly allied to kibbutz life and could not be fully comprehended if divorced from this. So ideological and practical training in Socialism and Zionism continued to be emphasized in the 1970s, as did the idea that children would grow up to be kibbutz members. Thus they were not trained for life in the city or anywhere else. They did not take the State examinations; they continued to take time out of school to work on their kibbutz; their lives were organized collectively, they were trained to organize themselves collectively and to take collective decisions. All these, therefore, are distinctive and persistent features of a kibbutz upbringing.

The main observable change between the two periods was a relaxation of the old notion of equality — everyone the same — which is usefully called formal equality. To an outsider, this kind of change may appear to threaten the system. Goshen's members did not see it that way. One pioneer explained the situation like this: "When we were poor," he said, "we all shared the same plate, and we were equal. Now times are better, we have one plate each, and we are still equal." In other words, he was emphasizing that there is more than one way of being equal. As outsiders, we should accept that kibbutz members can interpret equality as they wish; they developed the kibbutz way of life.

One type of change in the system which was occurring in the 1970s on other kibbutzim did worry members of Goshen. They saw the recent development of children spending nights with their parents as a change in the quality of the system. The relaxation which did not worry them was simply a change of quantity. Children spending the night with their parents threatened the integrity of the peer groups which was viewed as fundamental to the system. It was a basic alteration in the children's experience of collectivity. The change was not proposed in Goshen or any other Kibbutz Artzi kibbutz in the mid-1970s. It was simply considered out of the question. However, the fact that it was taking place elsewhere seems to explain why some members of Goshen were worried by the development of the "hour of love." The discussions suggested that people were not sure how radical a change this was, whether it was one of quantity or quality, and they were anxiously watching its effects. Those who were parents of young children at the time were very happy with the change, enjoying the opportunity of a break from work and a chance to visit their children.

## Making Decisions

The first major separation for members of a children's group came when they reached eighteen years of age and began their army service. Goshen's first children joined the army in the late 1960s, after the 1967 war at a time when the self-confidence of Israel and its army was high. The next group found its army service extended by the Yom Kippur War of 1973, a traumatic experience for them and a demoralizing one for Israel generally. Whenever they were home from army service, the groups continued to spend time together, maintaining strong mutual ties. These ties started to weaken when they began to decide whether or not to become members of Goshen and especially when they began to marry.

By the time I did fieldwork, three groups of children of Goshen had reached the stage of deciding whether or not to commit themselves to formal community membership. Of the first two groups born 1947-51, ten people remained. Group cohesion had tended to weaken as people had moved away, or stayed, married and started families of their own. The third group was in the process of deciding about membership and remained cohesive with a core of five members out of eleven spending most of their spare time together on Goshen. I have named them Anat, Ya'ir, Avi, Illan and Nitzan. Irella had married a member of Goshen and joined them sometimes, but she spent most of her time with her husband. Three more students living away from home (Sharon, Caramit and Maya) visited this core group regularly. Another (Hadass) visited very rarely; the last (Liora) never visited for she had married a Dutch volunteer and had gone to live in Holland.

Focusing on Goshen's third group of children illustrates the process of decision making and highlights factors that influence a decision one way or another. Some basic characteristics are shown in the table (below) including sex, parents' origins (if they were still living on Goshen in 1975), their siblings, and, in the final column, a summary of their residence and activities in 1975-6. The group is named "Cyclamen" following the kibbutz tradition of naming groups after a feature of the natural environment of Goshen. There were eleven members of the Cyclamen. Seven were female and four male. All were born in 1952 or 1953 with an age gap of about eighteen months between Maya, the eldest, and Nitzan, the youngest. All were children of pioneers of Goshen.

Despite the uniformity in their upbringing and the stress on formal equality, the members of the Cyclamen remained individuals, not only in personality but also in their social relationships and assets. Although the role of parents in a child's upbringing was played down ideologically and emphasis was given to community rather than family, parents were considered of great importance in the formation of a child's character in everyday life on Goshen. Some parents were able to further their children's careers through their position in the community. Some sabras had wider contacts with friends or relatives outside Goshen. Such contacts could provide material or nonmaterial help. Even though the kibbutz movement officially frowned on such help, many children of Goshen used it to useful effect.

A child born on Goshen was often referred to as *ben kibbutz* or *bat kibbutz*, a son or daughter of the kibbutz. The Cyclamen had known and been known to the members of their parents' generation since birth. Some of their former *metaplot* (nurses) and school teachers were still members in 1975-6 and continued to have close relationships with them.

# The Cyclamen

| Name | Sex | Resident Parents' Countries of Origin | | Siblings Sex | DOB | Situation 1975-1976* |
|------|-----|------|------|------|------|------|
| Maya | F | F | Egypt | M | 1955 | Outside Goshen |
| | | M | Tunisia | F | 1958 | working |
| | | | | F | 1964 | |
| Anat | F | F | Egypt | | | Student (also working |
| | | M | not resident | | | in Roses) |
| Caramit | F | F | Egypt | F | 1950 | Outside Goshen |
| | | M | Rumania | | | Student |
| Ya'ir | M | F | Rumania | F | 1955 | Working in cotton |
| | | M | Germany | F | 1964 | (planning to travel) |
| Illan | M | F | Egypt | M | 1948 | Student (also working |
| | | M | Poland | M | 1964 | in metal factory) |
| Avi | M | F | Israel | F | 1956 | Working in cotton |
| | | M | Israel | M | 1961 | (later travelling) |
| Nitzan | M | (not resident) | | | | Travelling (then working in cotton) |
| Sharon | F | F | Egypt | F | 1958 | Student |
| | | M | Italy | | | |
| Irella | F | (not resident) | | F | 1950 | Working with children and in kitchen. Married and pregnant. |
| Hadass | F | F | (not resident) | F | 1964 | Outside Goshen |
| | | M | Egypt | | | working |
| Liora | F | F | Poland | F | 1955 | In Holland; with |
| | | M | Israel | M | 1960 | spouse and child |

*Unless otherwise stated, each person was resident on Goshen and unmarried.

Generally, everyone was interested in the Cyclamen and keen for them to become members. Many people had even deeper bonds. In these more personal relationships, some of the Cyclamen were more popular than others, giving another source of variation in their assets. At this time, a certain ideal of the kibbutz child as physically good looking, clean living and intelligent was promoted. Someone unlucky enough to fall short of this ideal might attract disproportionate criticism.

# The Group

Maya, the first born member of the Cyclamen, had been somewhat unpopular. She was labelled "Maya in the clouds" because she rarely paid attention to what was going on around her. In high school, only Caramit would share a room with her. Maya's mother was often characterized by members of Goshen as "half mad." She was frequently very agitated over what others thought were minor issues and very anxious about her children. When talking about Maya, people would often refer to her mother as the reason for her behavior.

"Maya in the clouds" confessed to having been completely lost in the army and to having found the world outside the kibbutz strange and unwelcoming. Returning to the kibbutz afterwards however, she said she only did so because she felt there was no other choice. She worked in the kitchen, hating it, until an English volunteer encouraged her to further her education. She chose, and the kibbutz approved, training as a dental nurse. When her training was complete, she could be an assistant to the dentist who served several neighboring kibbutzim. But Maya was not settled. She soon moved away from Goshen and had a variety of jobs and addresses. Eventually, the renounced her kibbutz membership, and embarked on a drama course.

Maya's own view of things was that her parents had done something really worthwhile in founding a kibbutz. She spoke several times of going to a new kibbutz herself. Nothing materialized, however, and it is not clear that it was a realistic notion. It did demonstrate the success of her ideological education. Some of her problems were individual. Decision making was particularly difficult for her. Her problems were also generally those of a person whose social position was weak. As a child of Goshen, she might have expected help and support from her peer group, her family, and her family's supporters. Not only was she rather unpopular in the group, but her mother was also a liability. Maternal efforts to plead Maya's case often served to set it back rather than to advance it. Some of her difficulties outside Goshen resulted from lack of contacts elsewhere. Maya had to build these for herself; she found that struggle preferable to life in a community where her reputation had already been damaged.

Anat's parents had divorced when she was very young. Her mother had remarried and moved to another kibbutz where Anat had a young stepbrother and visited frequently. In 1975, she was training as a teacher, and her fellow group members expressed pleasure that she seemed to enjoy her work so much. As far as Goshen was concerned, she would one day teach at the high school. Anat's views, however, were not as clear. Like other students, she was expected to work one day a week on Goshen. She had been assigned to the roses. She resented this and frequently stated that her course was hard and that she needed a day of rest, etc. In expressing her dissatisfaction, she often referred to Goshen as "they." She was generally critical of Goshen's organization and what she saw as its members' colorless, narrow-minded existence. She specifically compared Goshen unfavorably to the kibbutz where her mother lived. Despite this, she knew she could benefit from Goshen's "defects," particularly the rather generous attitude towards outside resources. These helped Anat in two ways. Helped by rich relatives, she had been able to travel to America. In 1975 after the death of her grandmother, she inherited some money. Knowing of many others on Goshen who had done the same, she decided to keep this money in reserve despite rules about handing over such resources to the collective. She explained that she was unlikely to want to spend her whole life on Goshen and that if she decided to go, she would find it difficult to get established elsewhere. The inheritance gave her the chance to leave Goshen whenever she was so inclined.

Anat's position on the kibbutz was strong by comparison with Maya's. She was popular with the Cyclamen who could be relied on to support her. Although only her father lived on Goshen, she actually belonged to one of the larger kin groups. Her father's brother was a member and had a wife and two young sons. The wife also had a daughter from a previous marriage. Anat's contact with this family was limited, but they were certainly potential supporters who gave her indirect access to a range of people in different positions in the community.

Caramit was Anat's close friend and a popular member of the Cyclamen. Though commenting that "everyone hates the army," she admitted to having done well during her period of service, working in an important and prestigious job. After the army, she returned to Goshen to work for about six months before deciding that she would not stay. She left for the university, financing her studies independently of the kibbutz with the help of relatives outside and a part-time job. She explained her decision to leave with the following criticisms of Goshen. To her, people there were lazy and the kibbutz was badly organized. The General Assembly was a "bear garden." Caramit enjoyed her life in town where she lived near Maya whom she often helped through a continual series of crises. Maya's visits to her family on Goshen most weekends also helped her maintain contacts with the rest of the Cyclamen. She felt her future definitely lay elsewhere. She said she would probably become a teacher.

Like Anat, Caramit enjoyed the benefits of outside contacts. By 1975, she had already used hers to enable her to leave Goshen. Had she chosen to stay, her position would have been quite strong, since she would have enjoyed the support of the Cyclamen and also her family.

Ya'ir, too, was critical of Goshen. The kibbutz idea was good, but Goshen was a bad kibbutz. He was a popular member of the Cyclamen, although not regarded as especially clever. His affair with a foreign volunteer, who cheated him, confirmed his reputation as good-hearted but innocent. Some of his contemporaries blamed the kibbutz education system for making Ya'ir too trusting of others and therefore easily fooled. Ya'ir, however, knew how to bring his ambitions to fulfillment within the kibbutz. He wanted to travel abroad. With the support of the Cyclamen, he successfully persuaded the General Assembly to allow him to work outside and to save his wages towards the cost of the trip while continuing to enjoy all the facilities of his kibbutz membership.

Ya'ir did not talk much of his future beyond the proposed trip. The Cyclamen suspected that he was really looking for a wife, and that once he married, he would settle down to family life on Goshen. They explained that Ya'ir was an ordinary, simple kibbutznik well suited to kibbutz ways.

Ya'ir had no need of outside contacts with rich relatives. He had no difficulty securing a laboring job to earn his money, boasting of the reputation of kibbutzniks as good workers. On his travels, he planned to make use of the contacts with former volunteer workers he had cultivated over the years on Goshen. He had useful support on Goshen and knew how to present his saving scheme in a way that would gain acceptance. He also had the great advantage of being male. Goshen wanted to keep its sabras. Not only did people subscribe to the general view of the high value of men's productive work, but Goshen also faced a shortage of young, strong men.

Illan, according to Caramit and Anat, was desperate to find a wife, but he would fail because he was so chauvinistic. Even so, they often tried to "fix him up," though the women they chose never suited him. He was not generally popular and had inherited his parents' reputed selfishness and ambition. Illan also carried the burden as the younger brother of Goshen's first born child who was viewed as a total failure. Special significance had been attached to the first born. When he not only left Goshen but also joined a nonJewish Eastern religious sect thus radically rejecting his kibbutz background, members were appalled. "Would Illan go the same way?" people asked.

Illan considered that the kibbutz owed him the facilities to do as he wanted and openly stated that he aimed to get just that. Though he could not totally rely on the Cyclamen's support, he managed to get permission to study as a doctor with financial support from the General Assembly. People said he would one day be the kibbutz doctor, perhaps replacing the doctor who then served several nearby kibbutzim. Illan therefore looked relatively committed to Goshen and likely to stay.

Avi was in many respects the ideal sabra: tall, handsome, strong, intelligent, an ex-fighter pilot. He was popular in the group and also in the kibbutz. Great sympathy was accorded him and his parents due to their tragic family circumstances. Avi's sister was mentally handicapped, and his brother the victim of a progressively debilitating disease.

While in the army, Avi had had an affair with one of Goshen's eldest daughters. A match between these two would have delighted Goshen's pioneers—a son and daughter of the same kibbutz marrying would have been a source of great rejoicing. In this case, the joy would have been even greater. Avi was much loved and the woman was a divorcee with a young child who needed only a new husband to be a happy kibbutznik, according to general opinion. Unfortunately, it seemed that the marriage would not occur. Avi stayed on for an extra six months in the army, earning enough money to finance a trip abroad. He set off in August 1975 for a year's travel, intending to return afterwards to Goshen to make his life there.

Nitzan also conformed to the ideal, particularly with his good looks. He had acquired, and to some extent cultivated, an outrageous reputation. Much of this concerned women. Nitzan, it was said, never needed to look for girlfriends. He had only to open his door and they would all tumble in. He enjoyed antagonizing the older members of Goshen by wearing his hair long, dressing untidily, and generally conforming to their idea of a "hippy." He criticized them for being narrow-minded and ignoring how hard he worked. He insisted that appearances were not important in the kibbutz and that his critics were just being puritanical. Nitzan nevertheless managed to retain the general affection of the community, and most people were prepared to allow him to do as he wished. The consensus was that he was going through a rebellious phase and would grow out of it to become a good kibbutz member.

Nitzan was deeply affected by and anxious to talk about the 1973 Yom Kippur War. Such a profound experience, he felt, made him truly adult, and he resented kibbutz members who still looked on him as a child. He used his discharge money from the army plus some financial help from his father (who had long since left Goshen) to travel the world. With the Cyclamen's support, he received a year's leave and set off, returning to Goshen after a year and a half.

On his return, he was more critical of Goshen than ever. He even started to attack members of the Cyclamen saying that they should learn as he had done by travelling how boring and confined kibbutz life was. They resented this saying that Nitzan had no respect for ordinary life, that he did not realize that most people did not have the chance for excitement that he had had, and they worked hard for a living for themselves and their families.

Generally, it was clear that Nitzan remained committed to kibbutz life. Like Ya'ir, he would insist that he only criticized bad aspects of Goshen not the kibbutz ideal. He enjoyed his work in the cotton fields, the companionship of his workmates, and the congenial social life of the young people in the kibbutz, and he made an effort to participate in community decision making.

Irella appeared in 1975-6 to be the most settled of the Cyclamen in her decision to become and remain a member of Goshen, even though her childhood had not been altogether happy. Her father was the only person ever to have been expelled from Goshen. Irella's mother had stayed with her two young daughters before leaving to join her husband when she felt the children were old enough to fend for themselves. The first time the father returned to Goshen was to Irella's wedding in the Summer of 1975. Irella was a popular member of the Cyclamen who had special sympathy for her unfortunate family situation. When she lived with her boyfriend (the normal practice before marriage on Goshen), their room was a gathering place for the group, and the couple became the center of an extensive gossip network. Members of the Cyclamen used to say that if you wanted to know anything that was going on, you had only to ask Irella. After the marriage, people no longer assumed that they could drop in whenever they felt like it. The general attitude was that although living together and marriage were in some respects a continuum, married couples would want more privacy and more time to be a couple rather than part of the crowd. Irella nevertheless remained an important purveyor of information.

Irella had some problems getting settled in a job on Goshen, mainly because she lacked parental pioneer support. In Chapter 3, we saw her struggle with another daughter of Goshen for a job in the children's house and training as a *metapelet*. Like many women, she had work problems. In 1976, Irella became pregnant, and this decision to start a family is the factor which indicates her stability as a member. Movement statistics (Kibbutz Artzi 1972) show quite clearly that those least likely to leave a kibbutz are people with young families. People at this stage are extremely unlikely to interrupt their children's upbringing, having already decided to raise them on a kibbutz. Indeed Irella's own childhood illustrates this tendency. Her parents wanted their children to have the continuity of staying on Goshen, despite the community's action towards the father.

The three remaining members of the Cyclamen, Sharon, Hadass and Liora, had virtually given up contact with Goshen and the rest of their group. Liora had married and started a family abroad. By 1976, two years had passed since her last visit to Goshen. She was not expected to resume her membership. Her daughter had been given a Dutch rather than a Hebrew name which served to confirm this general opinion. Hadass had never been popular with the Cyclamen, and her family had fallen apart while she was in high school. She had not returned to Goshen after army service and was a very infrequent visitor in 1975-6. Sharon visited rather more often; she was a student studying philosophy. But she was very critical of Goshen, and the other members of the Cyclamen felt she would not return. "She isn't interested in ordinary life," they said. "She only wants adventure and excitement, and she can't get it here. So she won't stay."

## Decisions Made?

Two factors are immediately striking about the decision-making process described for the Cyclamen. One is that reaching a final decision took a long time, several years in some cases. The other is that the process illustrates the individuality of each member of the group. These very personal decisions are more comprehensible in terms of individual experience than collective factors. Nevertheless, some general factors do help explain both the length and the individuality of the decision-making process.

Until the 1970s, the kibbutz movement as a whole claimed great success in keeping its children as members. Until then, the children were born on veteran kibbutzim which historically suffered few recruitment problems and were particularly successful in economic terms. Billis' (1972) work is important for showing how the experience of veteran kibbutzim has been markedly different from that of the post-state "little kibbutzim" such as Goshen. One of the most important differences he identifies is that the "little kibbutzim" have had great difficulties keeping their children as members. This was becoming particularly clear in the mid-1970s when the second generation was reaching the stage of having young families. Having reached that stage, decisions were definitive if not irrevocable. Prior to this stage, as we have seen, there could be all sorts of vacillating, keeping one's options open, acting as a semimember, and so on. For the individual, this meant that the process could be drawn out so that a variety of opportunities could be tested. For the kibbutz and the movement, it offered hope that people would eventually settle as members and could be counted as successes. In the mid-1970s, it was becoming clear that the little kibbutzim's second generation was opting in large numbers not to stay. My evidence for this is ethnographic, from Goshen and other comparable kibbutzim; Billis' (1972) work supports the conclusion. At the time of fieldwork, the kibbutz federation was not publishing statistics relating to kibbutz born people staying or leaving, so I cannot offer support from that direction.

Also characteristic of the "little kibbutzim" as explained in Chapter 2 was a "generation gap." Few members existed between people of pioneer age and their children and children's contemporaries. Goshen's generation gap was particularly clear. For any new kibbutz member, there would be problems: getting to know everyone, getting established in a job, learning the local conventions of political participation, and so on. However, these matters were more difficult where there was a pioneer "mafia" still effectively controlling the community. When the mafia consisted of one's parents, former teachers and so on, the transfer of influence was likely to be even more difficult. Young people joining Goshen needed time to build a secure social position by utilizing whatever resources might be available to them. However secure they were able to become, they would have to recognize that the transfer of pioneer influence was likely to be slow at best and more likely a painful process. This experience as a new member would, of course, be entirely different from their parents' pioneering experience. It was often suggested that the stress on pioneering and socialist values in education may have made children more critical of their home kibbutz since it seemed impossible to recapture those basic values.

One factor must be recognized as crucial in the decision-making process: marriage. Looking at the case histories of the Cyclamen, one is often tempted to ask what they were waiting for. One answer to this question is certainly marriage. Marriage carried for kibbutz young people associations of settling down which was reflected in the tendency of young kibbutz families to stay put. On the kibbutz, young people had few opportunities to meet others they might consider potential spouses. Most would survey the field elsewhere: in the army, among visitors to the kibbutz, among fellow students, at work outside the kibbutz, at social events in town. As the Cyclamen case studies show, the community as a whole was particularly interested in their romantic involvements. There were risks for the kibbutz in allowing its children to range far and wide in their search for spouses. There was no certainty that nonkibbutz spouses would wish to live on a kibbutz. For a community needing members and unable to offer potential spouses from within, there was little choice. Marriage was generally considered more important for women, as we have already seen, and kibbutz women at the time were more likely to find fulfillment in their children than in their work. Maya's, Anat's, and possibly Caramit's apparent indecision seems to reflect at least partly their failure to find partners. Ya'ir, Illan, Avi and Nitzan, the four male members of the Cyclamen also remained single, yet they appeared more committed to kibbutz life than the women. The clearest decisions in 1975-6 had been made by the two married women; Irella who stayed and Liora who was gone for good.

Within the framework provided by these more general features of life in a little kibbutz, the Cyclamen also had their individual resources consisting of contacts and support inside and outside Goshen. Many of them in 1975-6 were using these resources to enhance their positions. It is difficult to weigh the relative importance of the individual and general factors in each case, but it is quite clear that the interaction of factors of both types would influence any decision about becoming kibbutz members. To place the Goshen ethnography in a wider context and a historical perspective, we can now examine some of the literature on kibbutz child-rearing and education, and relate it back to Goshen.

## Ordinary or Extraordinary?

Of all aspects of kibbutz life, the method of bringing up children has excited the greatest controversy. There appears to be nothing about the kibbutz more likely to agitate an outsider, particularly one from an affluent, western culture, than the fact that tiny children do not spend every minute of their days with their mothers and in many kibbutzim do not sleep in their parents' houses at night. Much of the research literature on the kibbutz has concentrated on child-rearing. Two of the most frequently recommended introductory treatises, Spiro's (1965) *Children of the Kibbutz* and Bettelheim's (1971) *The Children of the Dream* offer highly specialized accounts of child-rearing, drawing on culture and personality theory in cultural anthropology and psychoanalysis. I cannot think of another human society whose method of child-rearing has been scrutinized so minutely. The kibbutz movement itself has reflected at length on child-rearing. Debates about how to raise children to benefit both the community and the children are well documented. Recently, outside commentary and internal reflection have become somewhat blurred as research institutes closely connected with the kibbutz movement have been carrying out more sociological and psychological surveys.

There appears to be something extraordinary about the children of the kibbutz, arising from their upbringing. After reading some of the literature, a visitor might be forgiven for expecting to meet monsters, reared by books and theories. It is not difficult to find examples of practices which might seem outlandish to an outsider. Spiro (1965, 1979) reports that in the early days of Kiryat Yedidim, equal amounts of breast milk had to be given to all babies of the same age. Any baby whose weight suggested it was lagging would be "topped off" by another mother. Criden and Gelb (1974) report a phase when it was believed that mattresses were bad for children's backs, so all children slept on boards. Bettelheim (1971) suggests that kibbutz children were more likely to be bed wetters because they were not taught that property could be private (so they did not hold onto things, including their urine). Darin-Drabkin (1962) points to the difficulty kibbutz children experienced outside their communities, where they were shocked to find that the "real world" was different. Ben-Rafael and Weitman (1984) stress that children were considered children of the community rather than the parents and mention a case where children's names were chosen by the community as a whole and not by their parents.

When you meet the children of the kibbutz however, they appear quite human after all. As a young researcher in my twenties, I was the same age as Goshen's first generation of children. We communicated easily, got on well, and shared many interests in common. It was easy to share books, music, travel, discussion of ideas, particularly kibbutz ideas, and I became good friends with many of them despite the apparent total contrast in our upbringing. As I hope the ethnographic material I have presented indicates, we discussed their decision-making process deeply and at length, and it was easy to empathize with their thoughts and feelings. My friends' younger brothers and sisters, indeed all the children of Goshen, seemed no less human than children elsewhere. Some were happy-go-lucky, some more melancholy, some noisy, some quiet, some more aggressive, some more passive. In other words, they were as individual as children everywhere else. One less usual feature of their lives was that they wanted for nothing. The best food and lodging, toys, playmates, treats, parental love and the care and concern of all the community were theirs; they lived in pleasant countryside, totally safe wherever they went in the kibbutz. The children especially liked the farm, and days at work were sometimes interrupted by groups of small, inquisitive visitors out on their walks. All this seemed far away from the portraits of kibbutz children presented in literature.

So there are two pictures of kibbutz children. Books present an outsider with an extraordinary, even abnormal, impression. Firsthand experience suggests perfectly normal and ordinary children. The fact is that children in the kibbutz are like children in any other home. Some are accepted better than others, but one cannot say realistically whether they generally conform or do not conform to any absolute standard based on a "more desirable" method of upbringing. To understand new kibbutz generations, we must place their kibbutz experience in its own broad context.

# The First New Generation

The early kibbutz movement pioneers were very young, and many for a long time were rootless. Rubin (1986) refers to "communes of wandering youth" travelling around the country seeking work wherever it was to be found and living in decidedly rough conditions. In many cases, they had run away from—and certainly all had rejected—what they saw as the constricting Jewish family life in Europe. That family structure had been an important mechanism of survival under conditions of poverty and oppression. Diamond (1957:80) describes how that same structure "generated potentially explosive tensions" for its young members which awaited an outlet in the possibility of escape to Palestine. Diamond emphasizes how the early kibbutzim directly rebelled against old-fashioned Jewish life. Thus, the young pioneers were certainly not focusing on having children.

In Degania, the first kibbutz, some of the pioneers wanted only to carry on pioneering: founding one new settlement after another then handing it over to people who preferred a more sedentary life. "They accused themselves of living in idleness and luxury and they felt the desire in them to go elsewhere" (Baratz 1954:65). These people saw the possibility of children as a threat to their life-style. "They were afraid that children would detach the family from the group, that the life of the group would be less adventurous and its comradeship less steadfast" (Baratz 1954:65). Evidence like this must remind us that the kibbutz was not always the "child-centered society" to which many commentators refer. Many of those who pursued the pioneering life-style to its limit saw this as specialist activity for themselves and not for future generations. The argument against this, Baratz (1954) reports, was put in Degania by Joseph Bussell. He said that the first assault of a battle was indeed heroic, but that greater heroism was required to stand fast and to defend a position until it was secure. Bussell's supporters, who seem to have been in the majority, apparently saw children as a natural part of life. They might postpone families while living conditions were unsuitable, but they expected to raise children eventually. Quite soon, it became normal for kibbutz members to have children.

Along with the discussions about whether or not to have children, there were discussions about sexual morality and regarding the formalization of relationships between parents. Spiro (1970) reports that the pioneers of Kiryat Yedidim who arrived in Palestine in 1920 experimented with various ways of avoiding what they saw as bourgeois marriage, including "informal polygyny and polyandry" (p. 112). When they were expecting children, they underwent a legal marriage ceremony to insure legitimacy since illegitimate children were denied civil rights. Some writers say that early kibbutzim went through a period of misogamy, that is, being anti-marriage (e.g., Ben-Rafael and Weitman 1984). Early kibbutz marriages were, it seems, not celebrated in the communities. Couples did not spend much time together; indeed, they actively avoided doing so for fear of being thought "bourgeois." The terms ba'al and isha (husband or master, and wife) were not used. A male partner was a *chaver* (comrade) or a *bachur* (usually translated "young man") and a female *chavera* or *bachura*. More extreme misogamous practices are reported in the literature. For example, one kibbutz is said to have expelled a man who refused to do guard duty on his wedding night (Ben-Rafael and Weitman 1984). Despite misogamy however, it appears that the first children of the kibbutz were born to legally married couples.

There is thus plenty of evidence that the early pioneers did not want to live in the old-fashioned European type of family. Some pioneers wanted neither marriage nor children. These notions were probably not widespread and were surely not long-lasting. We must not overemphasize some of the more radical experiments. As Yosef Criden of Kfar Blum affirms (Criden and Gelb 1974:129), "free love" has interested outsiders far longer than it interested the kibbutz pioneers. He stresses that although they experimented, they were not the promiscuous bed-hoppers that some outsiders' reports have suggested. Given the harsh conditions, the hard work and the poor health experienced by the early settlers, there was probably little energy for sexual athletics. After a short period of some experimental efforts when questions of marriage and children were largely irrelevant, most came to hold the view that their communities did want children and that they would be born to married couples. Less clear was the way the children of the kibbutz would be reared.

Degania's first child was born to Joseph and Miriam Baratz and was named Gideon. Joseph (Baratz 1954) reports that the whole community fussed over the baby, worried at his every cry and was concerned with every new experience. Miriam carried the baby with her everywhere. When she came back to Degania from the hospital, she wanted to return to work and Gideon simply came too, lying in the fields, in the cowsheds or in the kitchen. Joseph reports that she simply decided for herself how he was to be cared for. No one in Degania had any knowledge or experience of babies. He points out that Miriam was doing two jobs — her kibbutz work and looking after the baby. When a second child was born to another woman, Miriam suggested the mothers might take turns caring for two babies and doing their other work. The new mother did not agree, "so both of them went on overworking" (Baratz 1954:67).

This account emphasizes the lack of planning characteristic of the early kibbutz. Trial and error was important in the development of the kibbutz way of life. It is clear that no one knew at first how kibbutz children would be brought up. As Miriam continued to overwork (she had a daughter less than two years after Gideon and again carried on with her other work), Joseph explains how the members of Degania realized they had to sort something out. They began to discuss how the children should be cared for. While they saw child care as women's responsibility, they decided that it should be a collective responsibility so that women could continue to do other work for the community and thus "share communal life" (Baratz 1954:67). This met the well-established collective orientation of the kibbutz and the asymmetrical notion of equality whereby women did traditional men's work but men did not do traditional women's work. The details of child-rearing in kibbutzim developed from these rather *ad hoc* beginnings in Degania and the other early settlements. The interchange of ideas between one community and another, particularly once the federations had been established in the twenties, fostered similar child care systems throughout the movement. Illustrating how the process occurred, Baratz (1954:69) describes Gideon as "a real pioneer among babies." At every stage of his development, the members of Degania had to discuss what was best for him. Soon this was being done in communication with other kibbutzim deciding on the care of their children. When Gideon reached school age, it was arranged for him to attend a school on a nearby kibbutz where there were more children.

## Growing Children

The system of child care in kibbutzim, as many other institutions of kibbutz life, developed gradually. There was no predesigned plan and there was no fixed way of doing things. Change was part of the system. People were searching for the best way to raise children for a kibbutz way of life, and they searched constantly for better ways of doing this. The particular course that the development of child care took was influenced by the requirements of the kibbutzim as seen by their members at different times. Baratz described this process when he spoke of the eventual decision to care for children collectively to allow mothers to do work other than child care. In that decision, kibbutz members were putting their ideas about women's necessary economic role into practice. Secondly, the development of child care was influenced by wider forces. An example of this can be seen in the use of the shtetl type family as a model to reject. The pioneers were sure that however their children would be raised, they would experience none of the stifling conditions of the old ways. Other influences would appear: some related to the involvement of the kibbutz movement in the wider Zionist movement and Israeli society, and some to an engagement with a particularly intellectual tradition of child care. Often, it is difficult to trace precisely how all these influences have operated. Of course, they interacted with one another. Recognizing their existence suggests areas to be investigated to understand kibbutz child care.

One feature of kibbutz child care particularly useful and instructive for an outsider investigator is its intellectual tradition. In the writings of kibbutz educators, we find important discussions of how children can best be raised in the kibbutz context. These discussions refer not only to exigencies of kibbutz life but also to theories of child development and training from the western European and American traditions. In drawing on such wider ideas, these discussions are similar in character to many other kibbutz debates. We have already seen how much the early approach to communal life drew on the European socialist tradition in discussions about the rights and wrongs of wage labor and the economic dependence of women on men. In this respect, the kibbutz movement's published debates about child care are part of a more general kibbutz movement approach to decision making about its life-style. However, a bibliographic search shows that child care and education in the kibbutz appear as the most popular topics in both academic and movement literature.

Explanations for this preoccupation with writing about kibbutz child care vary. Segal (1971) refers to the ideas of Robert Owen, the great English socialist, who saw education of the masses as the way to bring about a socialist society. Segal argues that the perpetuation and spread of kibbutz socialism must depend on kibbutz education. Spiro (1965), an outside researcher, argues that collective education was seen as essential to collective life; therefore, the kibbutz movement was bound to be particularly self-conscious about child care. Segal refers to the needs of socialism in general, Spiro to the kibbutz movement's interpretation of socialism. It is also important to recognize the degree of critical attention from the outside. Both non-Israeli as well as Israeli scientists (at a later date) have analyzed kibbutz education. Josef Criden (Criden and Gelb 1974:109) expresses some of the sensitivity of the movement to this attention:

> Though I am the father of two and have two grandchildren, I am not much of an authority in this area [child care]. Far more capable people — after seven weeks at a kibbutz — have written authoritative tomes on the subject of kibbutz children. They are great experts although they do not even know Hebrew; I can boast of only thirty years' experience with our youth.

Certainly, some of the movement literature on child care is related to outside responses. Sometimes the aim is to persuade outsiders that kibbutz upbringing and education is best for all children. Other times, the literature is written from a defensive posture.

However we account for this self-conscious intellectual tradition, we can learn from it much about how child care and education have developed in the kibbutz movement. Some examples will illustrate the interaction of all the influences identified.

Kibbutz theorists insist that the basis of everything has been the kibbutz way of life, and that all the practices adopted were thought to be best for kibbutz children. This continues the tradition described by Baratz (1954). Golan, a theorist prominent in the 1940s and 1950s, wrote (1961:21):

> Collective education is a necessary result of the special needs of the kibbutz and has been formed and shaped in accordance with these needs.

Hazan, a later contributor, argues (Rabin and Hazan 1971:4):

> The relationship between the educational system and the social essence of the kibbutz and its aspirations has endowed collective education with its form and content. Kibbutz society has given rise to an educational framework and reflects its way of life, its cultural and moral values.

Whatever nonkibbutz theories of child-training are drawn upon, writers invariably start from and return to this theme of kibbutz child-rearing as appropriate to kibbutzim. If a principle of kibbutz life can be found, this would be one, subscribed to continuously from the early days. Variation appears from time to time in what precise practice is considered correct for the kibbutz, but the stress is always on matching child care to kibbutz needs, however perceived.

There is, as I have indicated, some debate about whether kibbutz child care is right for all children, kibbutzniks or not. Writing in the 1950s, Golan (1961:43) suggested it was:

> . . . the fact that no delinquency, sexual aberrations or child neglect are to be found within its domain, that the incidence of emotional disturbances is low, that the physical, intellectual and ethical standards of the pupils are commendable, is a source of encouragement and evidence of substantial achievement. It is also our warrant for attempting to present communal education to a wider public.

Leon (1964:105) put a similar argument in a different vein:

> It is undeniable that nobody can love their children like parents, but far more doubtful whether this automatically makes them all the most suitable people to accept exclusive responsibility for educating them.

Hazan's viewpoint (Rabin and Hazan 1971) tends to the idea that the real point is to show that kibbutz upbringing should be appropriate for kibbutz children first and foremost. She quotes the argument of Erik Erikson, the prominent psychoanalytic theorist of cross-cultural child development, for support (see e.g., Erikson 1972). Erikson said that different cultures dealt in their own way with the learning experiences every child must face. There was no universally correct way of doing this, except that children in any particular culture would develop harmonious personalities (free from disturbing, unresolved conflicts) if the way they were raised met the requirements of the culture in which they must eventually function as adults.

The writers in Rabin and Hazan's (1971) collection of essays represent the child-rearing and educational tradition of the Kibbutz Artzi federation of kibbutzim to which Goshen belonged. Those of other federations have been somewhat different. More recently, they have increasingly diverged as non-Artzi kibbutzim have been accommodating children overnight in their parents' houses. To members of Goshen in the 1970s as I mentioned earlier, this was an interesting but generally undesirable development. They argued that collective child-rearing and education were essential to kibbutz life.

Describing the development of the educational system in the Kibbutz Artzi, Katz and Lewin (Rabin and Hazan 1971:30-31) identify several phases. Early on, they outline an "authoritarian" phase when children were trained very strictly in what were thought appropriate habits. This is probably the phase of Criden and Gelb's sleeping on boards and Spiro's strict breast-feeding regime. Then there was a libertarian phase when it was thought appropriate to leave children to develop more freely, without having onerous demands placed on them. After World War II, this more libertarian method was "consolidated" by the use of psychological theory, at least partly psychoanalytic, which emphasized "ego strength."

> Today, we consider the strengthening of the child's "ego" — for example, cultivating his senses, increasing his motor aptitudes, and understanding and improving his mental processes — the principal and most effective means of directing his instinctual drives into constructive social and human channels. . . . Kibbutz education advocates tolerance toward manifestations of instinctual drives, and attains its educational goals without resorting to pressure, threat or repression. (Katz and Lewin 1971:31-32)

General principles of this kind were seen as offering a basic rationale for what actually went on in the children's houses and school rooms. Further theoretical support was developed for more detailed matters, particularly the organization of the "children's society" and the school curriculum.

Discussing the "children's society" (age groups in which children spent most of their time) and how the groups were organized, Alon (Rabin and Hazan 1971), explains how older children were encouraged to act as leaders of the committees which ran the day-to-day cultural and social activities around the school. This measure was seen as part of their maturation and as training for kibbutz life which ran along similar collective lines. She also explains how, as they went through school, kibbutz children were encouraged to work both in the school itself taking turns at such tasks as cleaning up, serving meals, and gardening in the school grounds, and also in the wider kibbutz. Secondary school children particularly were required to work in the kibbutz economy, making a significant contribution to the community's economic effort. This practice was seen as maintaining a link between school life and community life. It reinforced the lessons about collectivism learned and experienced at school and offered training in kibbutz life.

Lavi (Rabin and Hazan 1971) examines the development of "methods of study and instruction at high school." He emphasizes that this was a gradual process and describes how the early educators looked for educational theories and methods which would harmonize with the kibbutz life-style. The ideas of American "progressive education" (he refers to Jerome Bruner's *The Process of Education*) proved particularly adaptable for kibbutz use, as did the experiences of some American and German experimental schools. A notable feature of the kibbutz schools was the project method which gave children a concrete problem to investigate and encouraged them to search in their own way and at their own pace for answers. After World War II, the early, heavy emphasis on projects was tempered somewhat. "Unsuitable" subjects (i.e., mathematics, languages, crafts and physical education) were taught by more conventional methods and a standardized curriculum was adopted for the whole Kibbutz Artzi federation.

Throughout, education has been nonselective and there are no examinations. Furthermore, the educational process is subject to constant review: Lavi writes (Rabin and Hazan 1971:159):

> Every method of education and instruction, however revolutionary and progressive, must be dynamic and sensitive to change, or else it is doomed to stagnation. Changes in objective conditions, accelerated scientific advances, and developments in the psychological and educational sciences demand constant reexamination of curricula and teaching methods . . . achievements and results must be retested in the light of our goals.

## Children for the Kibbutz

The key to understanding child-rearing on the kibbutz lies in an appreciation of its main purpose; to educate new generations ideologically and practically for kibbutz life. The system has been seen at its most successful in the veteran kibbutzim which have prospered in every way, including having their children become members. In the "little kibbutzim," evaluating the system is more difficult because of the more general numerical and economic decline of the kibbutz movement since 1948. These kibbutzim did far less well generally than the veteran settlements, as I explained in Chapter 3. It is not surprising that their second generation, inculcated with old-fashioned pioneering values, should grow up critical of the current version. Children of the "little kibbutzim" also faced practical problems such as lack of resources, unavailability of potential marriage partners, difficulty finding work and so on, which certainly reinforced their view of permanent kibbutz membership as only one of several options for their futures. These practical problems could be related back to more general difficulties of the "little kibbutzim" which were relatively poor, of low and transient population, and economically underdeveloped. One might say that for Goshen's children, collective education had worked too well. They knew what a "good" kibbutz should be, and many of them found Goshen wanting.

# - 7 -

# Ceremonies
# and Festivals

## New Year, New Ideas

According to the traditional Jewish calendar, the New Year, *Rosh Hashanah* occurs in the late Summer or early Autumn. On Goshen it was an occasion for celebrating the community's achievements. In 1975, there was a communal meal in the dining room followed by a review of the previous year. Members of the Secretariat and representatives of the economic branches conducted the meeting in a fairly jocular mood. The assembled company were informed about how much had been produced, how much profit had been made, and about any new developments in the year. In a lighthearted vein, a poll was held to select the "man of the year," "woman of the year," "dog of the year" and so on. There was also some musical entertainment provided by kibbutz members. The day following this evening celebration was a general day off work. As on Shabbat, only essential jobs were done.

Rosh Hashanah began Goshen's annual cycle of collective ceremonies. Although many of the ceremonies owed their origins to Judaism, an observant Jew would find the ceremonies and the rationale for their celebration offered by members of Goshen barely recognizable in many cases. As a member of the Kibbutz Artzi federation, Goshen had added atheism to the basic kibbutz tenets of socialism and Zionism. Like all kibbutzim of the federation, Goshen was involved in a process of developing new rituals (kibbutzim of other federations were agnostic, not atheist). Generally, the idea of this ritual construction was that Jewish tradition could be separated from religion and adapted to celebrate the history of the Jewish people and the annual cycle of an agricultural community. The regular ritual observances of Judaism such as prayer, *kashrut* (rules about food), purity rites for women and rules governing marital relations had long since been abandoned by kibbutz

129

members in all the secular kibbutz federations and were not followed on Goshen. Efforts were also made to adapt rites of passage, which mark changes in status at various points in an individual's life, to the requirements of an atheist community.

The field material from Goshen illustrates that all these modifications of traditional rituals entailed difficulties, as I will show later. Whatever the problems involved, Goshen and other Artzi kibbutzim remained committed to Jewishness, the Jewish people and the Jewish state, in a nationalistic sense. This meant that they could not reject the Jewish tradition wholesale. It had made them who they were, and formed the basis of their way of life. Given that commitment, their only real choice was to adapt tradition. While they were atheists, they were Jewish atheists living in a Jewish state, and the key to understanding their view of the world expressed in the symbols used at festivals and in daily life lies in understanding their relationship with this outside world. As we will see, Goshen's dialogue with Judaism exemplifies how closely the kibbutz was tied to the State and how its development and internal activities were intimately related to those of the State. The dialogue also stresses the inherent dynamic of kibbutz life, emphasizing once and for all that we cannot treat kibbutz ideas and actions as static or predetermined.

## Nationalist Festivals

Many people in Israel regard days of national commemoration as at least partly religious occasions. For some, the State is the fulfillment of religious prophecy. There is, however, no intrinsically religious content to the four nationalist festivals celebrated regularly by members of Goshen. Holocaust Day remembers the six million Jews who died through Nazi persecution. Memorial Day honors those who have died for Israel. Independence Day marks the declaration of the State in 1948. May Day celebrates the international workers' festival. All four occurred within a month in the Spring. The celebration of each one had a distinctly kibbutz quality but showed no marked dissonance with celebrations in the rest of the country. At the same time, each ceremony expressed some of the important themes of kibbutz life that we have already encountered.

Holocaust Day on Goshen in 1975 was marked by an evening gathering with poetry reading, solemn music, some speeches and silent contemplation. Not all the members of the kibbutz took part in the ceremony. Those of North African origin said it was not their concern; others, members of the second generation, felt that the Holocaust was better not dwelt on. The representation of members of European origin, particularly those who had themselves narrowly escaped death, was strong. At the ceremony, the speeches were made by a pioneer and by a member of the second generation. These speeches were intended to be formal, stressing the continuing memory of the Holocaust into new generations. However, the young man made what was considered a very inflammatory speech, questioning this continuing memory. Others felt they could not let such comments go unchallenged and a heated debate ensued. This episode was embarrassing for all those at the ceremony; it was not supposed to happen.

The selective attendance at the Holocaust Day ceremony represents two important divisions in Goshen that we have already encountered: the ethnic distinctions still important in the community and the generation gap. These were differences both of experience and interest. Failure to participate actively in the ceremony, while not universal, was widespread among the North Africans and the kibbutz born who had no experience of the Holocaust. Other observers have noted that elsewhere in Israel the Holocaust is generally less important symbolically to such groups than it is to those who remember it. Sherman (1982) suggests that the increasing self-confidence and numerical preponderance of the Oriental Jewish population of Israel may prompt renegotiation of the place of the Holocaust as a fundamental national symbol. Its meaning for Israeli and worldwide Jewry may be reassessed. Regarding differences of interest, the young man's comments at Goshen's ceremony can be seen as an expression of the challenge of its second generation to pioneer control. The pioneers' power and one of their basic symbols were being actively questioned. The pioneers defended their values in no uncertain terms showing their continuing effectiveness at the core of the community.

The Memorial Day ceremony was much more generally attended, and all participants were solemn and reverential. For Goshen, as for every such community in Israel, the day brought personal memories of people they had known and lived with as well as a more collective, national commemoration. There was no immediate debate about the meaning of an event which related so intimately to everyone's experience.

Independence Day (the day after Memorial Day) was a very popular occasion on Goshen, as in Israel as well. There was a big sit-down evening meal followed by singing, dancing and party games. For once, the singing and dancing was enthusiastic. In the morning, celebrations continued with a communal picnic in the woods, building shelters among the trees, and playing more games. This was another occasion deeply meaningful to all concerned.

May Day was a very low-key affair. In 1975, it was marked by a banner stretched across the dining room: "Long live May Day, festival of friendship for all workers." There was a coffee evening in the *moadon* (clubhouse) where records described as "workerist" songs were played. This was not a collective celebration; people simply turned up if they felt like marking the day with a sociable coffee. The symbolic red flag flew all day outside the *moadon* to mark the formal allegiance of Goshen to international socialism. On the following day, everyone who could be spared went out to work in the cotton fields, and participation was quite enthusiastic.

In the kibbutz movement, both the importance of May Day as a festival and the identification with international socialism have lessened somewhat, particularly in response to external events. Until the 1950s, the USSR was a model Socialist

State for the Kibbutz Artzi federation. The prominent celebration of May Day and the anniversary of the Russian Revolution in some kibbutzim such as Kiryat Yedidim (Spiro 1970) marked its symbolic importance. Stalin's purges and USSR policies towards the Jews made such symbols less resonant. The Russian Revolution in particular is no longer commemorated in the kibbutz movement. More recently, the Israeli context has influenced the formerly outward-looking socialism of the Kibbutz Artzi. Before 1948, the movement expanded rapidly, and there were heady dreams of a socialist state of Israel, full of kibbutzim. As we have seen before however, the foundation of the State proved a mixed blessing for the kibbutzim. In the State, they became numerically less significant. In addition, as part of the establishment, they lost some of their former autonomy both ideologically and practically. Now irrevocably committed to the State of Israel, they had to negotiate with other elements, notably those favoring a much less radical socialism plus the religious authorities. It became more difficult and less relevant to look to international socialism. The pressure of external events (in which the kibbutzim were involved) continued to erode the importance of its symbols.

## Reinterpreting Tradition

Succot, the Feast of Tabernacles, follows shortly after Rosh Hashanah in the Jewish calendar and lasts a week. The official kibbutz interpretation of Succot was that it was a harvest festival. This interpretation related to part of the traditional account (Schauss 1962) that Succot was indeed the ancient harvest festival of Palestine. Some elements of tradition such as pious religious pilgrimage were omitted from the new kibbutz version. This kind of selective use of tradition was characteristic of the process of ritual and symbolic reconstruction in Goshen and other kibbutzim. It emphasized both the continuity and the dissonance that kibbutzim saw between themselves and previous epochs of Jewish life. Religion was out, but Jewish history and the annual cycle of nature remained crucial to their new Jewish way of life. On Goshen during the Feast of Tabernacles, the traditional *succot* (booths made of branches) were built, and the school children held parties in them. The four ancient symbols of the festival, the citron, myrtle, willow and palm were also displayed.

It is a simple matter to point out how tradition was being used, to note the official meaning of the festival, to illustrate which of the old elements were rejected and which retained. More complicated is the interpretation of the meaning of it all to the ordinary kibbutznik. Generally, we find confusion and ignorance. Of course, an anthropologist should know that this is a usual response to ritual and symbolism among ordinary folk (that is, not religious specialists) in many societies. Charsley (1987) warns us against constructing elaborate accounts of symbolic structures which make us lose sight of the real place of ritual and symbolism in most people's lives. We should concentrate on the kibbutz members' own views and interpret these in context.

The schoolteacher on Goshen in 1975 explained to the schoolchildren that the citron, willow, myrtle and palm symbolized all the possible kinds of Jews in the world. Older members of the kibbutz could interpret these symbols in traditional ways specific to their countries of origin. The first generation of Goshen could not give accounts of their meaning because they had never been taught any. Each generation's view seems to reflect a different historical period in kibbutz development. The pioneers knew of the old traditions and could still give accounts of them even while rejecting religion. They had not thought it worthwhile to pass their knowledge on to the second generation raised at a time when rejecting religion meant ignoring it as much as possible and before the kibbutz alternative was much developed. Children of the 1970s were being taught in a much more structured way about the interpretation of symbols. I will be arguing later on that their experience reflected the changed environment of the kibbutz, and that the ceremonial cycle of Goshen needs to be seen as using and adapting the rituals of the wider modern society as well as looking back to an ancient tradition. It is also important not to take the ignorance and confusion at face value; they can be seen as an important element in kibbutz autonomy.

Ignorance of the traditional meaning of a festival could be seen at Hannukah, the Festival of Lights, occurring in December. Again, this was particularly noticeable among Goshen's second generation. One such person gave this typical account:

> Several things, including the Maccabees, are mixed up in it. And once, the Temple was destroyed; there was only enough oil left to burn for one day, and it burned for eight days. That was a miracle. In the kibbutz, it is a children's festival. My son loves it.

At the celebrations, the children acted a play about the Maccabees and took part in a procession carrying candles and sparklers. Each candle of the traditional nine-branched candlestick, the *hannukiah*, was lighted by a representative of a different category of people on Goshen. Following traditional practice, lights were not kindled directly but from the ninth candle, the *shammash*, servant light (Fishman 1973). The food included doughnuts, which people also said were "traditional at Hannukah." The children played with spinning tops inscribed with the Hebrew letters *nun*, *gimmel*, *heh* and *shin*.

It proved quite difficult to observe the actual ceremony at Hannukah and to talk to people about its meaning. Throughout the proceedings, people were chatting to one another so loudly that it was impossible to hear what was going on. Their main topic of conversation was how badly organized the whole thing had been. Afterwards, thinking that I was going to have problems getting good material on kibbutz ceremonies, I looked back at my notes on Succot. There had been a slide show of various kibbutz activities which had brought loud complaints from the audience. The slides were the same every year, the show was boring, and anyway, they were not even good slides. While the slide show was going on, people had been inattentive, and the commentary had been inaudible at times. At the time, I was concerned that I was missing important material and found myself quietly cursing the people of Goshen for preventing me from observing their festivals. Only later on, after repeated similar experiences at tradition-based festivals did I realize that the people's reactions had to be seen as an integral part of the proceedings. Their apparent lack of interest in what was going on was part of the process of ritual reconstruction.

At Tu Bishvat in January 1976, kibbutzniks gave me a clearer account of what was happening. This is a minor festival in religious terms. In modern Israel, it has been given greater national significance, particularly by association with State reforestation programs. Tu Bishvat is also called Rosh Hashanah Lailanot, the New Year of the Trees. On Goshen, there was a communal meal and musical entertainment, and the dining room was decorated with tree branches. People stressed to me that at Tu Bishvat, they ate dried fruits, nuts and seeds in the Sephardic custom, and recalled that many of Goshen's members had originally come from Sephardic communities. They also stressed that Tu Bishvat had become a Zionist more than a religious festival. Though this celebration did derive from tradition, it was clear that people were more comfortable with it than the others and that their attitude was as previously described towards the secular nationalist festivals. Ignorance, confusion and inattention did not appear.

Purim, in March was a day on Goshen for dressing up and displaying deliberately disorderly behavior. Schoolchildren would read the story of Esther, traditionally associated with the festival. I was unable to observe Purim, but people's views on it echoed some familiar themes. It was boring, they said; the jollity was forced, the spirit of Purim had been lost.

Pesach (Passover) (together with Rosh Hashanah one of the most important tradition-based festivals) was marked by a large meal called a *seder*. The meal was laid on long tables; while looking at the food, people waited to eat until the ceremonial part of the proceedings was over. As might be expected, they began to mutter and then to state loudly that it was a long time to wait when your meal was on the table in front of you. The ceremony involved a reading of the *Haggadah Pesach*, the Passover story, in an adapted version published by Sifrat Poalim, the publishing house of Hashomer Hatzair. Representatives of different sub-groups in Goshen stood up to read various sections of the story. As they read, some members of the audience chatted with one another. Other members said "shhh" very loudly with the result that some of the readings could hardly be heard. The traditional four toasts were drunk in wine, the last and most enthusiastically pronounced being "Leshanah haba'ah biyerushalayim" (next year in Jerusalem). Then there was a play acted by children telling the traditional long rhyming story about a kid, eaten by a cat, which was bitten by a dog, which was beaten with a stick . . . and so on, which is printed at the end of the book. There was some singing in which participation was limited and accompanied by much general conversation. The meal itself included *matzot* (unleavened bread) and bitter herbs, part of old tradition.

Shavuot follows seven weeks after Pesach, with the four national and religious festivals falling between the two. In 1975, people on Goshen complained that by this time, they were tired of celebrating. No member proved willing to organize the proceedings, so the secretary of the kibbutz was left to take charge. Although people were reluctant, no one suggested that Shavuot be abandoned. It had to be marked somehow. Again, there was a communal meal with entertainment. The secretary persuaded a group of Swiss volunteers to sing at the meal and arranged for members to tour the various branches of the economy. School children, organized by their teachers, went out to the fields during the day and read the Book of Ruth, traditionally associated with the festival. It appears that Shavuot had changed over the years on Goshen. In the early 1950s, people remembered that it had been a major event celebrated in the open air to mark the first fruits of the year.

The themes that emerge from an examination of Goshen's reworking of tradition are repeated elsewhere. The best comparative ethnography is Spiro's (1970) based on observations made in the 1950s. In particular, Spiro found that the people of Kiryat Yedidim were dissatisfied with the way their festivals were celebrated. They were not keen to participate. For example, the choir would not rehearse for Pesach until publicly shamed into it; the New Year entertainment was unenthusiastically received, and some people complained that the festivals were petit bourgeois.

## The Meaning of Festivals

Nationalist and tradition-based festivals celebrated in the kibbutz, past and present, express the community's integration with and autonomy from the wider society at the same time. The relationship is a dynamic one. We find changes over time in the celebration of festivals and the possibility for further change to occur. Given the ambiguity, confusion and debate regarding festivals, it is almost certain that future alterations will take place.

Kibbutz autonomy from the wider society is most clearly expressed by movement attempts to rework tradition to suit a developing kibbutz way of life, which rejects religion and promotes agricultural and historical aspects. Kibbutz members also assert kibbutz autonomy by their approach to the traditional-based festivals. They constantly challenge them, care little about the details of meaning, fail to participate as the form of ceremonies seems to dictate, and maintain criticism of the celebrations. Thus, they continuously disdain religion and assert their rejection of it. However, they still join in to celebrate their Jewishness and their alternative kibbutz way of life.

At all the festivals, the details of social interaction on the kibbutz came into play. As people sat down to a communal meal on Goshen, they formed a social map of the community. Strong kin groups, friendships and ethnic associations were marked; boundaries between insiders and outsiders, the integrated and the outcast were clearly evident. For days after such an occasion, the gossip network would discuss the details of who had sat with whom, and what this meant for their relationships. The details of interaction, of course, must vary from one kibbutz to another,but the way that they can be seen in play at festivals does not. In this respect then, we can think of kibbutz ceremonial as expressing internal features of community life.

At Goshen's nationalist festivals, people's behavior was rather different from that at the tradition-based ones. They still expressed their relationships in seating plans, they still revealed the divisions between them in their actions at celebrations, and they still gossiped afterwards. Generally speaking, their participation was more active, and their knowledge of and identification with festival symbols was much clearer. It is reasonable to say that nationalist celebrations on Goshen expressed greater integration into the wider society and emphasized the kibbutz as part of the nation.

It is too simple to say categorically that tradition-based festivals show autonomy while nationalist ones celebrations show integration. Most importantly, we have to understand how the reworking of tradition also integrates the kibbutz movement with Israeli society. At the most basic level, this occurs as the kibbutz movement uses the Jewish tradition and identifies itself with Israel and the Jewish people. The situation would be very different if, for example, the kibbutz members had decided to build their ritual on Buddhism or invent it from scratch. Once the commitment had been made to rework the Jewish tradition rather than construct a totally different alternative, it was inevitable that reconstructed "kibbutz Judaism" (Lilker 1982) should reflect establishment Judaism over time and match changes in Israeli Judaism. For example, since 1948, kibbutzniks had several different understandings of tradition-based festivals according to their generation. Children born in the early 1950s were particularly "ignorant," reflecting perhaps their parents' confidence in the kibbutz as an alternative way of life. They had enough faith in themselves for radical rebellion. Children of the 1970s were being taught more coherent accounts of festivals, reflecting perhaps the general weakening of the kibbutz movement's position in Israeli society and less confident rebellion. These corresponding changes in kibbutz Judaism and Israel's Judaism are particularly clear in rites of passage. This major component of kibbutz ritual provides a key to understanding the whole picture.

## Rites of Passage

Where possible, the kibbutz movement tried to construct secular alternatives to traditional religious rites of passage. After 1948 when certain religious rules became enshrined in law, this became difficult. In the post-State kibbutz, the celebration of rites of passage shows interesting compromises with the legal and customary rules of the wider society.

In Judaism, the *bar mitzvah* is a rite making a boy into a man which qualifies him to be part of the religious congregation of Jews. In the Kibbutz Artzi, this has been replaced by the ceremony of enrollment for boys and girls into the youth movement, Hashomer Hatzair. Here they learn ideological and practical training for kibbutz life. On Goshen, this ceremony was Zionist and Socialist and did not draw on religion. Despite the strongly secular atmosphere, enrollments were done at about *bar mitzvah* age (twelve or thirteen). Thus, the reference to tradition was made, expressing both the connection and disconnection between past and present, kibbutz and religion.

Funerals and memorial ceremonies on Goshen were marked by non-religious ritual. This was possible because the kibbutz had its own burial ground which was not subject to external religious authority nor the control of Orthodox burial societies. During my fieldwork, there was one death on Goshen. The elderly mother of a veteran member died. A non-religious ceremonial was held in the kibbutz cemetery, and the weekly film show was cancelled as a mark of respect. Some members commented that on a larger kibbutz the death of a "marginal" person would not have been collectively marked. Goshen was in the habit of holding memorial ceremonies for the dead, although people said that not all kibbutzim did so. These comparisons support Criden and Gelb's (1974) point that kibbutzim had as yet no established practice for marking death. They also found that this had been a source of unease for many kibbutz members. I did not find this on Goshen. However, the community had faced very few deaths. Also, it was an actively atheistic community. Agnostic kibbutzim may find the matter of death ceremonies more difficult.

Rubin (1986) has examined changes in "death customs" in the kibbutz movement from the early days. He reports that in the 1910s funerals involved song and dance which were spontaneous and varied from one funeral to another. From the 1920s until the 1950s, decorum and silence were customary. After 1950, there were attempts to rework some traditional aspects of funeral rites, constructing a kind of "secular religion." Rubin gives many interesting examples. Quoting Ben-Gurion he reports (1986:296):

> . . . the *kaddish* prayer, . . . one of the high points in burial ritual . . . which begins 'May the name of the Lord be glorified and sanctified' was sometimes reformulated as 'May the lust of life of the Hebrew man be glorified and sanctified.'

And he quotes a memorial prayer written by Katzenelson, a labor movement leader to replace the traditional "Let God remember the souls of his sons and daughters" with "Let Israel remember the souls of its sons and daughters" (Rubin 1986:296).

He attributes the development of alternative ritual using traditional symbols to changes in the kibbutz movement from the "stormy existence" (1986:300) of the early days which encouraged spontaneity. When this died down, only silence was appropriate. In the 1960s, kibbutz pioneers began to face their own inevitable deaths and to look for new rites. He feels the last phase may be a result of weakened ideological fervor, as the kibbutz had become an established way of life. Nevertheless, he emphasizes that the new rites are not religious. Kibbutzim seem to have taken the opportunity to construct alternatives to religion which still use religious symbols. The active use of religious symbols, he says, moves the kibbutz movement closer to the nation. The changes in death rites make kibbutz practice more similar to that of the wider Jewish society, but in fact in this rite of passage, the kibbutzim have managed to retain greater autonomy than in circumcision, marriage and divorce. Rubin perhaps underemphasizes the relative independence of kibbutzim in the matter of death.

On Goshen, all male babies underwent ritual circumcision which marked them, in the terms defined by traditional religion, as Jews. Like all Jewish Israelis, kibbutz members were subject to very strong pressure to circumcise their sons. Like the vast majority, the operation was carried out by the *mohel* (the religious circumciser) with religious ceremonial (Tamarin 1973). When asked why, as atheists, people did this, they explained that they did not want kibbutz boys singled out for ridicule as different from other boys. Tamarin (1973) says that in any case, if they did avoid circumcision as babies, the army would almost certainly "persuade" them to undergo the operation as recruits. Newly arrived immigrants to Israel who are uncircumcised meet the same fate.

In the matter of circumcision, kibbutzniks argued that they had no effective choice but to conform to tradition. They justified this by referring to the community of Israelis to which, as Zionists, they wished to belong. Although they could explain the custom, there were plenty of signs of unease over the apparent compromise. People were, I found, very unwilling to discuss circumcision. They would say "we do it because we must," then regard the subject as closed. Trying to press the question, I was sometimes told that kibbutz boys developed "complexes" about circumcision, but this would not be discussed in detail. This unease reflects the difficulty at the heart of the issue for kibbutzniks. Trying to separate nationalism from religion was particularly problematic where circumcision was concerned. Kibbutzniks would try to justify circumcision in national terms despite knowing that it was, and is, a very important sign of membership of the religious community.

I explained in the last chapter that marriage was the norm for kibbutz couples in the 1970s, particularly if they planned children. In the absence of civil marriage in Israel, and given kibbutzniks' desire to have their marriages recognized outside their communities, there was no choice but to have a religious ceremony. On Goshen, it was usual for couples to live together before being married, but marriage itself was seen as an important step, a true rite of passage marking a change in status. Criden and Gelb (1974:131) state that on Kfar Blum, couples would get married once the woman was pregnant. Implied is a lack of urgency about the issue. On Goshen in the seventies, marriage preceded pregnancy. Once a couple had married, they would start their family very soon. The practice on Kfar Blum is more like the old kibbutz attitude to marriage. In the past, the formal ceremony was thought much less important. Criden and Gelb (1974:141) report stand-in bridegrooms in the early days of Kfar Blum, deputizing at ceremonies for men away on army service, and add that "the rabbi wouldn't know the difference." Spiro (1970) feels that the formal ceremony in the 1950s simply acknowledged an existing union since the community considered cohabiting couples as permanent as married ones. He refers to people who got married sooner rather than later so that their unions would be recognized by the outside world they were entering if, for example, they were going to a university.

Only one couple on Goshen in the 1970s decided to have a child without getting married. They argued that the bourgeois institution of marriage had no place in a socialist community. Others thought them very strange, saying their views were old-fashioned and pointing out the problems the child might have in the outside world. "They write 'bastard' on the birth certificate," people said. Once the baby was born, however, the couple was treated no differently from other parents and the child no differently from other children. I know that at the time of my fieldwork many kibbutzim had a few members who held out for the old-fashioned rejection of marriage, but they were a tiny minority. We saw in Chapter 5 how kibbutz men and women looked forward to marriage.

For a wedding on Goshen, there would be a big party involving the whole community. Often, guests from outside the kibbutz would also attend. There would be lots of food and drink, singing and dancing and congratulations for the couple and their parents. The ceremony itself might immediately precede the party, or it might have taken place a few days earlier. On one occasion, the rabbi came to the kibbutz to perform the marriage. Normally the couple and their families went into town for a quieter ceremony. There was considerable social pressure to go to town; many kibbutzniks did not like the rabbi coming to the kibbutz. While they had no choice but to conform to religious practice, they felt it should not be made into a public spectacle in the community.

During my fieldwork, three Goshen couples were married abroad. Three men married volunteer workers. It was impossible for these marriages to take place in Israel because the women concerned were classified as Christians and no mixed-religion marriage was possible by law. People of Goshen responded to these marriages as equally valid as the Jewish ones. However, there was then considerable pressure placed on the women to convert to Judaism. On the surface, this appears very strange. An atheist community accepts new members, accepts their marriages, and then urges them to change religion. The conversion process first involved learning about Torah and Jewish observance, then there was an oral examination and the cleansing ritual bath (*mikvah*). Certainly the pressure can be partly explained by the fact that, in religious law, a Jew is the child of a Jewish mother. Goshen saw itself very much as a Jewish community. The suggestion is strengthened by the fact that two non-Jewish men on Goshen were not expected to convert.

In fact, one who expressed a wish to do so was mocked and accused of being "too religious." At least some of the explanation must lie in the fact that the knowledge acquired in the conversion course was a "cultural baggage" of Jewishness. As the women converted, they would acquire this as background for being atheist Jews, while a religious person acquired it for other purposes. They would know how to be Jewish atheists rather than simply atheists. The complete program of initiation into kibbutz life also involved Hebrew lessons and instruction in movement ideology.

## Everyday Life

In their everyday lives, kibbutzniks of Goshen would insist that religion did not affect them, stressing their atheism. They did not pray or attend synagogue; they did not observe religious pollution taboos relating to food (*kashrut*) or the human body; they did not conform to rules of modesty in dress or to traditional commensal ritual (ritual at meals) or to rules segregating the sexes to preserve their purity. Because they were in Israel, their lives were affected by religion. Because they were Jewish atheists, they reacted to it characteristically.

They almost always ate kosher meat, any other meat being difficult to obtain in Israel. When they did not, this was a cause for comment and a chance to stress their difference from the outside world. During my fieldwork, bacon fritters were served for lunch one day. The meal was accompanied by unusually lively banter about what a change it was to eat something really tasty for once. The underlying message emphasized that they were committing an anti-religious act. Many people seemed a little uneasy about flouting the rules of *kashrut*. This observation is supported by the kitchen manageress' strict instructions to workers serving supper that cheese and meat should be placed on separate tables "because some of the older people don't like to see them together." This was a gesture towards *kashrut*. The kibbutz kitchen was certainly not kosher. Other manifestations of *kashrut* could be seen in the bread eaten on Goshen. The bakery (on another kibbutz) produced only *matzot* (unleavened bread) at Passover and only *challah* (soft, white bread) at Shabbat. I doubt that members of Goshen would have enjoyed anything else, particularly at Passover. For them, conformity to some aspects of *kashrut* was a matter of Jewish custom and tradition, not a religious act or sign.

Shabbat (Friday evening to Saturday evening) was a day of rest for most people on Goshen. Anyone who had to work would "have their Shabbat" on another day during the week. If anyone wanted a day in town, they might volunteer to work Shabbat so that they could use public transportation. Because of religious influence, there was no public transport on Shabbat. Therefore, Shabbat was a day at home. On Friday night there was a special meal with tablecloths and hot food (usually schnitzel or chicken). When someone remembered to put them there, two lighted candles stood on the piano at the end of the dining hall. These were said to be "something Jewish"; there was no ceremony attached to them. During my fieldwork, there was a move to make some Friday nights more of an occasion by having a monthly sit down meal with entertainment provided by a kibbutz family. Three families participated. They organized singing and poetry reading and enacted satirical sketches about kibbutz life which proved particularly popular with the audience. After those three contributions, no other families volunteered, so things went back to normal.

Orthodox Judaism involves maintaining ritual purity by adhering to a set of pollution taboos (details are given by Zborowski and Herzog 1962). These were not generally observed on Goshen. We saw, for example, how boys and girls shared showers and sleeping accommodations. Married couples did not observe the taboos about sexual contact in marriage. Women of Goshen went to the *mikvah* (ritual bath) perhaps once in their lives before their marriage ceremonies. A rabbi would refuse to carry out the marriage unless the woman was ritually pure. The women who were converting to Judaism would go at the end of their course. This is a marked contrast with orthodox practice which prescribed that women should go every month after their menstrual period and after childbirth. Women of Goshen did not care to talk about the *mikvah*, reflecting the widespread distaste for and discomfort about its virtual compulsion among nonreligious Israeli women (Tamarin 1973). Their attitudes and actions were rather similar to those I described relating to circumcision: "we do it because we must." The reason they must do it comes from their engagement with Judaism and their identification with Israel.

## A Culture of Unbelief

We can make more sense of all the material on kibbutz ritual if we use the concept of a "culture of unbelief" put forward by Caporale and Grumelli (1971) whose work is concerned mainly with helping the establishment of the Roman Catholic Church to understand nonbelievers. In their book, Luckmann (1971:36) argues that unbelief is "constituted by institutional definition." He explains that unbelief is only found in societies where religion is a specialist activity, and there are religious specialists to define the boundaries of belief. Unbelievers are outside this boundary. By contrast, in an undifferentiated society where religion is embedded in everyone's life, there are no opportunities for unbelief. The idea of a culture of unbelief is useful where people are actively organizing a movement contrasting with institutionalized belief. They do more than just ignore religion; they try to set up an alternative. The kibbutz movement is a particularly interesting example because it involves not simply opposition to established ideas but attempts to adapt them to different purposes: not rejection but reworking. Thus the movement cannot escape from the established alternative but must continually conduct a complex dialogue with it. The kibbutz culture of unbelief is a balance of external influence in the form of institutionalized traditional religion and internal ideology in the form of kibbutz atheism which rejects God but not history or custom.

Over the years since 1948, the influence of religious agencies in Israel generally has increased (Frankel 1980), particularly since religious political parties have held the balance of power in the Knesset and have influenced the law. For example, when completing official forms, all Israelis are asked for their *leum* which translates literally as "nation" but actually represents a religious identification—Jew, Moslem, Christian or Druze (Ghilan 1974). The legal definition of a Jew is religious and orthodox. Kibbutzniks adhere to this, as we have seen. Religious influence has insured that there is no civil marriage in Israel. Not only must all marriages be religious (Jewish, Moslem, Christian or Druze) but the couple involved must be of the same religion. Divorce also involves a religious element, according to tradition. Circumcision for males is part of the religious definition of Jewishness and is therefore difficult to avoid.

Not only law but custom also helps support religious influence in the State. The wars of 1967 and 1973 have helped to reinforce religion's customary power. In 1967, the Israeli army entered the West Bank, Gaza, Sinai and East Jerusalem. On reaching the Western Wall in Jerusalem, young soldiers reported that they felt an upsurge of Jewish feeling for the first time (Near 1970). They reflected a countrywide excitement about and renewed interest in Jewishness, stimulated by the victory. The Yom Kippur War of 1973 was, by contrast, seen as a defeat and a sign that Jewry was threatened yet again in its history. It was followed by further religious revivalism primarily concentrated on settling the occupied territories which more and more people were starting to consider Israel's historical right.

Liebman and Don-Yehiya (1983) have written a comprehensive review of the relationship between traditional religion and the state in the Yishuv and Israel. They discuss the "civil religion" of the state defined as (1983:ix) "the ceremonials, myths and creeds which legitimate the social order, unite the population and mobilize the society's members in pursuit of its dominant political goals." They identify three phases. The first was Zionist socialism (1919-1945) which conformed broadly to the ideology of the early kibbutz movement with its focus on class-based politics and its rejection of religion. Though so-called "revisionists" challenged Zionist socialism with a more radical nationalism and greater interest in religion, they made little headway. The second phase, Statism (1948-1956) saw the elevation of the State itself to a dominant symbol. At least this was what the Zionist socialist politicians of the new Israel intended. It became clear, however, that their strategy was potentially dangerous and socially divisive, particularly as the Oriental immigrants arriving in large numbers in the 1950s did not find the State a particularly meaningful symbol. From 1956, the "new civil religion," the third phase began to appear. The State began to make increasing use of traditional religious symbols. These had to be modified say Liebman and Don-Yehiya (1983) because traditional religion per se was inappropriate. Many of its symbols conflicted with the notion of the state; it insisted that everything came from God (and therefore nothing from the state); it was transnational, and not all Jews adhered to it. Liebman and Don-Yehiya (1983) give much detail on the process of reinterpretation which is not relevant here. Suffice it to say that in recent years, both state and kibbutz have been reinterpreting religion. The state has shifted from valuing secularism and tolerating religion to tolerating secularism and valuing religion. The trend which began in the late 1950s gained greater momentum from the wars of 1967 and 1973 and had a profound effect on the kibbutz culture of unbelief.

Following Luckmann's (1971) argument about the necessity of an institutional definition of religion for a culture of unbelief to appear, we should expect that as the institutional definition changes, so must the culture of unbelief. Looked at like this, changes in the kibbutz culture of unbelief seem to parallel those in the State civil religion. Though kibbutz members express things in terms of changing reinterpretations of traditional religion, it is quite clear that their dialogue is also with civil religion, the aspiring dominant ideology of the wider society they inhabit.

In the early years of the kibbutz movement, kibbutzniks were part of the mainstream Zionist socialist movement, confidently rejecting religious rites and symbols and creating their own alternatives. With the foundation of the state — and Goshen — came Statism, still broadly compatible with Zionist socialism and therefore with kibbutz ideas. At this period in Goshen, the culture of unbelief confidently rejected religious symbols. Children, as we have seen, were brought up ignorant of them. Festivals were reinvented. Succot, for example, became the open air harvest festival, Shavuot an enthusiastic celebration of the first fruits, and so on. In everyday life and rites of passage, religion intruded only where it was unavoidable. Otherwise, it could be ignored. At this time, nationwide control of kashrut and Shabbat observance were weaker than they were later to become and so there were fewer dietary and travel restrictions. In rites of passage, there were thoughts of civil marriages; kibbutz funerals were silent and secular.

We should not forget that in the early years of the State, the kibbutz movement was part of the establishment, directly involved and represented at the highest governmental and trade union levels. The movement not only had ideas compatible with Statism, but its representatives were involved in promoting it. They were also involved in the compromises with religious political parties which helped maintain the Labor Party and its allies in government. These compromises combined with custom helped to maintain the religious cast of Israeli Jewish life. At the kibbutz level then, traditional religion was secularized and used to kibbutz ends. At the State level, compromises were made which helped retain and enhance its national influence.

The "new civil religion" appeared as "a response to the failure of Statism to provide a meaningful symbol system" (Liebman and Don-Yehiya (1983:223) for the mass of Jewish Israelis, particularly the growing proportion of Oriental immigrants. Its rise coincided with the decline of the kibbutz movement and the Labor Party as influences in Israeli society. In the kibbutz movement, the culture of unbelief began to change as institutional definitions of religion began to change. As more religious symbols were used at the State level, so atheists in the kibbutz movement had to define their position in relation not only to traditional religion per se but also to the new civil religion. In effect, the kibbutz culture of unbelief, like State ideology, was under constant critical review, reworking its relationship with its reference point.

In the 1970s at the time of my fieldwork, the influence of religious symbols in wider Israeli society was increasing, and the kibbutz culture of unbelief was getting more elaborate. For example, the disdain for some festivals seems to have strengthened. Purim and Shavuot were less popular than formerly. The practice of making commotion during ceremonies was well established, and there was some argument about national festivals. Rites of passage also were altered with a more serious approach to weddings (clearer on Kfar Blum than Goshen), more complicated funerals directly addressing religion (again, the comparative evidence is strong), and on Goshen, the conversion of Christian brides to Jewish atheists. In everyday life, religious influence was getting stronger. There was more enforced kashrut observance and less movement on Shabbat. The response to those changes was constant discussion and criticism of religious influence.

These complicated patterns of interaction between the kibbutz and the wider society over ideological and meaning systems parallel those we have seen earlier in the book. Economically, politically, as well as in terms of gender roles and reproduction, the kibbutz has developed as part of the wider society of Israel. As an isolated commune, it is bewildering. As part of Israeli society, it begins, I hope, to make some sense.

# - 8 -

# Studying the Kibbutz

## Further Questions

For some readers, this book has been an account of life on a kibbutz and an attempt to explain some of its hows, whys and wherefores. In giving the fullest account I could and offering the wide-ranging type of explanation I did, I hoped to satisfy people's curiosity about the kibbutz as a way of life in Israel. For other readers, I hope it has been a temptation to learn more. In this last chapter, I want to suggest how this might be done by looking at some current issues in the kibbutz and reviewing the development of kibbutz studies. The sheer volume of material already published about the kibbutz may suggest there are no uninvestigated topics and no more questions worth asking. My view is that this is not so if only because the kibbutz, like all human societies, is dynamic and enigmatic. Previous research, including my own, may have flaws — methodological, empirical, even ideological. This means that we look not only for new data but also for new ways of collecting and interpreting it. The questions I will raise here develop from my own research and are therefore not exhaustive. I do think they are worth asking.

An important way to find out more about the kibbutz and to develop new questions to ask about it is to tackle the immense literature. Its volume is daunting, but it can be made more manageable with the understanding that it can be classified into several groups, each offering a rather different type of material. In reviewing the literature, I concentrate on social scientific work and generally exclude publications from the kibbutz movement itself. The line between the two is not always clearly marked, however. I also concentrate on books rather than journal articles which can be highly specialized and difficult to obtain. While some key articles offer particularly helpful insights, it would be quite impossible to deal with every piece of work ever published about the kibbutz movement. Rather, I have concentrated on a series of items which represent the various traditions of kibbutz studies. The critical remarks I make about them are intended to alert readers to their limitations and also to help reveal more of the thinking behind this book. To any kibbutz researcher whose work has been omitted from this review, I can apologize. The work reviewed here represents important influences on the development of my own analysis and can also serve as essential background for any kibbutz study.

## Early Studies

Infield's *Cooperative Living in Palestine* first appeared in the USA in 1944 offering itself as a sociological study of the kibbutzim. Infield wrote (1946:2):

> At the very least, sociology ought to help men shape their relations more purposefully, so that they may forget that sorriest of all excuses for disastrous blunders, namely, that they did not know what they were doing.

He heralded a theme which was to recur in kibbutz studies: the idea that there were lessons to be drawn from kibbutzim for humankind in general. I can share Infield's hopes for sociology, but I find it difficult to agree with him that the kibbutz is more instructive than any other type of community. I will return to this matter later on.

Infield's study was a basic account of the development of the kibbutz movement up to the 1940s, particularly stressing the pioneers' aims and investigating their practicality. Generally, he seems to have found the ideals laudable and the practice falling somewhat short because "men lag behind their postulates" (Infield 1946:111). In the communities, he found social ambition, clique formation, individualism and laziness to be "dissociative" factors, but his account always puts greater emphasis on the inherently associative character of kibbutzim and praises them.

Landshut's work, *The Communal Settlements in Palestine* (1944) echoes Infield's approval, referring to the "national mission" (p.640) of kibbutzim as the foundation of a revolutionary way of life. He particularly emphasizes the importance of looking at the place of the kibbutzim in the wider society and pinpoints the importance of examining the effects of their economic orientation on the development of their moral stance. Both these themes would recur in later studies, as they have in this book.

These early studies are, of course, of great historical interest. Although lacking the immediacy of accounts based on more modern participant observation, they nevertheless show us something of what kibbutzim were like just before the great turning point in their history brought about by the foundation of the State. They are also valuable because they ask questions which are still important, the discussion of which we can follow through subsequent kibbutz literature.

## The 1950s: Key Studies

After the Second World War, Palestine was in turmoil. The expiration of the British Mandate in 1948 was immediately followed by the Declaration of the State of Israel and the War of Independence. This upheaval meant, among many other things, that no outsiders published major kibbutz studies for some years. The next large group of studies written by people not involved in the movement appeared in the 1950s. These represented a break with Infield and Landshut and directly stimulated much modern research. Many of them are classics of kibbutz studies.

Yonina Talmon was one of the most important people in kibbutz studies during this period. From 1955 until her death in 1966, she directed a research project involving combined sociological and social anthropological investigations into the kibbutz movement. In his introduction to her collected essays (Talmon 1974), the distinguished Israeli sociologist, S.N. Eisenstadt, explains that Talmon's work was strongly influenced by British social anthropologists like Evans-Pritchard, Fortes, Gluckman and Nadel. This influence is clear in Talmon's own description of the project. A wide range of topics were investigated: "basic values, work, consumption, public life, the family, the second generation" (Talmon 1974:243) which reflected the holism characteristic of social anthropology. Child-rearing, the collective education system, was excluded because Talmon felt it to be a topic for long-term psychological investigation and therefore beyond the scope of her project. Methods of data collection included participant observation, various standard anthropological types of interviewing including life histories and intensive focused interviews, examination of movement records and internal publications, and a systematic statistical survey.

Publications from the project relate to more specific topics and tend to be primarily statistical or structural functional. That is, they concentrated on building a picture of kibbutz society as a somewhat static system of functioning parts. Important as they are as individual pieces, they are disappointing because they do not, for the most part, reflect Talmon's breadth of vision. Erik Cohen (1976), one of Talmon's pupils and now himself a distinguished sociologist, explains that Talmon was somewhat unhappy with her early work and always intended to write broader ranging pieces to synthesize all the different aspects of and types of material collected by the project. Unfortunately, she died before she was able to do so. Her published papers tend to be open to criticism relating to the use of the survey method and their structural functionalist orientation. Frequently, the reader will find a somewhat mechanistic view of the kibbutz and its ideology, a rather limited perception of the various manifestations of basic structural features, failure to consider actual social relations, and problems identifying and explaining social persistence and the processes of social change.

Erik Cohen has developed the synthesis that Talmon herself was prevented from achieving and explains (1976) that he does so in the spirit she intended. He has written two particularly important papers. One (Cohen 1966) traced ideological contradictions and their impact on kibbutz development; the other (Cohen 1976) systematically tracked and accounted for various paths of social structural evolution in kibbutzim.

At the Hebrew University, Talmon trained Cohen and many other important Israeli social scientists. Two whose work has been influential in recent kibbutz studies are Joseph Shepher, coauthor of the sociobiological *Women in the Kibbutz* (Tiger and Shepher 1975), and Menachem Rosner, who has specialized in the statistical study of kibbutzim and is a key figure in the development of the kibbutz movement's own research effort. His most frequently cited works are about women (Rosner 1967), the second generation (Cohen and Rosner 1975) and work (Leviatan and Rosner 1980).

While the work of Talmon and her pupils was proceeding in Israel, a number of American sociologists and anthropologists were conducting independent research projects on the kibbutz. They included Stanley Diamond, Eva Rosenfeld and Melford Spiro (Diamond 1957). All of them did participant observation in kibbutzim for one or two years and published their findings during the 1950s and early sixties. Their publications reflect various currents of thought in sociology and anthropology at the time. By far the most prolific and influential of these fieldworkers was Spiro whose work still receives widespread citation.

His first book *Kibbutz-Venture in Utopia* first appeared in 1956 and has had two new editions (1972, 1975) and many reprints. It is his famous ethnography of Kiryat Yedidim, a veteran Kibbutz Artzi community, based on participant observation. It remains extremely valuable as an account of kibbutz life in the 1950s and is certainly required reading for any student of the kibbutz. As a source, it may be limited by its use of a psychological approach and the consequent failure to offer full sociological explanation. This problem is particularly clear in the historical section. The early stages of movement history are considered psychologically; the settlers' old European way of life which preceded the period and their newly established kibbutz which followed it are examined sociologically. The shifts of viewpoint create difficulties for a reader trying to understand the processes at work. Spiro's ethnography is revealing although his explanations are generally psychological and thus not always useful for a social anthropologist or sociologist. His second book, *Children of the Kibbutz* (1958), is a study of child training and personality in Kiryat Yedidim and continues in the psychological vein including more explicit use of psychoanalysis. Spiro himself acknowledges (in the Preface to the 1964 edition) that psychoanalysis biased his study in two important ways. It overemphasized genetic determinants of behavior at the expense of environmental ones and it focused too heavily on unconscious rather than conscious motivation. However, the book remains the richest source of material about kibbutz children of the period, particularly for its detailed, direct observation.

In the 1970s, Spiro returned to the study of the kibbutz with the publication of an afterword to *Kibbutz-Venture in Utopia* and later with a book about kibbutz women, *Gender and Culture* (1979). In *Gender and Culture*, Spiro reveals a change of mind about kibbutz women. When he first did fieldwork, he explains, he would have insisted that gender roles were culturally determined. After a return visit to the kibbutz in the late 1960s, he decided that there was also some biological determination at work. The reader will have realized that I have little sympathy for this view, but I must acknowledge that for the kibbutz, no one presents it with greater subtlety or depth of understanding than Spiro. Indeed, so careful is his argument that at times a reader will wonder whether he really does adhere to a biological determinist position.

By comparison with Spiro, Diamond and Rosenfeld were less prolific. Diamond's (1957) comparison of the kibbutz and shtetl shows the former as a startlingly perfect mirror image of the latter, insisting that historical viewpoint is essential for understanding the kibbutz movement. Rosenfeld's most important work (1951-2, 1957) is about the process of differentiation and stratification in kibbutzim. She also published (1958) an account of fieldwork on a kibbutz, one of the very few available. In it, she reveals the kinds of challenges a kibbutz researcher must face if s/he is to carry out participant observation.

## The Heritage

I have already mentioned Talmon's influence on Israeli social science as a whole and on kibbutz studies in particular. Kibbutz research by her students has not always followed Talmon's own approach. Except for Erik Cohen, they seem to concentrate on particular aspects of it, especially the questionnaire survey. Both Rosner and Shepher do this, Shepher adding biology when other forms of explanation appear incomplete (Tiger and Shepher 1975:260-281).

Immediately influenced by Spiro was Bettelheim's popular and widely available book, *The Children of the Dream*. Bettelheim set out, acknowledging inspiration from Eisenstadt, Talmon and Erikson (a psychoanalyst specializing in the cross-cultural study of child development), to write a critique of Spiro's work on kibbutz children. Based on only seven weeks' field research in Israel, his book presents a number of difficulties. Early on he explains that the kibbutz is a ready-made experimental situation. His presentation and discussions of field material therefore tend to ignore the role of the kibbutz movement in Yishuv and the State and the mutual influences of movement and environment that I have argued are so important. Bettelheim's analysis is strongly psychoanalytic, belonging to a tradition entirely different from this book. He ventures into cross-cultural analysis (a potentially anthropological enterprise) via Erikson's (1972) model of personality development, well outside mainstream anthropology and sociology. Though Bettelheim's work is widely read, his basic view of the kibbutz as an experiment and his psychoanalytic viewpoint limit its contribution to the advancement of social scientific study of the kibbutz movement.

## Committed Research

The kibbutz movement itself has long had its own research branches aimed at studying problems defined by the movement itself, as well as disseminating its findings to a wider audience. Material from this source will surface very quickly in any literature search. Much of it is useful, much of it not. In any case, it is important to recognize that it starts with a basic commitment to the kibbutz as a way of life and concentrates on presenting it in a positive light. The same can be said of accounts written by individual kibbutz members.

Blasi (1980) and Lilker (1982) are useful examples of "internal" research. Blasi's study of "Kibbutz Vatik" is questionnaire based and adopts a social psychological perspective. He explains (1980:2):

> . . . the aim of this work is a critical examination of one kibbutz as a model of integrative community on a small scale, where changes in the quality of life can be brought about without continuing the process of atomization in our society or the dangerous road of government centralization and programs.

Following the survey and discussion of some of the strains and stresses of Vatik, Blasi concludes that the kibbutz is no perfect utopia but describes it as "a good try" (1980:221) at an alternative life-style, certainly suggestive of a better life for humankind.

Lilker's (1982) study is a review of the development of an alternative-agnostic or atheist-Judaism in the kibbutz movement. As such, it is a unique and valuable piece of work. It is clear that Lilker would like to see more Judaism in kibbutzim, and he offers explicit argument to that effect. Observing the kibbutz movement's general failure to mark Yom Kippur, he writes (1982:154):

> To a community for whom a healthy collective conscience is a vital necessity, Yom Kippur is the ideal and most important of all the holidays. It is indeed strange that this day should be rejected by those in greatest need of it.

Examples of accounts written by individual members are Leon (1964) and Criden and Gelb (1974). Leon's account is a committed political discussion, focusing particularly on ideological problems and practical dilemmas faced by the kibbutz movement at the time of writing. As a critical review by a participant in kibbutz life, it is unsurpassed. For an outsider, it clearly explains what the ideological debates are all about. Criden and Gelb (1974) are members of Kfar Blum, a veteran kibbutz, and their book is written as a conversation between them about contemporary kibbutz life. They frequently comment, often acidly, on outsiders' misinterpretations and offer a corrective, insiders' point of view. Their work is of enormous value to the ethnographer. It not only offers direct, comparative material on many aspects of kibbutz life but it also communicates some of the atmosphere of everyday life and relationships.

## The Kibbutz and the Wider Society

Stern (1965) and Rayman (1981) appear to have worked independently of mainstream kibbutz studies and of commitment to the movement. Their work has one important feature in common. They both examine the kibbutz as part of a wider society. Stern's work is a critical review of the kibbutz movement as a whole and can serve as a useful counterbalance to some of the less questioning research. In 1965, he saw the kibbutz movement in retreat, even in crisis and wrote (1965:151):

> Kibbutzim . . . can put an end to the existing political strife and divisions inside the movement . . . regain their lost prestige and resume their important role as a dynamic force in the social and economic life of Israel only if they can free themselves from the stranglehold of the political parties and the antiquated Marxist doctrines.

Rayman's (1981) study is based on firsthand field research in the 1970s in a veteran kibbutz she calls Har. She gives little detail of the research experience itself and presents her material in a depersonalized manner. She works more in a sociological than an anthropological tradition. Although basically ethnographic, her study does not include case studies which can add so much color to a basic structural account. The account itself is strongly historical, perhaps to the detriment of presentation of field material. Nevertheless, her study provides valuable information on conditions in a kibbutz in more recent times and on links between that kibbutz and the wider society.

## The Bernstein Project and the Manchester School

The studies I have reviewed so far represent a variety of ways of trying to understand the kibbutz movement. They examine and analyze their data differently. Methods of collecting information include reflections on personal experience, a broad overview of historical developments in the kibbutz movement, questionnaire survey research of one or several kibbutzim, structural functional study of the kibbutz as a social system, and more flexible participant observation. Approaches to data analysis have included political and ideological discussion, quantitative work on survey results, the application of psychological models including psychoanalysis and a form of social psychology, structural functional commentary, and more personal and anecdotal discussion. There is a multitude of varied precedents for a prospective researcher to follow. However, each of the approaches has certain flaws. We will now examine some work which immediately precedes my own study from which I have drawn considerable inspiration. In my opinion, it overcomes many of the earlier difficulties.

The work was part of the Bernstein Israel Research Project which began in 1963 at the University of Manchester, England under the joint direction of Professor

Max Gluckman and Emanuel Marx (Marx 1975). The wide-ranging project focused on the topic of the "ingathering of exiles." Ten studies by anthropologists in different types of community in Israel were involved. There were four moshav studies (a moshav is a family farm cooperative), three of new towns, one of a sheltered workshop for the elderly, and two of kibbutzim, by T.M.S. Evens (1970, 1975, 1980) and I. Shepher (1972, 1980, 1983). Together, they are an important group of studies in the social anthropology of modern Israel. All are based on intensive fieldwork, participant observation of at least one year's duration, and all use some version of the approach to anthropological study developed at Manchester in the 1960s.

The Manchester school of anthropology developed from a critique of traditional British structural functional theory originating among fieldworkers in Africa, especially at the Rhodes-Livingstone Institute in Zambia. Workers there found the material they were collecting in the heterogeneous, rapidly-changing communities in the Copperbelt towns simply did not fit the rather rigid and static approach of structural functionalism (Kuper 1983). The critique quickly became more general, and there was a call for a new approach in all anthropological field study. The new approach entailed a focus on the individual as a social actor (not a personality as in the psychological view) to complement a focus on social groups and categories. Mitchell (1969) argued that anthropological research must focus on structural, categorical and personal orders of social relationships and give accounts of how these were integrated. Thus, studies would be more dynamic and would show individuals living and working in societies rather than freezing them into a static picture of a system. There were several ways of dealing with the new kind of material including the treatment of social situations and extended cases (Van Velsen 1967), social dramas (Turner 1957) and social networks (Mitchell 1969). In Shepher's and Evens' work, the case study was particularly important. It provided strong, truly ethnographic support to their more general analysis. Their work gives a flexible (and therefore more realistic) picture of the kibbutz and offers greater insight into the social processes at work.

Shepher's two main contributions have concerned work roles (1972, 1983) and social boundaries (1980). The study of work roles, using much extensive case material, was the first to come fully to grips with the implications of permanent jobs for kibbutz members and to show how their existence had implications for the whole kibbutz way of life. It has been a valuable foundation for my own work on the kibbutz economy. Shepher's (1980) discussion of social boundaries breaks down the rigidity of considering the kibbutz as an isolated community of members. It explores ethnographically various ways that the kibbutz is bounded and how the different boundaries are crossed. The discussion suggests therefore how the anthropologist can begin to examine the interconnections between a kibbutz and the wider society. The strength of Shepher's work derives both from the detailed, long term ethnographic study and from his use of an analytical approach in the Manchester tradition.

Evens' doctoral thesis (1970) deals with the question of the relationship between ideology and actual social relations. The main argument of his long theoretical section is that Manchester school theory has sometimes overdone the focus on the individual social actor at the expense of considering more collective aspects of social life such as shared ideas. He insists that both collective and individual dimensions must be studied, and the relationship between them should be carefully traced. His case material in the thesis is somewhat limited, as he admits. However, Evens later work on social control (1975, 1980) shows how productive a focus on case material can be. The papers both discuss the same case of a kibbutz deviant, someone the community he calls Timem did not want. The later paper is a more developed version of the earlier one. Evens traces how the case can reveal the structural character of kibbutz social relations, the interpretation of ideological principles and many of the dilemmas faced by the contemporary kibbutz. It is interesting that Evens feels it necessary to devote a long footnote to an apology for having written the paper, revealing the strains and tensions of kibbutz life and, by presenting this particular case (whose details he has changed), showing the kibbutz in a bad light. One of the main strengths of his work, however, is that it reveals at last that kibbutz people are like other people. I hope that the book I have written does the same.

## New Issues and Problems

To talk about the kinds of questions that future kibbutz research might investigate, it is useful to draw a distinction between issues for study and problems for the kibbutz movement. Issues for study are questions I have found repeatedly raised in my own and others' work on kibbutzim. Some are more important than others; some are certainly matters of greater concern to outsiders than to the kibbutzim themselves. An issue may relate more to internal social processes of a kibbutz or be concerned more with the place of the kibbutz in the wider society, but its investigation necessarily involves examining both internal and environmental factors, as I have argued throughout the book. Outsiders often assume that an issue they find interesting to research is a problem the kibbutz movement must solve. This is, of course, an ethnocentric assumption which fails to consider the kibbutz movement's own definitions of the problems it faces and the way internal research and discussion proceeds. Objectively, an issue may be a problem for the movement if it means kibbutzim lose members (actually or figuratively), if destructive divisions appear in the communities, if the movement does not reproduce itself. Subjectively, the kibbutz movement has its own views about problems, and these perceptions themselves are an important part of a social scientific exploration. One issue for investigation which is not a problem for kibbutzim, either objectively or subjectively, is the process of social change. Outsiders frequently feel it is a problem. I have argued throughout this book that social change has been essential for movement survival. Indeed, one of the kibbutzim's greatest assets has been their ability to adapt to new circumstances.

During the course of researching Kibbutz Goshen and writing a doctoral thesis, several articles and this book, I have examined a range of research issues and some problems. Once my original misconceptions had been corrected (as explained in the first chapter), it was possible to see more clearly what questions I should be asking. As I collected more and more field material, new issues arose all the time which lead into areas of investigation I had not anticipated. When it came to the process of actually writing up the research, my perspective has developed over the years. In the thesis (Bowes 1977), I spent a long time sorting out very basic theoretical matters which dealt not only with the kibbutz but with social scientific explanation in general. In later papers, there is less explicit theoretical discussion, and greater weight is given to the interpretation of field material. The later the article, the wider ranging the interpretation becomes. As I have been writing the book, I have found myself returning to material I had already examined before and wanting to develop more elaborate ways of explaining it. This kind of personal research development parallels, I think, the development of research generally, particularly the last part where "old" issues are examined with a fresh perspective.

If we are looking, then, for directions for future kibbutz research, it is true that all the issues dealt with in this book are worth further examination. Deeper understanding of social processes in the kibbutz, exploration of new kinds of theoretical argument, incorporation of new sets of data, and examinations of the interconnections between kibbutz life and the wider society are ready topics. I want to concentrate, however, on some issues and problems which arise directly from the book and form the next stage in this particular research process. The issues fall under three main headings: family issues, economic issues and issues of comparison. The problems, which are of great concern to the contemporary kibbutz, are the roles of women and the movement's recent loss of its establishment position.

In some respects, these issues and problems are general to the kibbutz movement, faced by each kibbutz and by the movement as a whole. In other respects, they are more particular, because my choice of these questions has arisen from a distinctive ethnography. My discussion of them is influenced by the ethnographic and analytical process I have described. A different ethnography might alter the issues and problems in form but not, I think, in substance. Like any self-respecting anthropologist, I have to insist that the ethnographic foundations of the discussion strengthen it. The detailed examination of one case should in the end enhance our grasp of more general questions. Therefore, the proposals for study made here are proposals for further ethnographic work, using participant observation as the main method of data collection.

## Family Issues

As kibbutzim develop a demographic structure more like other communities with several generations and a wide and complete age structure, so the network of kin relationships within communities becomes more complicated, particularly if marriages are internal to the community (anthropologists call this endogamy). In traditional British social anthropology, kinship was often seen as the key to understanding community structure. It formed the basis of social relations in so many small scale societies. Until very recently, such a view of kibbutzim would have been mistaken; there was no web of kinship spreading through the community. Plenty of recent commentators repeat remarks about a return to familism, the resurgence of the nuclear family and so on, but ethnographic study of kibbutz kinship is lacking. There is no systematic picture of attitudes to kin in kibbutzim, of regularities (or otherwise) in their social relationships, of how kin relationships interweave with other types of relationships of the extent to which webs of kinship may have political, economic and symbolic aspects. Clearly, the question is of most relevance for veteran kibbutzim, which should yield the richest data. The investigation of newer ones might also show a process of building kin networks. My own field material on this is weak. My only excuse is that I did not think it was an important or interesting question at the time.

Another set of long-term family issues relates to the development of communal child care which is continuously monitored by the movement itself. As I discussed in Chapter 6, ideological argument about this is of great importance to the movement, and social scientists can watch the development of thinking at that level through the history of communal child care. The relationship between ideology and practice is highly complex but an important area of investigation. Anthropologically, it is helpful to think in terms of a developing social construction of childhood in the kibbutz movement and to consider its ideological and practical manifestations and interaction with other aspects of kibbutz life. The most recent change in communal child care has been the change of children's sleeping arrangements in some kibbutzim, and the insistence in others that the old arrangements are best. People on Goshen saw this change, as I explained, as a threat to communal child care, going against ideological principles at the levels of theory and practice. For them, it was wrong and dangerous. For a social scientist, the questions must be about what difference the change has made, not only to the kibbutzim which have implemented it but also to those which now find themselves having to defend arrangements once taken as universally right and proper. I was indeed interested in this issue on Goshen and have noted how members defended the old ways. The comparative ethnographic material which would enable this to be viewed in a wider perspective was, in general, simply not available.

It is, however, possible to comment more generally on the effects on the kibbutz of the privatization of family life. I mean by this the increasing tendency for people to spend more time with their nuclear family than formerly. The examples of recreation and family meals when food would be taken from the communal kitchen for consumption in a couple's flat, often with children home from secondary school or the army, and sometimes with other relatives illustrated this change. Time spent like this was time away from more communal activities like collective social events and shared meals. Cohen (1976) has argued that the privatization of the family in kibbutzim weakens ties between individuals and the collective by reducing communication between them and setting up alternative networks to which communication resources are diverted. In the association (the very large kibbutz), individuals barely relate to the collectivity, focusing their attention on these alternative networks particularly within their families. This reduces people's ability to participate in the collective life of the kibbutz, especially economic management and political activity. This makes a significant difference to social organization and relationships. Cohen (1976) points out that the majority of kibbutzim, having seen the association type, have deliberately tried to resist developing that way, particularly by restricting numbers (not difficult after 1948). They have, he relates, found it more difficult to restrict people's family activities and Goshen was no exception. Certainly, there were members who did not participate in collective life, preferring to devote their energies to their families. Cohen's conclusions were based largely on work done by Talmon's project. Clearly, a systematic comparison of more recent ethnography in this area would clarify the kinds of kibbutz life now brought about by these trends.

When I wrote about "new generations" in Chapter 6, I focused on the young. As a kibbutz develops, it eventually produces another new generation, the old. In kibbutzim there is no retirement; there are no sharp distinction between "old" people and others in work terms. Old people who can work in the kibbutz economy continue to do so, perhaps moving to less physically demanding jobs or reducing their hours if necessary. People do still age, and again, ethnographic work in this area is lacking. On Goshen, it was simply not possible because no one was particularly old. I would like to see how old people are regarded in the contemporary kibbutz, how they participate in community life, and to understand their sense of belonging to their communities. Furthermore, aged members of veteran kibbutzim have lived through the history of the movement, and social scientific work on this very special experience would undoubtedly prove rewarding.

## Economic Issues

I have returned repeatedly to the study of the economic aspects of kibbutz life, finding them some of the most rewarding and illuminating issues. So many developments in the contemporary kibbutz are connected with economic aspects and there is no doubt that future kibbutz studies must continue to monitor the development of kibbutz economies and their links with other aspects of kibbutz life. There are some key questions which every investigator must ask. The answers, in a series of different historical circumstances, are essential elements in building an understanding of kibbutz life. Many of them are closely related to movement ideology, and the implementation of this ideology has often, as we have seen, affected the practicalities of kibbutz economic efforts. Scientifically, the issues vary in importance, that is in the degree to which they really do affect kibbutz life.

One area often discussed by outsiders is private property; the development in kibbutzim of individual ownership of objects, material things, consumer goods. In my experience, outsiders feel that as kibbutz members become more "materialistic," they become somehow "less pure" kibbutz members. Such a view not only entails a value judgment about what is a good kibbutz member but also conflicts with kibbutz members' own assessments of the same developments. Furthermore, it obscures some interesting questions. Members of Goshen were keen to improve their life-style, as they saw it, through the acquisition of material things like nice clothes, nice furniture, refrigerators, stereos, and so on. As such items came to Goshen, the community would try to insure fair shares and equal access. From their point of view, there was nothing intrinsically wrong with material things like these and no reason why kibbutz members should not enjoy them if they could afford to do so. From a social scientific point of view, the effects of different items of private property on kibbutz social relations are interesting to consider. Nice clothes and furniture for all had little effect on the institutional or relational aspects of kibbutz life, but television sets in people's flats tended to cut down on mutual socializing. More generally, we can consider questions relating to the role of private property in a collectively owned and controlled economy. It is likely that in the last analysis, the effects of collective ownership and control of the means of production prove more profound for kibbutz life than fairly shared consumer items which represent, after all, collective enjoyment of the fruits of collective endeavour.

Throughout movement history, kibbutzim have given manual labor ideological and practical importance above nonmanual, service labor. This view has profoundly influenced their economic planning, and its consequences have profoundly affected kibbutz life. Its most important result has been the distinction drawn between "productive" and "nonproductive" work. I have discussed the issue at some length in the book because of its relationship with gender roles in the kibbutz; men are "productive" and women are "nonproductive." In any kibbutz study, questions about the differential evaluation of different kinds of work must be fundamental. Quite simply, people's work makes a great difference to their lives and to the kibbutz as a way of life.

Kibbutzim continue to face the issue of hired labor, something with which they have lived, albeit uncomfortably, for many years. Although considered undesirable theoretically and ideologically, the use of hired labor (and to a lesser extent volunteer labor) has allowed kibbutz members to pursue a particular form of communalism involving equality based on specialization and indispensability in jobs. For future studies, it will be important to continue examining the role of hired labor in kibbutz economies and how kibbutzim continue to find ways of continuing to hire or ways of lessening their dependence on outside sources. Studying this issue in the case of Goshen revealed much about the structure of the kibbutz economy, the practical use of ideological principles, and the conduct of interpersonal strategies and relationships. The findings should aid comparison with any kibbutz and the analysis should have general applicability. Goshen had a relatively small hired (and volunteer) workforce, a result of its status as a little kibbutz. Ethnographic data from a veteran kibbutz with more nonmember labor would undoubtedly add further insight. Undoubtedly, it would be much more difficult to collect.

The very large kibbutz, with more than a thousand members is a rarity, but there are many kibbutzim of sufficient size and appropriate relationship type to conform to Cohen's (1976) definition of the "association" where relationships are generally impersonal and individuals can participate in communal life only minimally. Cohen comments on the lack of studies of such kibbutzim and urges that they be done. I can only repeat his remarks and argue that any future study should pay particular attention to the economic factors which have proved so important in developing an understanding of Goshen.

## Issues of Comparison

There is a powerful tradition in kibbutz studies—especially those sponsored by the kibbutz movement itself—which sees the kibbutz as a social scientific laboratory. Findings from kibbutz studies are used to offer lessons for societies everywhere and solutions to theoretical problems in social science. A recent paper in this tradition (Leviatan 1984) lists the theoretical and social issues to which kibbutz studies are thought capable of contributing. The theoretical topics are role theory, the sociology of work, the sociology of aging, demography, achievement motivation, social interactionism and systems theory. The empirical topics are gender roles, the effects of nonretirement on old people, longitudinal studies, collection of accurate data on individuals, holistic studies, informal social controls, and the use of experimental methods in social scientific investigation.

I cannot deny the validity and importance of comparative study, which is indeed the basis of social anthropology. Nor can I deny the intrinsic interest of the kibbutz way of life. I must, however, question the use of the kibbutz as a laboratory because I cannot agree that it presents us with laboratory conditions. I have insisted throughout the book that the kibbutz movement is linked to its environment and has developed while interacting with it continuously. It has depended upon and influenced Yishuv and State and simply cannot be cut off from them and thought of as an independent utopia. I hope I have traced enough precise ways in which kibbutz and environment are linked to convince the reader that a program like Leviatan's (1984) is simply untenable. Kibbutzim are no more social laboratories than any other types of community, and their self-orientation towards an experimental life-style should not mislead us otherwise. Therefore, their place in comparative studies is not distinctive. They have a contribution to make, indeed, but they cannot be definitive test grounds.

## Kibbutz Problems

Finally, I must pinpoint two problems the contemporary kibbutz movement faces. These are matters which can affect the future of kibbutzim, even their ultimate survival especially in their present form. They are objective difficulties, perceived in this case by insiders and outsiders. The two problems are the role of women in kibbutzim and the role of kibbutzim in Israeli society.

That the role of women remains a problem for kibbutzim is not really surprising when one understands that movement success was often achieved at the expense of women. Women were, as I have explained, systematically, undervalued. Their preferences were placed second to matters considered more pressing such as the maintenance of national level political power. Within the kibbutz community, their work was devalued; they were effectively deprived of legitimate political power and found themselves virtually unable to participate in running the kibbutzim of which they were members. As the movement developed, women repeatedly voiced dissatisfaction with their lot. Many were believed to be leaving communities because of this. In the 1970s, women seemed to be trying to alter things for themselves by asking for more time with their children. The full results of such changes remain to be ascertained.

It is likely that dissatisfaction among women members will continue because of the other major problem the movement faces today and the likelihood that historical precedent will be followed. The problem of women is likely to be subordinated to a matter thought more pressing: the movement's loss of establishment position in Israel as a whole. Since the election of the first non-Labor government of Israel in 1977, the kibbutzim have been under attack from a newly confident opposition. Years of previously unheard criticism have come out into the open. The entrenched power of the kibbutz movement as part of the Labor governing elite can no longer be taken for granted, and the movement has been put on the defensive. Faced with political, economic and ideological insecurity it is undergoing renewed self-examination. The future no longer promises the continuing march of socialism but a period as a somewhat beleaguered minority in an unsympathetic society.

# Bibliography

Abarbanel, Jay, 1972. "The Dilemma of Economic Competition in an Israeli Moshav." In Moore, S.F. and B.G. Myerhoff (eds.), *Symbol and Politics in Communal Ideology*, pp. 144-165. Ithaca and London: Cornell University Press.

Agassi, Judith B., 1980. "The Status of Women in Kibbutz Society." In Bartölke, K., T. Bergmann, and L. Liegle (eds.), *Integrated Cooperatives in the Industrial Society: The Example of the Kibbutz*, pp. 118-130. Assen, Netherlands: Van Gorcum.

Amitai, M., 1966. *Together.* Israel: English Speaking Department, World Hashomer Hatzair.

Arian, A., 1968. *Ideological Change in Israel.* Cleveland: Case Western Reserve University Press.

Baratz, Josef, 1954. *A Village by the Jordan.* London: The Harvill Press.

Ben-David, J., 1964. "The Kibbutz and the Moshav." In Ben-David, J. (ed.), *Agricultural Planning and Village Community in Israel*, pp. 45-57. Paris: UNESCO.

Ben-Rafael, Eliezer and Sasha Weitman, 1984. "The Reconstruction of the Family in the Kibbutz." *Archives Européennes de Sociologie*, 25(1):1-27.

Berler, Alexander, 1972. *Strengthening Absorption in Development Towns and their Rural Hinterland.* Rehovot: Settlement Study Centre.

Bettelheim, Bruno, 1971. *The Children of the Dream.* London: Paladin.

Billis, David, 1972. "Membership Stability and Structural Developments in Israel's Collective Settlements in the Sixties." *International Review of Community Development*, 27-28:239-254.

Blasi, Joseph R., 1980. *The Communal Future: The Kibbutz and the Utopian Dilemma.* Norwood, Pennsylvania: Norwood Editions.

Borochov, Ber, 1948. *Selected Essays in Socialist Zionism.* London: Rita Searl.

Bowes, Alison M., 1975. *Ideology and Communal Society: The Israeli Kibbutz (Working Papers in Social Anthropology No. 1).* Durham: Department of Anthropology, University of Durham.

**161**

Bowes, Alison M., 1977. *Ideology and Communal Society: The Israeli Kibbutz.* Ph.D. Thesis, University of Durham.

Bowes, Alison M., 1978. "Women in the Kibbutz Movement." *Sociological Review* (N.S.), 26(2):237-262.

Bowes, Alison M., 1980. "Strangers in the Kibbutz: Volunteer Workers in an Israeli Community." *Man* (N.S.), 15(4):665-681.

Bowes, Alison M., 1986. "Kibbutz Women: Conflict in Utopia." In Ridd, R. and H. Callaway (eds.), *Caught Up In Conflict: Women's Response to Political Strife,* pp. 138-162. Basingstoke and London: Macmillan.

Buber, Martin, 1949. *Paths in Utopia.* London: Routledge and Kegan Paul.

Caporale, R. and A. Grumelli (eds.), 1971. *The Culture of Unbelief.* Berkeley and Los Angeles: University of California Press.

Central Bureau of Statistics, State of Israel, 1975, 1976, 1986. *Statistical Abstract of Israel.* Jerusalem: State copyright.

Charsley, Simon, 1987. "Interpretation and Custom: The Case of the Wedding Cake" *Man* (N.S.), 22(1):93-110.

Cohen, Erik, 1966. "Progress and Communality: Value Dilemmas in the Collective Movement." *International Review of Community Development,* 15-16:3-18.

Cohen, Erik, 1970. *The City in the Zionist Ideology (Jerusalem Urban Studies No. 1).* Jerusalem: Institute of Urban and Regional Studies, Eliezer Kaplan School of Economics and Social Sciences, Hebrew University.

Cohen, Erik, 1976. "The Structural Transformation of the Kibbutz." In Zollschan, G.K. and W. Hirsch (eds.), *Social Change: Explorations, Diagnoses and Conjectures,* pp. 703-742. New York: Wiley.

Cohen, Erik and Menachem Rosner, 1970. "Relations between Generations in the Israeli Kibbutz." *Journal of Contemporary History,* 5(1):73-86.

Cohen, Reuven, 1972. *The Kibbutz Settlement.* Israel: Hakibbutz Hameuchad Publishing House.

Criden, Yosef and Saadia Gelb, 1974. *The Kibbutz Experience: Dialogue in Kfar Blum.* New York: Herzl Press.

Davis, Uri, 1977. *Israel: Utopia Incorporated.* London: Zed Press.

Deshen, Shlomo A., 1980. *Immigrant Voters in Israel.* Manchester: Manchester University Press.

Diamond, Stanley, 1957. "Kibbutz and Shtetl: The History of an Idea." *Social Problems,* 5(2):71-99.

Don, Yehuda, 1977. "Industrialization in Advanced Rural Communities: The Israeli Kibbutz." *Sociologia Ruralis,* 17(1-2):59-74.

Drabkin, H. Darin, 1962. *The Other Society.* London: Gollancz.

Durkheim, Emile, 1964. *The Rules of Sociological Method.* New York: Free Press of Glencoe (first published 1938).

Eisenstadt, S.N., 1967. *Israeli Society.* London: Weidenfeld and Nicolson.

Elon, Amos, 1983. *The Israelis: Founders and Sons.* Harmondsworth: Penguin (first edition 1971).

Erikson, Erik H., 1972. *Childhood and Society.* Harmondsworth: Penguin.

Evens, Terence M.S., 1970. *Ideology and Social Organization in an Israeli Collective.* Ph.D. Thesis, University of Manchester.

Evens, Terence M.S., 1975. "Stigma Ostracism and Expulsion in an Israeli Kibbutz." In Moore, S.F. and G.B. Myerhoff (eds.), *Symbol and Politcs in Communal Ideology,* pp. 166-209. Ithaca and London: Cornell University Press.

Evens, Terence M.S., 1980. "Stigma and Morality in a Kibbutz." In Marx, E. (ed.), *A Composite Portrait of Israel,* pp. 179-210. London: Academic Press.

Fishman, Aryei, 1983. "The Religious Kibbutz: Religion, Nationalism and Socialism in a Communal Framework." In Krausz, E. (ed.), *The Sociology of the Kibbutz,* pp. 115-123. New Brunswick and London: Transaction Books.

Fishman, P. (ed.), 1973. *Minor and Modern Festivals.* Jerusalem: Keter Books.

Frankel, William, 1980. *Israel Observed: An Anatomy of the State.* London: Thames and Hudson.

Ghilan, Maxim, 1974. *How Israel Lost Its Soul.* Harmondsworth: Penguin.

Gluckman, Max, 1963. "Gossip and Scandal." *Current Anthropology,* 4(3):307-316.

Golan, S., 1961. *Collective Education in the Kibbutz.* Merchavia, Israel: Education Department of the Kibbutz Artzi Hashomer Hatzair.

Grayzel, Solomon, 1968. *A History of the Jews.* New York: Mentor.

Hardyment, Christina, 1984. *Dream Babies: Childcare from Locke to Spock.* Oxford: Oxford University Press.

Hashomer Hatzair, 1963. *With Strength and Courage.* New York: Machleket Chinuch.

Hazelton, Lesley, 1977. *Israeli Women.* New York: Simon and Schuster.

Herzl, Theodor, 1967. *The Jewish State.* London: H. Pordes (first published 1896).

Infield, Henrik, F., 1946. *Cooperative Living in Palestine.* London: Kegan Paul, Trench, Trubner and Company.

Kanovsky, E., 1966. *The Economy of the Israeli Kibbutz.* Cambridge, Massachusetts: Harvard University Press.

Katzenelson-Rubashow, R., 1976. *The Plough Woman: Records of the Pioneer Women of Palestine.* Westport, Connecticut: Hyperion Press (first published 1932).

Kibbutz Artzi, 1972. *Mifkad Haocclusia (Census of Population).* Tel Aviv: Hakibbutz Haartzi Hashomer Hatzair, Department of Statistics (in Hebrew).

Kuper, Adam, 1983. *Anthropology and Anthropologists: the Modern British School.* London: Routledge and Kegan Paul.

Lahav, Pnina, 1977. "Raising the Status of Women through Law: The Case of Israel." *Signs,* 3(1):193-209.

Landshut, Siegfried, 1967. "The Communal Settlements in Palestine: A Sociological Study." In Viteles, H., *A History of the Cooperative Movement in Israel Book Two: The Evolution of the Kibbutz Movement,* pp. 323-324, 429-431, 510-511, 640-641. London: Vallentine Mitchell.

Larkin, M., 1971. *The Six Days of Yad Mordechai.* Israel: Yad Mordechai Museum.

Leon, Dan, 1964. *The Kibbutz: A Portrait from Within.* Tel Aviv: "Israel Horizons" in collaboration with World Hashomer Hatzair.

Leviatan, Uri, 1973. "The Industrial Process in Israeli Kibbutzim: Problems and their Solutions." In Curtis, M. and M.S. Chertoff (eds.), *Israel: Social Structure and Change,* pp. 159-172. New Brunswick, New Jersey: Transaction Books.

Leviatan, Uri, 1984. "Research Note: The Kibbutz as a Situation for Cross-cultural Research." *Organization Studies,* 5(1):67-75.

Liebman, Charles and Eliezer Don-Yehiya, 1983. *Civil Region in Israel: Traditional Judaism and Political Culture in the Jewish State.* Berkeley, Los Angeles, London: University of California Press.

Lilker, S., 1982. *Kibbutz Judaism: A New Tradition in the Making.* New York: Cornwall Books.

Luckmann, Thomas, 1971. "Belief, Unbelief and Religion." In Caporale, R. and A. Grumelli (eds.), *The Culture of Unbelief,* pp. 21-37. Berkeley and Los Angeles: University of California Press.

Maimon, Ada, 1962. *Women Build a Land.* New York: Herzl Press.

Marx, Emanuel, 1967. *Bedouin of the Negev.* Manchester: Manchester University Press.

Marx, Emanuel, 1975. "Anthropological Studies in a Centralized State: Max Gluckman and the Bernstein Israel Research Project." *Jewish Journal of Sociology,* 17:131-150.

Mednick, Martha S., 1975. *Social Change and Sex Role Inertia: The Case of the Kibbutz.* Givat Haviva, Israel: Publications Department.

Mitchell, J. Clyde (ed.), 1969. *Social Networks in Urban Situations.* Manchester: Manchester University Press.

Near, Henry (ed.), 1971. *The Seventh Day: Soldiers' Talk About the Six-Day War.* Harmondsworth: Penguin.

Paine, Robert, 1967. "What is Gossip About? An Alternative Hypothesis." *Man* (N.S.), 2(2):278-85.

Peretz, Don, 1977. "The 'Earthquake': Israel's Ninth Knesset Elections." *Middle East Journal,* 31(3):251-266.

Rabin, A.I. and Bertha Hazan, 1973. *Collective Education in the Kibbutz: From Infancy to Maturity.* New York: Springer Publishing Company.

Rayman, Paula, 1981. *The Kibbutz Community and Nation-Building.* Princeton, New Jersey: Princeton University Press.

Rein, Natalie, 1980. *Daughters of Rachel: Women in Israel.* Harmondsworth: Penguin.

Rokach, A., 1964. "Agricultural Planning Since the Establishment of the State of Israel." In Ben-David, J. (ed.), *Agricultural Planning and Village Community in Israel,* pp. 31-44. Paris: UNESCO.

Rosenfeld, Eva, 1957. "Institutional Change in the Kibbutz." *Social Problems,* 5(2):110-136.

Rosenfeld, Eva, 1958. "The American Social Scientist in Israel: A Case Study in Role Conflict." *American Journal of Orthopsychiatry,* 28:563-571.

Rosner, Menachem, 1967. "Women in the Kibbutz: Changing Status and Concepts." *Asian and African Studies,* 3:35-68.

Rubin, Nissan, 1986. "Death Customs in a Non-religious Kibbutz: The Use of Sacred Symbols in a Secular Society." *Journal for the Scientific Study of Religion,* 25(3):292-303.

Saltman, Michael, 1981. "Legality and Ideology in the Kibbutz Movement." *International Journal of the Sociology of Law,* 9:279-302.

Schauss, Hayyim, 1962. *The Jewish Festivals.* New York: Schocken (first published 1938).

Schwartz, Richard D., 1954. "Social Factors in the Development of Legal Control: A Case Study of Two Israeli Settlements." *Yale Law Journal,* 63:471-491.

Schwartz, Richard D., 1976. "Law in the Kibbutz: A Response to Professor Shapiro." *Law and Society Review,* 10(3):439-442.

Segal, M., 1971. "Collective Education: The Background." In *Kibbutz: A New Society?* pp. 167-170. Tel Aviv: Israel: Ichud Habonim.

Shapiro, Allan E., 1976. "Law in the Kibbutz: A Reappraisal." *Law and Society Review,* 10(3):415-438.

Shatil, J., 1966. "The Economic Efficiency of the Kibbutz." *New Outlook,* 9(7):33-39.

Shepher, Israel, 1972. *The Significance of Work Roles in the Social System of a Kibbutz.* Ph.D. Thesis, University of Manchester.

Shepher, Israel, 1980. "Social Boundaries of the Kibbutz." In Marx, E. (ed.), *A Composite Portrait of Israel,* pp. 137-177. London: Academic Press.

Shepher, Israel, 1983. *The Kibbutz: An Anthropological Study.* Norwood, Pennsylvania: Norwood Editions.

Sherman, Neal, 1982. "From Government to Opposition: The Rural Settlement Movements of the Israel Labour Party in the Wake of the Election of 1977." *International Journal of Middle Eastern Studies,* 14:53-69.

Shur, Shimon, 1972. *Kibbutz Bibliography.* Israel: Higher Education and Research Authority of the Federation of Kibbutz Movements; Department of Higher Education, Executive Committee of the Histadrut Israel and the Van Leer Jerusalem Foundation.

Spiro, Melford E., 1970. *Kibbutz: Venture in Utopia, 2nd Ed.* New York: Schocken (1st Ed., 1956, 3rd Ed., 1975 by Harvard University Press).

Spiro, Melford E., 1971. *Children of the Kibbutz.* New York: Schocken (first published 1958).

Spiro, Melford E., 1979. *Gender and Culture: Kibbutz Women Revisited.* Durham, North Carolina: Duke University Press.

Stern, B., 1965. *The Kibbutz That Was.* Washington, D.C.: Public Affairs Press.

Talmon, Yonina, 1974. *Family and Community in the Kibbutz.* Cambridge, Massachusetts: Harvard University Press.

Talmon-Garber, Yonina and Erik Cohen, 1964. "Collective Settlements in the Negev." In Ben-David, J. (ed.), *Agricultural Planning and Village Community in Israel,* pp. 58-95. Paris: UNESCO.

Tamarin, Georges R., 1973. *The Israeli Dilemma: Essays on a Warfare State.* Rotterdam: Rotterdam University Press.

Tiger, Lionel and Joseph Shepher, 1975. *Women in the Kibbutz.* New York: Harcourt Brace Jovanovich.

Turner, Victor W., 1957. *Schism and Continuity in an African Society.* Manchester: Manchester University Press.

Van Velsen, J., 1967. "The Extended Case Method and Situational Analysis." In Epstein, A.L. (ed.), *The Craft of Social Anthropology,* pp. 129-149. London: Tavistock.

Viteles, Harry, 1967. *A History of the Cooperative Movement in Israel Book Two: The Evolution of the Kibbutz Movement.* London: Vallentine Mitchell.

Viteles, Harry, 1968. *A History of the Cooperative Movement in Israel Book Three: An Analysis of the Four Sectors of the Kibbutz Movement.* London: Vallentine Mitchell.

Wershow, H.J., 1973. "Aging in the Israeli Kibbutz: Growing Old in a Mini-Socialist Society." *Jewish Social Studies,* 35(2):141-148.

Zborowski, Mark and Elizabeth Herzog, 1962. *Life is With People.* New York: Schocken.

Zureik, Elia T., 1979. *The Palestinians in Israel.* London: Routledge and Kegan Paul.